ALBERT AND VICTORIA

Albert and Victoria

The Rise and Fall of the
House of Saxe-Coburg-Gotha

Edgar Feuchtwanger

hambledon
continuum

Hambledon Continuum
A Continuum imprint

The Tower Building,
11 York Road,
London SE1 7NX,
UK

80 Maiden Lane,
Suite 704,
New York, NY 10038
USA

First Published 2006

ISBN 1 85285 461 8

A description of this book is available from the
British Library and from the Library of Congress.

Typeset by Carnegie Publishing, Lancaster,
and printed in Great Britain by MPG Books Ltd, Cornwall.

Contents

Illustrations

Between Pages 204 and 205

Text Illustrations

Illustration Acknowledgements

The author and publishers are grateful to the Royal Archives for permission to reproduce illustrations 8, 9, 12, 14, 15, 16, 18, 19 and 21.

Preface

Saxe-Coburg-Gotha was one of the smallest of the forty or so German states that survived the Napoleonic Wars. Along with quite a few others, it was rightly called a dwarf state. Yet during the nineteenth century its ruling dynasty spread its tentacles throughout Europe. Princes of Saxe-Coburg-Gotha sat on the thrones of Belgium, Portugal and eventually Bulgaria. Other Coburg princes and princesses came to figure prominently among European royalty by judicious marriages. The biggest prize of all was won by Prince Albert of Saxe-Coburg-Gotha. Born in 1819, the second son of Ernst I, the reigning Duke of Coburg, he married his first cousin, Queen Victoria, in 1840. Victoria, three months older than Albert, was herself the daughter of another Princess of Coburg, Victoire, a sister of Ernst I, who, through marriage to George III's fourth son, had become the Duchess of Kent.

In the first half of the nineteenth century most of Europe's hereditary rulers still wielded almost absolute power, scarcely limited by parliaments and constitutions, let alone democratic electorates. The great exception was Britain, where the prerogatives of the Crown were limited by the powers of Parliament. British monarchs, however, were still deeply involved in politics and far removed from the politically neutral stance later required of them. The transition to constitutional monarchy was only beginning when Victoria married Albert, but from the moment of his arrival in England Albert played an important role in this transition. For the next twenty years, until his death in 1861, the Queen and her Consort transacted the business of the Crown in partnership, with Albert as the driving partner.

While he was a supporter of constitutional monarchy, Albert was also a monarchical activist, making his views felt in every aspect of domestic and especially of foreign policy. It made him into the target of much criticism, which often extended to his wife. When attacks on him reached their climax, at the outbreak of the Crimean War in 1854, crowds collected to see him brought to the Tower as a traitor. They thought he had used his position as Consort of the Queen to undermine Britain's efforts to stand up to the Tsar of Russia. Normally, however, such attacks were less strident and came from within the establishment as much as from the populace at large.

Albert remained all his life an alien, however hard he laboured for the benefit of his adopted country. He had been brought up in a small German court, seen by much of British opinion as a reactionary remnant fit only for the dustbin of history. With his many relations dotted about the royal houses of Europe, his outlook remained centred on Coburg, and, so it was argued, he could never understand the interests of Britain, the superpower of the age. The Coburg connection, sometimes called the Coburg intrigue, took on menacing proportions in many minds, including that of Bismarck, and was meat and drink to conspiracy theorists.

In 1858 Victoria and Albert's eldest daughter, Vicky, the Princess Royal, married Frederick William, destined to become King of Prussia. The two major Protestant powers of Europe, England and Prussia, thus became closely linked through their royal houses. It was hoped by many in England, including Albert and Victoria, that Prussia would follow England's example and become a moderately liberal constitutional monarchy. Such a hope was doomed to failure, with tragic consequences for Europe and the world. With the premature death of Albert in 1861, at the age of forty-two, its most potent proponent had gone. A few months later Bismarck became Prime Minister of Prussia. He more than any other man ensured that Prussia, and later a united Germany, did not become a liberal state, but continued to be ruled by a powerful monarchy closely linked with the army.

The fate of Germany, however, also depended on the accident of longevity. The accession of Frederick William and Vicky to the throne of Prussia-Germany was delayed beyond expectation by the long reign of his father William I, the first German Emperor. When William I died in March 1888, two weeks short of his ninety-first birthday, Frederick William, now Emperor Frederick III, was himself dying and his reign lasted only fourteen weeks. It was now too late to turn Germany into a liberal state. Worse was to come. Vicky's son, and Victoria's grandson,

William II, the Kaiser, now ascended the throne, ruling until the defeat of Germany in 1918 drove him into exile. His attitude to his mother and his English heritage was deeply ambivalent, one of the many personality problems that made him unstable. This instability was highly dangerous in a man who wielded so much power.

Queen Victoria, even as a widow living in seclusion, remained until her death a formidable matriarch, much loved but ruling her far-flung and often dysfunctional family with a rod of iron. In British politics her powers were increasingly limited by the rise of a democratic electorate, but her immediate descendants occupied the most important thrones in Europe. The Kaiser was her grandson, and Alicky, her granddaughter, became the Tsarina of Russia when she married Tsar Nicholas II in 1894. Bertie, the Prince of Wales, who succeeded his mother as Edward VII in 1901, was their uncle. King George V, King from 1910, was the first cousin of both Kaiser William II and Tsar Nicholas II, to whom he bore a striking physical resemblance. These close dynastic relationships did not prevent the outbreak of the First World War, which led to the fall of the monarchies of both Germany and Russia, as well as to that of Austria-Hungary, but they added an important additional dimension to the complex web of diplomacy, power and commercial rivalry that brought about the catastrophe of 1914. It is a theme well worth exploring.

I would like to thank my publisher Martin Sheppard and my wife Primrose for their sustained efforts to improve this book.

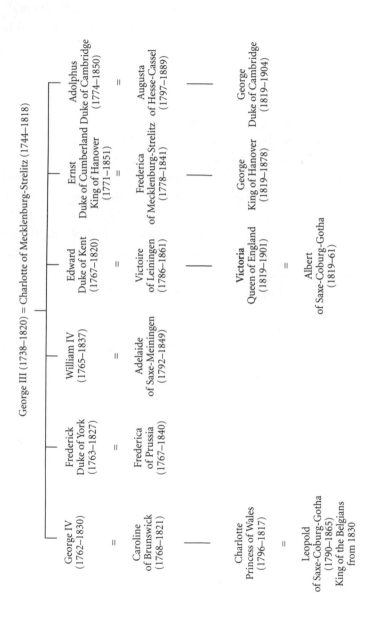

George III (1738–1818) = Charlotte of Mecklenburg-Strelitz (1744–1818)

George IV
(1762–1830)
=
Caroline
of Brunswick
(1768–1821)

Charlotte
Princess of Wales
(1796–1817)
=
Leopold
of Saxe-Coburg-Gotha
(1790–1865)
King of the Belgians
from 1830

Frederick
Duke of York
(1763–1827)
=
Frederica
of Prussia
(1767–1840)

William IV
(1765–1837)
=
Adelaide
of Saxe-Meiningen
(1792–1849)

Edward
Duke of Kent
(1767–1820)
=
Victoire
of Leiningen
(1786–1861)

Victoria
Queen of England
(1819–1901)
=
Albert
of Saxe-Coburg-Gotha
(1819–61)

Ernst
Duke of Cumberland
King of Hanover
(1771–1851)
=
Frederica
of Mecklenburg-Strelitz
(1778–1841)

George
King of Hanover
(1819–1878)

Adolphus
Duke of Cambridge
(1774–1850)
=
Augusta
of Hesse-Cassel
(1797–1889)

George
Duke of Cambridge
(1819–1904)

Victoria's family tree.

Dramatis Personae

Aberdeen, 4th Earl of, George Hamilton-Gordon (1784–1860), Foreign Secretary 1828–30 and 1841–46, Prime Minister 1852–55.

Adolf, Prince of Schaumburg-Lippe (1859–1916), married in 1890 Victoria, 'Moretta', second daughter of the Dowager Empress Frederick.

Affie, *see* Alfred, Duke of Edinburgh.

Albert, Prince of Saxe-Coburg-Saalfeld, from 1826 Saxe-Coburg-Gotha (1819–1861), second son of Ernst I, Duke of Saxe-Coburg-Saalfeld, and of Louise of Saxe-Gotha-Altenburg (1800–31), married Victoria, Queen of England, in 1840. Title of Prince Consort formally conferred in 1857.

Albert Edward, Prince of Wales, Edward VII (1841–1910), 'Bertie'. Albert and Victoria's eldest son.

Albert Victor, Duke of Clarence (1864–1892), eldest son and heir of the Prince of Wales, later Edward VII, 'Eddy'. Engaged to Mary of Teck (1867–1953), 'May', when he died.

Alexander II, Tsar of Russia (1818–1881), married to Princess Marie of Hesse-Darmstadt, the Tsarina Marie Alexandrovna, the aunt of Princes Louis, Alexander and Henry of Battenberg.

Alexander III, Tsar of Russia (1845–1894), 'Sasha', married to Dagmar, Princess of Denmark, the Tsarina Marie Feodorovna, 'Minnie', sister of Alexandra, Princess of Wales.

Alexander, Prince of Battenberg (1857–1893), Prince of Bulgaria, 'Sandro'.

Alexandra, Princess of Denmark, Princess of Wales, Queen of England (1844–1925), 'Alix', married to Albert Edward, Prince of Wales, sister of Marie Feodorovna, Tsarina of Russia, 'Minnie'.

Alexandra, Princess of Hesse-Darmstadt, the Tsarina Alexandra Feodorovna of Russia (1872–1918), 'Alicky'.

Alfred, Duke of Edinburgh, Duke of Saxe-Coburg-Gotha (1844–1900), 'Affie', married in 1874 Grand Duchess Marie Alexandrovna of Russia, only daughter of Tsar Alexander II. Albert and Victoria's second son.

Alice, Princess of England, Grand Duchess of Hesse-Darmstadt (1843–1878). Albert and Victoria's second daughter.

Alicky, *see* Alexandra, Princess of Hesse-Darmstadt.

Alix, *see* Alexandra, Princess of Denmark.

Arthur, Duke of Connaught (1850–1942). Albert and Victoria's third son.

Augusta auf Reuss zu Ebersdorf (1757–1831), married to Duke Franz Anton of Saxe-Coburg-Saalfeld, grandmother of Victoria and Albert.

Augusta, Princess of Saxe-Weimar, Queen of Prussia and German Empress (1811–1890).

Augusta Victoria, Princess of Schleswig-Holstein-Sonderburg-Augustenburg, Crown Princess of Germany, German Empress (1858–1921), 'Dona', daughter of Fritz Holstein and granddaughter of Victoria's half-sister Feodora.

Beatrice, Princess of Great Britain, Princess Henry of Battenberg (1857–1944). Albert and Victoria's youngest daughter.

Bernhard, Prince of Saxe-Meiningen (1851–1928), married to Charlotte, eldest daughter of Crown Prince Frederick William of Prussia and Victoria, 'Vicky', Princess of Great Britain.

Bethmann Hollweg, Theobald von (1856–1921), German Chancellor 1909–17.

Bismarck-Schönhausen, Otto von (1815–1898), Count (Graf) 1865, Prince (Fürst) 1871, Prime Minister of Prussia 1862, Chancellor of North German Confederation 1867, of Reich 1871–90.

Bülow, Bernhard von (1849–1929), German State Secretary (Foreign Minister) 1897–1900, Chancellor 1900–9.

Cambridge, George Duke of (1819–1904), Victoria's first cousin, uncle of Mary of Teck, later Queen Mary, Commander-in-Chief of the British Army 1856–95.

Caprivi, General Leo von (1831–1899), German Chancellor 1890–94.

Charles Edward, Duke of Albany, later of Saxe-Coburg-Gotha (1884–1954), 'Charlie Albany', posthumous son of Leopold, Albert and Victoria's fourth son.

Charlotte, Princess of Belgium, Empress of Mexico (1840–1927), daughter of Leopold I, King of the Belgians.

Charlotte, Princess of Prussia (1798–1870), sister of Frederick William IV and William I of Prussia, married Tsar Nicholas I, the Tsarina Alexandra Feodorovna.

Charlotte, Princess of Prussia (1860–1919), eldest daughter of Vicky and sister of the Kaiser, married Prince Bernhard of Saxe-Meiningen.

Charlotte, Princess of Wales (1796–1817), George IV's only daughter, married to Leopold of Saxe-Coburg-Saalfeld, Victoria's 'Uncle Leopold'.

Christian, Prince of Schleswig-Holstein-Sonderburg-Augustenburg (1831–1917), brother of Fritz Holstein, married to Helena, Albert and Victoria's third daughter.

Constantine, Crown Prince, later King of Greece (1868–1923), 'Tino', married to Sophie, daughter of Frederick III and Vicky and sister of the Kaiser.

Dagmar, Princess of Denmark, *see* Marie Feodorovna, Tsarina of Russia.

Disraeli, Benjamin (1804–1881), Chancellor of the Exchequer and Leader of the House of Common 1852, 1858–59, 1866–68, Prime Minister 1868 and 1874–80. Created Earl of Beaconsfield in 1876.

Dona, *see* Augusta Victoria, Princess of Schleswig-Holstein-Sonderburg-Augustenburg.

Ducky, *see* Victoria Melita.

'Eddy', *see* Albert Victor, Duke of Clarence.

Elizabeth of Hesse-Darmstadt (1864–1918), 'Ella', second daughter of Alice, married to Grand Duke Sergei of Russia (1857–1905). He was assassinated, she was murdered.

Ella, *see* Elizabeth of Hesse-Darmstadt (1864–1918).

Ernst I, Duke of Saxe-Coburg-Gotha (1784–1844), Albert's father.

Ernst II, Duke of Saxe-Coburg-Gotha (1818–1893), Albert's elder brother.

Ernst, Grand Duke of Hesse-Darmstadt (1868–1937), son of Alice, Princess of England, and grandson of Albert and Victoria, married to his cousin Victoria Melita, 'Ducky', daughter of Alfred, Duke of Edinburgh and Saxe-Coburg-Gotha.

Eugénie, Empress of France (1826–1920), wife of Napoleon III.

Feodora, Princess of Leiningen, later of Hohenlohe-Langenburg (1807–1872), Victoria's half-sister.

Ferdinand, King of Rumania (1865–1927), 'Nando'.

'Fischy', *see* Prince Friedrich Karl of Hesse-Cassel.

Frederick (Friedrich) William, later Frederick III, German Emperor (1831–1888), 'Fritz', husband of Vicky and son-in-law of Victoria.

Friedrich, Duke of Schleswig-Holstein-Sonderburg-Augustenburg (1829–1880), the Augustenburger, 'Fritz Holstein', son-in-law of Feodora, Victoria's half-sister.

Friedrich, Grand Duke of Baden (1826–1907), son-in-law of King William I of Prussia, later German Emperor.

Friedrich Karl, Prince of Hesse-Cassel (1868–1940), 'Fischy', husband of Margaret, 'Mossy', son-in-law of Vicky, Empress Frederick.

Fritz, *see* Frederick (Friedrich) William, later Frederick III, German Emperor.

Fritz Holstein, *see* Friedrich, Duke of Schleswig-Holstein-Sonderburg-Augustenburg.

George V, King of Great Britain and Emperor of India (1865–1936), second son of Edward VII and Queen Alexandra, married to Mary, Princess of Teck.

George V, King of Hanover (1819–1878), blind, forced to abdicate in 1866, first cousin of Victoria, son of the Duke of Cumberland who became King Ernst August of Hanover in 1837.

George, Prince of Schleswig-Holstein-Sonderburg-Glücksburg and of Denmark (1845–1913), from 1863 King of the Hellenes, brother of Queen Alexandra of England and of the Tsarina Marie Feodorovna, wife of Tsar Alexander III.

Gladstone, William Ewart (1809–1898), Chancellor of the Exchequer 1853–55 and 1859–66, Prime Minister 1868–74, 1880–85, 1886, 1892–94.

Helen, Princess of Waldeck-Pyrmont (1861–1922), wife of Leopold, Duke of Albany, Albert and Victoria's youngest son.

Helena, Princess of Great Britain (1846–1923), 'Lenchen'. Albert and Victoria's third daughter.

Henry, Prince of Battenberg (1858–1896), 'Liko', married to Beatrice, Victoria's youngest daughter.

Henry, Prince of Prussia (1862–1929), brother of the Kaiser, married to Irene (1866–1953), third daughter of Alice of Hesse-Darmstadt.

Lehzen, Louise (d. 1870), Baroness of Hanover 1827, governess of Feodora of Leiningen and Princess, later Queen Victoria of Great Britain.

Leiningen, Prince Charles of (1804–1856), Queen Victoria's half-brother, briefly Prime Minister in the Frankfurt Parliament of 1848.

'Lenchen', see Helena, Princess of Great Britain.

Leopold I, King of the Belgians (1790–1865), uncle of both Albert and Victoria, son-in-law of Louis-Philippe. Earlier Leopold of Saxe-Coburg-Saalfeld and previously married to Charlotte, Princess of Wales.

Leopold, Duke of Albany (1853–1884), married Helen, Princess of Waldeck-Pyrmont (1861–1922). Albert and Victoria's youngest son.

'Liko', see Henry, Prince of Battenberg.

Louis, Prince of Battenberg (1854–1921), married Victoria of Hesse-Darmstadt in 1884, father of Lord Mountbatten.

Louischen, see Louise, Princess of Prussia.

Louise, Princess of Great Britain (1848–1939), fourth daughter of Albert and Victoria, married Marquess of Lorne, Duke of Argyll (1845–1914).

Louise, Princess of Prussia (1860–1917), 'Louischen', married to Arthur, Duke of Connaught (1850–1942), Albert and Victoria's third son.

Margaret, Princess of Prussia (1872–1954), 'Mossy', daughter of Emperor Frederick III and Vicky, sister of the Kaiser, married to Friedrich Karl of Hesse-Kassel, 'Fischy'.

Marie, daughter of Alfred, Duke of Edinburgh and of Saxe-Coburg-Gotha, 'Missy' (1878–1938), married to Ferdinand, 'Nando', King of Rumania (1865–1927).

Marie Feodorovna, Tsarina of Russia (1847–1928), married to Alexander III, Tsar of Russia, 'Minnie'. Earlier Dagmar, Princess of Denmark.

Mary, Princess of Teck, Queen of England (1867–1953), 'May', married to King George V (1965–1936).

May, *see* Mary, Princess of Teck.

Melbourne, 2nd Viscount, William Lamb (1779–1848), Prime Minister 1834 and 1835–41.

Mensdorff-Pouilly, Alexander von (1813–1871), Austrian Foreign Minister 1864–66, first cousin of Victoria and Albert.

Minnie, *see* Marie Feodorovna, Empress of Russia. Earlier Dagmar, Princess of Denmark.

Missy, *see* Marie, daughter of Alfred, Duke of Edinburgh and of Saxe-Coburg-Gotha.

'Moretta', *see* Victoria, Princess of Prussia.

'Mossy', *see* Margaret, Princess of Prussia.

'Nando', *see* Ferdinand, King of Rumania.

Napoleon III (Prince Louis Napoleon) (1808–1873), President of Second French Republic 1848–52, Emperor of the French 1852–70, nephew of Napoleon I.

Nicholas II of Russia (1868–1918), 'Nicky', married to Alexandra, Princess of Hesse-Darmstadt, the Tsarina Alexandra Feodorovna of Russia (1872–1918), 'Alicky'.

Nicky, *see* Nicholas II of Russia.

Palmerston, third Viscount (Irish), Henry John Temple (1784–1865), Foreign Secretary 1830–34, 1835–41 and 1846–51, Home Secretary 1852–55, Prime Minister 1855–58 and 1859–65.

Peel, Sir Robert, second Baronet (1788–1850), Home Secretary 1822–27 and 1828–30, Prime Minister 1834–35 and 1841–46.

Rosebery, fifth Earl of, Archibald Philip Primrose (1847–1929), Foreign Secretary 1886 and 1892–94, Prime Minister 1894–95.

Russell, Lord John (1792–1878), first Earl Russell 1861, Prime Minister 1846–52; Foreign Secretary 1859–65; Prime Minister 1865–66.

Salisbury, third Marquis of (1830–1902), Lord Robert Cecil until 1865, Viscount Cranborne 1865–68, Foreign Secretary 1878–80, Prime Minister 1885–86, 1886–92 and 1895–1902, also Foreign Secretary 1886–92 and 1895–1900.

'Sandro', *see* Alexander of Battenberg.

Sophie, Princess of Germany (1870–1932), Queen of Greece, daughter of Frederick III and Vicky, married to Constantine, 'Tino', Crown Prince, later King of Greece (1868–1923).

'Tino', *see* Constantine, Crown Prince, later King of Greece.

Victoria, Princess of Hesse-Darmstadt (1863–1950), eldest daughter of Alice, married Prince Louis of Battenberg in 1884. Lord Mountbatten was their son.

Victoria, Princess of Prussia (1866–1929), 'Moretta', had a long attachment to 'Sandro', Alexander of Battenberg, married Adolf of Schaumburg-Lippe.

Victoria, Princess Royal (1840–1901), 'Vicky', Crown Princess Frederick William of Prussia, Empress Frederick of Germany. Eldest daughter of Albert and Victoria.

Victoria, Queen (1819–1901), only child of Edward, Duke of Kent, fourth son of George III, and Victoire of Saxe-Coburg-Saalfeld, widow of Emich, Prince of Leiningen. Heir Apparent to the British Throne 1830, Queen 1837, Empress of India 1876, married Albert of Saxe-Coburg-Gotha in 1840, four sons, five daughters.

Victoria Melita (1876–1936), 'Ducky', daughter of Alfred, 'Affie', Duke of Edinburgh and Saxe-Coburg-Gotha, married Grand Duke Ernst of Hesse-Darmstadt in 1894.

William (Wilhelm), Prince of Prussia (1797–1888), later King William I of Prussia and German Emperor.

William (Wilhelm), Prince of Prussia (1859–1941), 'Willy', later William II, German Emperor, the Kaiser.

Victoria

It was early in the morning of Tuesday, 20 June 1837, when Victoria learnt that she had become Queen. The old King William IV had died at Windsor during the night. In the early hours William Howley, the Archbishop of Canterbury, and Lord Conyngham, as Lord Chamberlain a principal officer of the Royal Household, hastened from Windsor to Kensington Palace, where the young Princess, heiress to the throne, had lived with her mother, the Duchess of Kent, since her birth on 24 May 1819. The death of the seventy-one-year-old King was not unexpected, for his life had hung in the balance for at least a month, but it was only during this time that Victoria had reached her eighteenth birthday and come of age for the purposes of the succession. She was now capable of exercising the full powers of the Crown without the need for a regency by her mother. The scene when Howley and Conyngham fell on their knees and kissed the hand of the young girl, a dressing gown hastily flung over her shoulders, was commemorated in innumerable pictures and prints. It became an iconic moment as the beginning of the Victorian age. By inheriting the Crown Victoria escaped the constant and oppressive tutelage in which her mother and the Duchess's adviser and confidant, Sir John Conroy, had kept her.

Many accidents of birth and death had conspired to bring Victoria to the throne. George III, the first ruler of the House of Hanover who could be regarded as British, had no fewer than fifteen children with his wife Charlotte of Mecklenburg-Strelitz, but by 1817, three years before his death, there were no survivors in the third generation. Offspring from the many illegitimate unions of George III's sons there were aplenty, but they were out of the running for the succession to the Crown. George III's one surviving legitimate granddaughter, Princess Charlotte, had died in November 1817 after giving birth to a stillborn son. She was the product of the only night that the Prince of Wales, later Prince Regent and George IV, could bring himself to spend with his wife, Caroline of Brunswick. By all accounts personal hygiene did not rank high with this German princess, so that the Prince of Wales, when first setting eyes upon her after their arranged betrothal, asked immediately for a glass of brandy. Princess Charlotte, their daughter, became the darling of the nation, the one ray of light among the sleazy and unpopular members of the royal family. Her eventual accession to the throne was eagerly anticipated. She had married, in May 1816, Leopold of Saxe-Coburg-Saalfeld (which became Saxe-Coburg-Gotha in 1826), later the uncle of Victoria and King of the Belgians. It was a match strongly opposed by her father, the Prince Regent, who had wanted his daughter and heir to marry the Hereditary Prince of Orange, due to become the King of the Netherlands. It would have been a politically useful match and a marriage treaty was under negotiation. Charlotte, an impulsive, headstrong girl, refused adamantly to marry the Prince of Orange, even when her father dismissed all her household and put her under house arrest. In the meantime she had met Leopold of Coburg when he came to London in the entourage of the Tsar in 1814 and, after a slow start, fell in love with him. Eventually the Prince Regent had to bow to the inevitable, but he never liked his son-in-law and called him *le Marquis peu à peu*. Leopold was ponderous, and always cautious and on his guard, but he could be charming.

The death of Charlotte left the succession to the British throne wide open. A race began among the surviving sons of George III to produce an heir in the third generation. For those who were, like the third son, the Duke of Clarence, or the fourth son, the Duke of Kent, in long-standing liaisons with mistresses, the incentive was above all financial. They were mired in debts and, unless they entered a union capable of sustaining the succession, Parliament would not loosen the purse-strings. None of those appropriately married, like the second son, the Duke of York, or the fifth, the Duke of Cumberland, were fancied runners in the succession stakes. York's health was weak, he lived separately from his wife, no progeny was any longer expected from his marriage, and the Duchess of York, a Hohenzollern princess, died in 1820. Cumberland had a fearsome reputation as the blackest of reactionaries, aggravated by a facial disfigurement suffered in battle. His own succession in the socially tense years after Waterloo would have been disastrous. The sixth son, Sussex, was in a childless marriage and the youngest, Cambridge, was Regent in Hanover and had not yet married.

There remained the possibility that the Prince Regent would either manage to divest himself of Caroline of Brunswick or she would be removed by natural causes and he would then marry again. After his accession as George IV he attempted to rid himself of Caroline, who was now his Queen Consort. Only annulment of the marriage was possible, for divorce was not an option for the Head of the Church of England. This plunged the monarchy into one of its most damaging scandals and the ministry of Lord Liverpool into one of its greatest crises. Fierce public opposition forced the withdrawal of the Act of Parliament annulling the marriage. Neither George nor Caroline was a model of monogamy, but such was the King's unpopularity that no parliamentarian wanted to be seen taking his side. When he went to the opera at Covent Garden, and rose in his box to acknowledge what he thought was the acclaim of the audience, he found that the applause was meant for his estranged wife who had just appeared in another box. Soon, following the failure of the Act of Annulment, Queen Caroline conveniently died. After years of dissipation George IV was now, however, no longer interested in remarrying, a disposition encouraged by his current mistress Lady Conyngham.

As for the succession, it came down to this: Clarence, Kent, Cumberland and Cambridge all rushed into marriages with Protestant German princesses. Any male offspring from these unions would inherit their place in the order of succession from their fathers and would have precedence over a female offspring from the same father. Cumberland was first off the mark in fathering a male child, but fortunately was well down the pecking order. Clarence, the front-runner, divested himself of his long-standing companion Mrs Jordan, a well-known London actress, who had not only borne him ten children but had also helped to keep him afloat financially. He married Princess Adelaide of Saxe-Meiningen.

Edward, Duke of Kent, his younger brother, had been trained for a career in the army, but it had ended in disgrace. He had acquired a reputation as a brutal disciplinarian, who ordered four hundred lashes to be administered for the slightest offence. In Canada he was accused of 'bestial severity'. After being recalled from Gibraltar in 1803 his elder brother York, the Commander-in-Chief, accused him of provoking mutiny by conduct which 'from first to last was marked by cruelty and oppression'. No more military commands would be forthcoming. Greville called him 'the greatest rascal that ever went unhung' and the Duke of Wellington regarded him with derision. He probably reserved his brutality for his troops. With his social equals he could be charming and affectionate: for Princess Charlotte he was her favourite uncle and he had an easy friendship with Mrs Fitzherbert, the Catholic wife to whom the Prince Regent was illegitimately married. Kent was fond of music and, in spite of his never-ending debts, supported many charities. He considered himself hard done by, both in his frustrated military career and in being denied the funds appropriate to his royal station.

The mistress of the Duke of Kent was not in the same league as Clarence's Mrs Jordan. She was a French woman of dubious provenance, several years Edward's senior, known as Mme de St Laurent, which was not her real name. The Duke had, however, lived with her, it seems happily, since about 1790, but she had borne him no children. Latterly they had for financial reasons lived an almost bourgeois existence in Brussels. Even before the death of Princess Charlotte, the Duke of Kent had been looking for a legitimate bride, in order to escape his straitened financial circumstances and reduce his debts. His search for a bride had to be conducted circumspectly, so as not to alarm Mme de St Laurent and to keep his elder brother, the Prince Regent, in the dark. It was probably the Duke's brother-in-law Leopold, the husband of Charlotte, who had directed Edward's attention to Victoire, Leopold's widowed elder sister. At the age of seventeen Victoire of Coburg, born in 1786, had married Prince Emich of Leiningen, whom she had borne two children. Leiningen was one of several hundred German principalities abolished by Napoleon. Only a small area around the moated castle of Amorbach, south east of Frankfurt, remained to the Princes of Leiningen. Emich died in 1814 and his widow resided and ruled in Amorbach.

The Duke of Kent's suit for Victoire became urgent in November 1817, after Charlotte's death in childbirth. Rumours of his suit had already reached the London press, from which, then as now, few secrets could be kept. When Mme de St Laurent read in the *Morning Chronicle*, a fortnight after Charlotte's death, that England would hail a union

of the Duke of Kent with one of the sisters of the bereaved Prince
Leopold with 'rapturous delight', she fainted over the breakfast table.
The Duke's efforts to reassure his 'poor faithful partner' did not deceive
her and soon she left for Paris. Edward was guilt-ridden and remained
concerned for her welfare. She was given a pension. In a letter to a
friend, which he hoped she would see, he wrote 'our unexpected separation arose from the imperative duty I owed to obey the call of my
family and my Country to marry, and not from the least diminution in
an attachment which had stood the test of twenty-eight years'.[1]

Edward now pressed the Dowager Princess of Leiningen for a positive
response, but it was not an easy decision for Victoire to make. The Duke
was nineteen years her senior; and she was giving up house, home and
an income for a man laden with debts, which might or might not be
alleviated by Parliament, and whose country she had never seen. Nevertheless, by January 1818 plans for the marriage could go ahead. It was
celebrated according to Lutheran rites in Coburg on 29 May 1818. Six
weeks later there was a second Anglican ceremony at Kew Palace, a double wedding, when Edward married Victoire and his elder brother, the
Duke of Clarence, married Princess Adelaide of Saxe-Meiningen. The
royal dukes had expected that Parliament would now prove generous
and increase their allowances, but they were to be disappointed. It was
on this occasion that the Duke of Wellington famously remarked:

> By God, there is a great deal to be said about that. They are the damnedest
> millstone about the necks of any Government. They have insulted – person-
> ally insulted – two thirds of the gentlemen of England, how can it be
> wondered at that they take revenge upon them when they they get them in
> the House of Commons?[2]

In spite of all the inauspicious circumstances, the marriage of Edward
and Victoire seems to have been happy. The Duchess became pregnant
with commendable promptitude and a baby was expected in May 1819.
If the child was one day to inherit the throne of England, something a
gypsy had many years previously predicted to the Duke, it had to be
born in England. Preparations needed to be made to bring the pregnant
Duchess from Amorbach to England and to house the family in suitable
style. The Prince Regent was entirely unhelpful. He had never had much
time for his brother and would have preferred it if Edward and Victoire

had stayed in Germany. He was in the end prevailed upon to make apartments available in Kensington Palace and a yacht for crossing the Channel. The Duke had to borrow money for the journey and for the redecoration of the apartments. At the end of March 1819 a caravan of carriages set off from Amorbach and arrived after about a month, via Cologne, Calais and Dover, at Kensington Palace. There the future Queen Victoria was born on 24 May 1819, after a labour of six hours, a healthy baby, 'plump as a partridge'.

When Victoria was born she was fifth in line of succession after her father's three elder brothers and the Duke of Kent himself, but for the moment she was the first in the third generation. The probability was that she would soon drop down in the pecking order. Clarence, of proven fertility with Mrs Jordan, was likely to have children. Victoria's parents were likely to have more children and a boy would take precedence over her. When it came to her baptism at Kensington Palace, everything depended on the whim of the Prince Regent, who was far from pleased that Kent might have fathered his eventual successor. It had particularly annoyed him when a few years earlier his younger brother had promoted the Coburg marriage of his daughter Charlotte and had acted as a *postillon d'amour* between Charlotte and Leopold. The Prince Regent did not fix the date for the baptism, 24 June 1819, until three days before. He forbade the use of his own name, in the form of Georgiana, and that of his deceased daughter Charlotte, and of Augusta, another name customary in the royal family. This left Alexandrina, after one of the godfathers, Tsar Alexander I, who could not be present. A royal child should have at least two names, so, as the Archbishop of Canterbury held the baby over the font, the irritated Prince Regent said 'give her the mother's name then, but it cannot precede the name of the Emperor'. So it was Alexandrina Victoria and the possibility of a Victorian age had arrived. Victoria had not hitherto been a usual English girl's name. It was to be left to this baby to rescue the monarchy from the contempt into which it had fallen under the House of Hanover.

When the baby Princess was only eight months old the Duke of Kent died at the age of fifty-two in January 1820, of a chill contracted at Sidmouth, where the family were spending the winter to save money. Thus

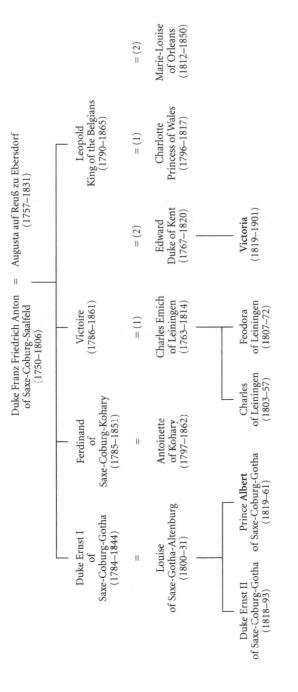

Duke Franz Friedrich Anton = Augusta auf Reuß zu Ebersdorf
of Saxe-Coburg-Saalfeld   (1757–1831)
(1750–1806)

Duke Ernst I
of
Saxe-Coburg-Gotha
(1784–1844)

Ferdinand
of
Saxe-Coburg-Kohary
(1785–1851)

Victoire
(1786–1861)

Leopold
King of the Belgians
(1790–1865)

= Louise
of Saxe-Gotha-Altenburg
(1800–31)

= Antoinette
of Kohary
(1797–1862)

= (1) Charles Emich
of Leiningen
(1763–1814)

= (2) Edward
Duke of Kent
(1767–1820)

= (1) Charlotte
Princess of Wales
(1796–1817)

= (2) Marie-Louise
of Orleans
(1812–1850)

Duke Ernst II
of Saxe-Coburg-Gotha
(1818–93)

Prince **Albert**
of Saxe-Coburg-Gotha
(1819–61)

Charles
of Leiningen
(1803–57)

Feodora
of Leiningen
(1807–72)

Victoria
(1819–1901)

House of Coburg family tree.

Alexandrina Victoria never knew her father, but the possibility that she might lose her place in the succession to a brother had gone. Her upbringing was therefore entirely in the hands of her mother. The Duchess of Kent was a foreigner in England and knew hardly any English, so that public pronouncements had to be written out for her phonetically. She was still encumbered by her husband's debts and in urgent need of advice and support. She got a good deal of it from her Coburg connections. Her widowed brother Leopold had not given up the £50,000 annual allowance Parliament had voted him when he was consort to the heir to the throne, a fact which did not make him popular. He gave some financial support to his sister, £3000 a year, but it was hardly generous. He also had an estate, Claremont near Esher, where Victoria spent much time in her childhood. With the increasing likelihood that her daughter would eventually inherit the throne, the position of the Duchess became less isolated and financially more secure. The Clarence marriage, the most likely source of a rival, had no surviving offspring. There was a still-born daughter, then another in December 1820 who lived only three months. Adelaide of Saxe-Meiningen was only twenty-eight at the time, twenty-seven years younger than her husband, but she could not match the fecund Mrs Jordan.

Victoria in later life described her childhood as isolated and unhappy. This may reflect her memory of the years after 1830, when as heiress presumptive to the throne she was subjected to pressures that few experience in adolescence. As a small child, however, she lived a fairly normal life away from the public gaze. She had the company of a few other children, mostly of her half-sister Feodora of Leiningen, who was twelve years older, and of Victoire and Jane, the two daughters of her mother's adviser Sir John Conroy. She had no great love for the Conroys and saw their father as the evil spirit of her childhood, which again may have coloured her view of her earliest years. When she was five years old Louise Lehzen, who had been Feodora's governess, became hers and the most important influence in her life until her accession. Lehzen was the daughter of a Lutheran pastor in Hanover and was made a Hanoverian baroness in 1827. The almost entirely German surroundings of the little Princess, who might one day inherit the throne, was one probable reason for keeping her out of the public eye. In fact her upbringing was very much that of an English upper middle-class girl of that period, so that when she was on the throne her instinctive reactions often matched those of her subjects, rather more so than those of some of the aristocratic politicians who served her. English was her first language and her clear feminine enunciation was one of her attractive personal characteristics. Despite her German surroundings, she began to learn German only at the age of seven.

Her moral universe was formed Hannah More and Maria Edgeworth, whose ideas also governed the nurseries of her contemporaries. Right and wrong were absolutes and righteousness always prevailed in the end. From the age of eleven so-called Behaviour Books were kept for Victoria by Lehzen and submitted to her mother. In it the Princess had to admit her own lapses, which she often did with the greatest of emphasis: 'very very very very horribly naughty!!!!!'[3] Victoria liked to write her own childish stories in the style of Maria Edgeworth, in which naughty little girls test the limits, get away with it, but some melodramatic eventual dénouement threatens. Drina, or Vickelchen as she was more often called, was a headstrong little girl, inclined to get her own way, but incapable of dishonesty or untruthfulness, emotional and fond of melodrama. These attributes remained with her for the rest of her life, magnified by her unique position as a female sovereign. It was not the most appropriate beginning for a future constitutional monarch.

There were exceptional pressures on Victoria, which increased as she grew older and came nearer to the throne. Many of them stemmed from Sir John Conroy. He was a minor Anglo-Irish landowner who had been the Duke of Kent's equerry. He became the Duchess's closest adviser and was suspected, by the Duke of Wellington among others, to be her lover, though this seems improbable. He realised that control over Victoria was his and her mother's biggest asset and appears to have tried, when the Duke of Kent lay dying, to extract a document from him making him Victoria's guardian. He was the author of what Victoria's uncle Leopold called the 'Kensington System', the close control over the Princess and her education, which immediately before her accession amounted almost to an attempt to imprison her. It was fuelled by a certain amount of paranoia, the fear that those further down in the succession, particularly Cumberland, might try to kidnap and kill her. The counterbalance in Victoria's life to the Conroyals, as the Duchess and her adviser became known, was her uncle Leopold and her governess

Lehzen. Leopold could only act intermittently and mostly from a distance, but in these years he filled something of the role of the father that Victoria never had. An especially poignant moment in the fraught relationship between the Princess and Conroy occurred in 1835, when Victoria was seriously ill with typhoid. Conroy and her mother tried to make her sign a document that he would become her private secretary on her accession. She adamantly refused.

Another aspect of the manipulation of the Princess by the Conroyals was the distance they created between her and her uncle William IV, when the latter became King in 1830. It was almost a tradition in the House of Hanover that the heir to the throne should favour the political faction opposed to those favoured by the King. The Duchess kept close to the Whig government that came into power in 1830 and which passed the Act of Parliament appointing her Regent for her daughter, should Victoria come to the throne before coming of age. William IV was unhappy with the Whigs and opposed to their most important policy, reform of the franchise. He tried unsuccessfully to bring back Wellington and the Tories in 1831, which would have scuppered the Reform Bill that eventually passed in 1832. William and Queen Adelaide were, unlike George IV, well disposed towards Victoria and would perhaps have liked to treat her as the daughter they never had. The Duchess, however, advised by Conroy, wanted to present her child to the public independently of the Royal Court, not least to dispel rumours, fostered by her seclusion, that she was physically handicapped. From 1832 onwards the young Princess was made to embark upon a number of journeys through the country, during which she began to perform some public duties, such as laying foundation stones, and was shown off to crowds of her future subjects. The King objected to this kind of royal progress, particularly as it involved frequent stays in the country houses of the Whig aristocracy, but he could not stop it.

During these journeys Victoria also encountered something of the poverty and hardship of the burgeoning industrial working class. In her journal, which she was made to keep, she described one of her first public journeys in 1832 through midland mining districts: 'The grass is quite blasted and black. Just now I saw an extraordinary building flaming with fire. The country continues black, engines flaming, coals, in abundance, everywhere burning and smoking coal heaps, intermingled with wretched huts and carts and little ragged children.'[4] No doubt, at the age of thirteen, she knew little of the industrial revolution and its significance for the country over which was to rule.

The ill-feeling between the King and the Duchess of Kent reached an embarrassing climax at dinner given at Windsor in celebration of the King's seventy-first birthday on 21 August 1836. In his speech William IV said:

> I trust to God that my life may be spared for nine months longer, after which period, in the event of my death, no Regency would take place. I should then have the satisfaction of leaving the royal authority to the personal exercise of that Young Lady, the Heiress Presumptive of the Crown, and not in the hands of a person now near me, who is surrounded by evil advisers and who is herself incompetent to act with propriety in the station in which she would be placed.[5]

And a good deal more in that vein. The Princess burst into tears; a terrible scene ensued when the guests rose and the Duchess announced her immediate departure from the castle. A reconciliation was patched up and she was prevailed upon to stay until the next day. When, shortly before her eighteenth birthday, the King, with the agreement of Prime Minister and Cabinet, offered the Princess £10,000 a year and a household of her own, she was forced by her mother and Conroy to refuse the offer.

The tension between Victoria, supported by Leopold and Lehzen, and her mother and Conroy reached a climax in the four weeks that elapsed between her eighteenth birthday and the death of the King. Thus her accession was for the Princess not only a public event but the escape from a personal bondage that had become intolerable. But these were indeed uncharted waters that Victoria now embarked upon, as a girl of eighteen with a sheltered and in many ways deliberately restricted upbringing. There had not been a female sovereign since the days of Queen Anne in the early eighteenth century, and since then both the position of the monarchy and of women had changed out of all recognition.

It fell to Lord Melbourne, the Prime Minister, to become Victoria's guide and mentor in this great adventure. It soon became evident that a bond had developed between them that far transcended that of sovereign and first minister. They found in each other a substitute for relationships that both had missed in their lives: Victoria had never had a father and Melbourne had never had a daughter. The Prime Minister, aged fifty-eight, was a man who presented few rough edges to the world, but there had been much unhappiness in his private life. As William Lamb his marriage to Lady Caroline Ponsonby, remembered for her hysterical attachment to Byron, had been famously turbulent. She had died in 1828 after years of mental illness. The son of the marriage was epileptic and had also died a few years earlier. Only a year before Victoria's accession Melbourne had nearly been brought down by scandal. He was accused of what was then called criminal conversation by the husband of Caroline Norton, one of the three beautiful daughters of the playwright Sheridan. Norton was himself a violent reprobate, who had once beaten his wife so badly that she suffered a miscarriage. But it could not be disputed that Melbourne was a frequent visitor to Mrs Norton's boudoir and he got off only by the skin of his teeth.

This was the worldly-wise man who now spent a great deal of his time in the company of the young and inexperienced Queen. It was a task such as had fallen to no subject since the days of the Protector Somerset in the reign of Edward VI in the sixteenth century. For the sake of it, and for the emotional satisfaction it gave him, Melbourne, accustomed to the most brilliant company society had to offer, was prepared to endure interminable hours of boredom in the monotonous Court surrounding the young Queen. This is Greville's description: 'She sits at a large round table, and Melbourne always in a chair beside her, where two mortal hours are consumed in such conversation as can be found, which appears to be, and really is, very up-hill work.' Of the changes in Melbourne's ways he wrote: 'Instead of indolently sprawling in all attitudes of luxurious ease, he is always sitting upright; his free and easy language interlarded with "damns" is carefully guarded and regulated with the strictest propriety, and he has exchanged the good talk of Holland House for the trivial, laboured, and wearisome inanities of the royal circle.'

Politically Melbourne was a Whig by family connection, but he had first held office in the Tory government of Canning in 1827 as Chief Secretary for Ireland. Since the French Revolution of 1789 British politics had been dominated by the task of preventing revolution at home, and

to fighting the revolution and its successor, Napoleon, abroad. To advocate reform of British institutions had almost become tantamount to
treason. This conservative constellation had prevailed, first under the
Younger Pitt, then under his successors. Canning's short-lived government was a step in the gradual realignment of politics that brought the
Whigs to office in 1830 and put parliamentary reform fairly and squarely
back on the agenda. In November 1830 Lord Grey formed a Whig government, which, although one of the most aristocratic of the century,
was committed to reforming the franchise.

This opened the gate to many other changes. Melbourne was Home
Secretary, responsible for the maintenance of law and order. These were
years that brought the country perhaps closer to violent upheaval than
it has ever been in modern times. Great grievances had failed to be
addressed for too long, at a time when the country was changing more
rapidly than ever before. Melbourne's tenure of the Home Office is
remembered chiefly for the transportation of the Tolpuddle Martyrs in
1834. They were rural labourers who were imitating their industrial
brothers in forming a trade union, alarming to the landowning class to
which Melbourne belonged. When in the spring of 1834 Grey tired of
keeping his factious colleagues together, Melbourne was chosen as his
least contentious replacement. He is said to have remarked to his secretary that it was 'a damned bore', but the latter encouraged him by saying
that even if it did not last long it was a position such as no Greek or
Roman had ever held.

When a few months later the succession of Lord Althorp to the
Spencer earldom left an awkward vacancy in the Cabinet, William IV
took the opportunity to ask for Melbourne's resignation and installed a
Tory government under Sir Robert Peel and the Duke of Wellington.
Melbourne offered little resistance to this royal move, which amounted
to a dismissal. When Peel in the spring of 1835 appealed to the electorate
he increased his following, which had been decimated in the first election under the reformed franchise, but still lacked a majority. This
precipitated a renewed rally of all the forces that had kept the Grey and
Melbourne Cabinets in office, Whigs, Radicals and Irish Repealers.
This so-called Lichfield House Compact can be regarded as an early
version of the later Victorian Liberal Party. The course of events demon-
strated that after 1832 the support of the monarch was no longer

sufficient to keep a ministry in office. The Crown could not dismiss a Prime Minister who had a majority in the House of Commons.

Melbourne returned to the premiership, even though his role had been hardly proactive. It was in fact an emollient and personally charming figure like him that was required to keep together the loose parliamentary connection sustaining his government. Although a Whig, Melbourne's temperament was profoundly conservative. He did not really believe that politics or politicians could or should change anything very much. At a moment of particularly severe political controversy he was reported to have exclaimed: 'Damn it, why can't everybody be quiet!' Melbourne was not untypical of the Whigs of his generation and there was no great ideological gulf between Whigs and Tories. The great Whig political families, like the Russells and the Cavendishes, were motivated by the consciousness that it had always been their historical task to carry out revolutions from above, when these became necessary. It was this that had made them the proponents of reform in 1830, but such reform should never go further than was needed to prevent a revolution from below.

On a personal and emotional level it was a great boon for Victoria that she had a man like Melbourne as her first Prime Minister, but it was less beneficial politically. He was hardly the man to explain to her how the ability of the monarch to exercise political choices had become limited by the reform of the franchise and early developments of the party system stemming from it. It was unlikely that he was himself fully aware how great a change in constitutional practices and assumptions had been brought about by the Reform Act of 1832. He was far from wishing to spoil the young girl's enjoyment of her new freedom and power, thereby perhaps endangering the exceptionally close relationship and great influence he had with her. For the Queen the emotional friendship with Melbourne became a kind of template for what she expected of her Prime Ministers, however much circumstances and the passage of years changed the situation. It was only during the twenty years of her marriage to Albert that an alternative source of support was available to her.

Yet Melbourne did not save the young Queen from errors of judgement that soon drained the reservoir of public good will with which she had come to the throne. To have an innocent young girl as the

head of the nation was at first like a breath of fresh air. The tawdry, frequently scandalous members of the House of Hanover, who made up the
majority of the royal family, could at last be forgotten. The symbiotic
relationship between the British monarchy and the media was, however,
just entering a new and more intensive phase. Newspaper readership was
expanding fast and new technology was making the wider dissemination
of visual images, prints and engravings possible. Nothing could have
been more opportune in stimulating this market than the arrival of a
pretty and innocent young girl on the throne. It sent an almost sexual
frisson down a great many spines.

At the time of her coronation in June 1838 Greville wrote in his diary:
'She never ceases to be a Queen, but is always the most charming, cheer-
ful, obliging, unaffected Queen in the world.' It was a phenomenon that
posed a dilemma for those with anti-monarchist leanings, but the implications of which were more serious in the late 1830s than they are now.
The political powers of the monarchy, even if in decline after 1832, were
still great, but even greater were the tensions in the social system of
which the Crown was the apex. The Chartist movement was about to
plunge the country into a degree of turmoil that might end in revolution. The royalist fervour generated by the accession of Victoria grated
on the nerves of those who were hoping for a radical overhaul of the
political system. Their hope was that progress would be achieved by the
spread of reason and education to ever wider sections of the populace.
They were to find to their cost that the apparently irrational appetite of
the public for irrelevant crumbs of information about the personal lives
of royalty remained insatiable for a long time to come. But there was
also a dilemma for those who wished to preserve the aura of mystery
that from time immemorial had surrounded the wearer of the Crown.
In making the person of the young Queen familiar to her subjects, there
was the risk that the mystique of the anointed sovereign would wane.

The populace at large had only a blurred picture of what went on in
the narrow world of Court and Cabinet, and the more widely dissemi-
nated news media could enlighten them only in a limited and
sometimes distorting way. The Whig sympathies of Victoria's mother
were, however, common knowledge. The Whigs were still the party of
reform, loosely allied to the more radical reformers in Parliament. The
Whig image as reformers was, however, by this time seriously tarnished.

The biggest reform they had introduced, the reform of the franchise in 1832, had proved a damp squib for the mass of the people. It left the vast bulk of the population more excluded than ever and still not recognised as full citizens. The poorer of them felt the sharp end of the other major Whig reform, the introduction of the New Poor Law in 1834. When they were without a job and in old age they suffered incarceration in the work houses, the hated bastilles, which were now, at any rate officially, the only places were poor relief could be granted.

In spite of all disappointment and disillusionment, the arrival on the throne of Victoria, a 'Whig' Queen, revived hopes of reform and relief. The accession of a new sovereign still precipitated a general election in those days and Victoria's accession was the last time an election was brought on in this way. The Whigs, the Radicals and even those who would have preferred a republic made use of the Queen's name as an election cry. The political neutrality of the Crown, soon seen as an essential concomitant of constitutional monarchy, was not yet a familiar concept. The monarchy was so inextricably woven into the national fabric that even those who would have preferred to see the last of it, the republicans, could not simply wish it away. The language of radicalism was very often couched in terms of constitutional rights: the ancient rights of the people, enshrined in law since time immemorial in famous enactments like Magna Carta, had been ignored in settlements such as that of 1832, through which the moneyed and propertied classes, 'Old Corruption', had conspired to secure their own privileges. The monarchy was part of a much more ancient and just order, so ran the popular myth. What better than to invoke the name of an innocent young Queen as a sympathiser with reform and the rights of the people. The Tory-inclined *Blackwood's Magazine* commented caustically:

> 'The Queen' echoed all the Whig Radicals, from John o'Groats to Land's End; 'the Queen' faintly murmured the Radicals hypocritical of the metropolitan boroughs, of sanctified Manchester and Unitarian Manchester; 'the Queen' bellowed O'Connell and his satellites through all the bogs of Ireland ... Queen or no Queen 'that is the question', whispered the more Really honest and truly destructive Radicals of Bath, of Westminster, and of Southwark.[6]

The presence of a 'Whig Queen' on the throne, however, reversed the natural political order for the Tories. They were the party of altar and throne, the upholders of the royal prerogative, the guardians of the traditional constitutional order. They were now forced to attack the actions of the monarch, something they could only do with conviction by claiming that the innocent young girl on the throne, scarcely out of the nursery, had fallen into the hands of unscrupulous Whig advisers.

The sense of a new beginning engendered by Victoria's accession did not last. Two events in 1839 seriously tarnished the Queen's reputation and popularity, the case of Lady Flora Hastings and the Bedchamber Crisis. Lady Flora, the daughter of the first Marquess of Hastings, had for some years been a member of the Duchess of Kent's court. Appointed to reinforce the 'Kensington System' and to lessen the influence of Lehzen, she was disliked by the Princess as a creature of Conroy. Late in 1838 or early 1839 the size of her figure made it look as if she must be pregnant. There were rumours that Sir John Conroy was the father and the Queen was only too ready to believe them. It was only after much delay that Lady Flora was prepared to submit to a medical examination to establish the truth. It required two doctors and a heavy presence of chaperones. Evidently she was found to be a virgin, but one of the doctors, Sir Charles Clarke, remarked to Melbourne that pregnancies could occur despite the appearance of virginity. When the Queen discussed the matter with Melbourne, and said that Lady Flora had not been seen for some time and might be sick, the Prime Minister repeated 'Sick?' with what the Queen described as a significant laugh. Clearly Melbourne did nothing to discourage the scurrilous rumours swirling round Lady Flora, who was in fact suffering from cancer of the liver.

It was late in the day when the Queen made conciliatory gestures and neither Lady Flora, and even less her family, were ready to forgive. They were Tories and the scandal had political overtones. It also gave Sir John Conroy a chance to discredit Melbourne. The whole hornets' nest of long-standing animosities in the Court was stirred up and relations between the Queen and her mother became more tense than ever. There were letters from the Hastings family, including Lady Flora, to the newspapers, and the scandal formed the staple diet of many London dinner tables for weeks on end. Although the finger of blame was pointed at Melbourne more than at the Queen herself, she was made to look an inexperienced, headstrong and manipulated young girl. Much of this was true, for Victoria was never one to give up an opinion once formed. To her the Hastings family, and particularly Lady Flora's mother, remained the villains of the piece. Feelings were by no means assuaged when Lady Flora died in early July, at the age of thirty-two. Victoria, unrepentant, had paid her a brief visit as she lay dying.

The scandal was still in full flood when the even more serious Bedchamber Crisis blew up. Melbourne's parliamentary position had been progressively weakened. When in May 1839 his majority dropped to four on an important division he felt compelled to resign. The Queen was in tears in her discussions with Melbourne, who advised her to consult Wellington, who would probably suggest that Sir Robert Peel should be sent for. The outgoing Premier warned her that she might find Peel's manner stiff and awkward; although 'a very gifted and able man ... he was an underbred fellow ... not accustomed to talk to Kings and Princes', as Melbourne himself was.[7]

Peel's father, the first Sir Robert, was indeed a textile manufacturer, an early example of how industrialism could produce enormous wealth for some. He was made a baronet, sent his son to Harrow and Christ Church, and got him into the House of Commons by buying him a pocket borough. The second Sir Robert, who like many at this time retained traces of his regional accent, was indeed a man of great ability and at the age of twenty-four had become Chief Secretary of Ireland, effectively the ruler of John Bull's Other Island. His stern treatment of Irish Catholics earned him the nickname Orange Peel. He had entered the inner citadel of the ruling class, but he was not entirely comfortable there, being shy and difficult to approach. That was just as the Queen found him, like a dancing master who in his embarrassment hopped uneasily from one foot on to another. It was a situation made for misunderstandings. Peel asked that a few changes should be made in the Royal Household. A few Tories should be appointed, so that its complexion would not remain too exclusively Whig. Constitutionally it was a perfectly proper request, for the incoming minister needed a visible assurance that he had the confidence of the sovereign. The Queen, however, remained adamant in refusing to change any of her ladies-in-waiting. If she hoped that this might induce Peel to give up his commission and bring back Melbourne, this was exactly what happened. Proud of having kept her composure, she wrote to Melbourne: 'I never saw a man so frightened ... I was very calm and decided and I think you would have been pleased to see my composure and firmness ... The Queen of England will not submit to such trickery. Keep yourself in readiness for you may soon be wanted.'[8]

Melbourne was somewhat embarrassed when he realised that Peel had only asked, as an entirely reasonable sign of royal confidence, that some ladies-in-waiting be changed and that Victoria had refused to change any. Even Wellington had been unable to move her. The self-willed young girl on the throne, up to a point aided and abetted by Melbourne, had kept a government of one particular political colour out of office and allowed one of the opposite persuasion to carry on for what proved to be another two years. It was something that the Queen no longer had the power to do in her later years, much as she may have wanted to. Even in 1839 such an action was not without danger to the future of the monarchy. The social tensions of the time were starkly exposed when the Chartist movement reached its first peak in the presentation of a mass petition to Parliament. The House of Commons took little notice, for those who had massed behind the symbol of the Charter were mostly still excluded from the political nation. The six points of the Charter were demands for inclusion (nearly all, except the demand for annual Parliaments, realised in due course), but they were at this time still outside the realm of practical politics. The monarchy was a symbol that reached beyond the political nation; it could be a factor for stability, but once tarnished would add to the sense of instability and be itself engulfed by it. These were issues of which Victoria could only have been dimly aware, but there was no one to instruct her how she could play her role to more positive purpose. The political and symbolic weight heaped upon the young girl on the throne was formidable.

Sooner or later Victoria would have to marry and speculation about who might fill the bill had always been lively even before she came to the throne, at home and abroad, in newspapers, round dinner tables and in the street. The difficulties in which the Queen had become embroiled made the question of her marriage more urgent, but she resented too much pressure in so personal a matter, even when it came from her favourite Uncle Leopold. There were moments when the early euphoria of being Queen had somewhat waned, but on the whole she was still enjoying herself immensely. To be always the centre of attention, the focus of pomp and ceremony, to be the queen of her own balls and dance into the early hours, with great and handsome kings, grand dukes and princes, was meat and drink to her. As for marriage, even a Queen of England could not entirely escape the fate of her female contemporaries. Marriage must mean a degree of subordination and loss of freedom. As for pregnancy and childbirth, Victoria was hardly likely to forget the fate of the unfortunate Princess Charlotte. Melbourne was not among those pressing her to decide on a husband, for it could only diminish his own position. With him restored to her, she could afford to wait for a while. She could not know that love and sexual arousal were awaiting and would change her intentions.

2

Coburg

Germany in the seventeenth and eighteenth centuries was choc-a-bloc with small and tiny statelets. The Germans called it *Kleinstaaterei*, little statism. Even after Napoleon, with his tidy mind, had cleared nearly three hundred of these dwarf sovereignties away in 1803, mediatising them as the technical term went, there were still nearly forty left after 1815. Saxe-Coburg-Saalfeld, ruled by Leopold's brother Duke Ernst I, was one of them. It formed part of the area known as Thuringia, in central Germany, where a number of small principalities had made their appearance in the late fifteenth century. Dynastic ambition required consolidation, by conquest, marriage or inheritance, and this was how the Habsburgs and later the Hohenzollerns had risen to eminence. But the Saxon branch of the Guelph dynasty, or the House of Wettin, as the Germans called it, went in the opposite direction and split up their territories. The first division came in 1485 and thereafter the family had two branches, the Ernestines, located in Thuringia, and the Albertines, with most their territories further east in Saxony. Both branches were among the foremost supporters of Luther and the Reformation in the sixteenth century. In consequence, they became involved in fierce conflict with the Habsburg Emperors. Until 1552 the Ernestines had the rank of Elector (*Kurfürst*), one of the seven German rulers entitled to elect the Holy Roman Emperor, but they then lost the title to the Albertines, who were known henceforth as Electors of Saxony. The habit of subdivision took root amongst the Ernestines and small pieces of territory were shunted to and fro between different branches of the family. Princes could dispose of their territories like private property. There was a mind-boggling profusion of dukes, with names like Albrecht, Friedrich and Joachim, sometimes qualified with sobriquets like the Good, the Wise, the Steady and the Magnanimous. Many of them were interested in magic and alchemy, but they were also stout supporters of Lutheranism.

The best remembered was probably Johann Casimir, who reigned in Coburg in the late sixteenth century. In 1592 he invited to his court an Italian magician and adventurer, Jeronimo Scotto, who had the reputation of being able to cure childless women of their infertility. The Duke intended him to use his magic on his young Duchess, Anna, who after several years of marriage had failed to produce any offspring. Scotto promptly managed to ingratiate himself with the young Duchess, often neglected by her husband, who preferred to spend his days hunting. The wily Italian not only insinuated himself into her bed, but appropriated her jewellery and then disappeared without trace. Before doing so he had introduced the Duchess to another lover, a young courtier by the name of Ulrich von Lichtenstein. When this affair was discovered by the Duke, he divorced the Duchess and imprisoned her for the rest of her life, another twenty years, in a succession of fortresses, including the castle in Coburg. Lichtenstein remained separately incarcerated for nearly forty years. After the death of the Duke he was pardoned, only to die a few days later. Eighteenth-century dukes still felt compelled to exorcise the ghosts of the lovers, Anna and Ulrich.

In the later eighteenth century the Thuringian duchies had acquired a quite different claim to Europe's attention. They became beacons of the German Enlightenment and havens for the heroes of the classical period of German culture, Goethe and Schiller foremost among them. This transformation owed much to one or two female rulers, who acted as regents for their infant sons. The most famous was Anna Amelia of Weimar-Eisenach, who ruled on behalf of her son Carl August until he reached the age of eighteen in 1775. Anna Amelia had engaged Christoph Martin Wieland, a significant figure in the German literary world, as tutor for her son. One of the first acts of Carl August, when he took over the reins, was to call to his court the young Goethe, then aged twenty-six and already famous as the author of *The Sorrows of Werther*, a seminal text of literary romanticism. Initially Goethe was, with the Duke, one of a group of young men who, regardless of rank, were bent on defying convention by wild behaviour in the romantic mould. Soon, however, he became a principal administrative official in the small duchy and later its chief minister. Schiller, ten years younger than Goethe, was called to the duchy's university in neighbouring Jena and was eventually joined there by Hegel. Thus Weimar-Eisenach harboured some of the most famous stars of German classical literature and philosophy.

Saxe-Coburg, at the southern edge of Thuringia, was not quite in the same league in the cultural stakes. Ducal extravagance had landed it in financial problems, though even Weimar-Eisenach did not have enough money to pay the professorial salaries of Schiller and Hegel. From 1773 Coburg had to submit its finances to the scrutiny of an imperial commission headed by the Duke of Saxe-Gotha-Altenburg, then the most considerable of the Thuringian principalities. Nevertheless, the Coburg dukes were not without cultural pretensions. Albert's grandfather, Franz Friedrich Anton, who ruled as Duke of Coburg from 1800 to 1806, collected etchings, and Gotha, which was later to join Coburg, had one of the finest coin collections in Europe. At any rate the Thuringian princes hung on to their patrimony, unlike the neighbouring Margrave of Ansbach-Bayreuth, who sold his territory to Prussia so that he could live with his mistress, Lady Craven, in London. Even worse was the habit, for which neighbouring Hesse-Cassel was particularly notorious, of selling subjects as soldiers to the perpetually warring larger powers of Europe. In this market Britain, financially more potent than any other power, was an especially active buyer. Hessians filled the ranks of the British armies fighting in North America and elsewhere.

When the avalanche of the French Revolution and the Napoleonic wars overwhelmed Europe, it left the minor German sovereignties like Saxe-Coburg battered like small rowing boats in a storm. Hitherto the Holy Roman Empire had provided some framework of law and legitimacy for their existence, even if no real protection. It now lost all meaning and by 1806 had even as a formality disappeared into the dustbin of history. Rulers like the Thuringian princes had to arrange themselves as best they could with the all-powerful French Emperor, but woe betide them if they were too slow in changing sides, either when he was on his way up or when his power disintegrated in the snows of Russia. Coburg survived the storm more by luck than good management. Besides the link with Russia, there was a link with the Austrian camp: Frederick Josias, the great uncle of Ernst, Albert's father, was an imperial field marshal who had fought in the Turkish wars in the late 1780s and then in the war against revolutionary France.

The small scale of affairs in Coburg itself – the town had only 8500 inhabitants in 1827 and the whole duchy of Saxe-Coburg and Saalfeld only 57,300 in 1812 – meant there were no great social tensions. It was a hierarchical society, but differences of rank counted for less than they did in larger territories. Albert's great-grandfather, Duke Ernst Friedrich, who ruled until 1800, used to sit in the window of the castle in Coburg, the Ehrenburg, and chat to the passers-by, whose names and circumstances were all familiar to him. In turn the inhabitants knew what the Duke liked to eat and sent him his favourite dishes for his birthday or for other feast days. The young Princes and Princesses wore carefully darned clothes and their elders gossiped with the wives of the more prominent citizens. When Albert later, as consort of the mighty English Queen, still believed that dwarf states like Coburg had a right to survive, it was this kind of patriarchal idyll that filled his mind.

Not that the idyll was entirely undisturbed. Albert's grandfather, Franz Friedrich Anton, was induced by the financial difficulties of the duchy to bring in a Prussian administrative official, Kretschmann, as minister to clear up the mess. His drastic measures drove Coburg's placid citizenry to the brink of revolt and in 1803 the Duke had as a pre-caution to borrow a company of dragoons from neighbouring Saxony in case of disorder. There was a miniature constitutional conflict and Kretschmann's dismissal was demanded, but he did not actually leave till 1807. In fact Kretschmann was a moderniser, like other similar, sometimes imported French administrators in minor German states. Some of his proposals diminished the influence which the quasi-feudal bigger landowners had acquired in a traditional society like Coburg and he would have gone further in the direction of the French model of a political system based on individual citizen rights. Soon after Ernst, Albert's father, succeeded to the dukedom in December 1806 he got rid of Kretschmann, for he was keen to run his own show.

By this time Napoleon had defeated the Austrians at Austerlitz in 1805 and Coburg was in process of negotiating its adherence to the Federation of the Rhine, Napoleon's league of German puppet rulers. Then the Prussians were crushed in their turn at Jena in 1806. The tide of war lapped at Coburg's doorstep. A succession of troops, some of them on the Prussian side, some on the French, passed through the duchy demanding billets and provisions. The French occupation became espe-cially onerous, exacting heavy impositions of money and goods. The old imperial Field Marshal Frederick Josias managed to persuade his fellow soldier, Napoleon's Marshal Augereau, once his opponent, not to give over the city of Coburg to plunder. Wars were still fought with a modicum of chivalry. Nevertheless, the citizens of Coburg suffered severely and even the ducal family sometimes had not enough to eat or enough fuel to keep warm. Augusta, the mother of Duke Ernst and the grandmother of Queen Victoria and Prince Albert, travelled to Berlin to intercede with Napoleon personally, but he would not receive her. Her son Ernst was not in the duchy at the moment of his accession, for he had first thrown in his lot with the Prussians and then sought refuge in Russia, where he fell severely ill. In May 1807, when he was already the Duke, he crept secretly back to Coburg and hid in his widowed mother's small castle, but then the situation changed again. Russia and Napoleon became allies at the Peace of Tilsit and Ernst's Russian relations managed to get his restoration as Duke accepted by the French. In July 1807 he entered Coburg as Duke amid great rejoicings.

Ernst now hoped for aggrandisement by grace of Napoleon. He had his eye on the neighbouring Prussian territory of Ansbach-Bayreuth, but Napoleon gave it to Bavaria. Ernst also hoped to assume the title of grand duke, but of the Thuringian princes only Carl August of Weimar-Eisenach achieved such a promotion. To advance his quest Ernst had to spend time in Paris, together with his younger brother Leopold, at the time only sixteen. In the French capital Ernst was more successful in affairs of the heart than in affairs of state. He acquired a mistress, Pauline Panam, a French actress of Greek extraction, known as *La Belle Grecque*, who soon bore him a son. It was the beginning of an ongoing scandal that dogged Ernst for years and was not laid to rest by his many subsequent liaisons. Coburg's quest for aggrandisement in Napoleonic Europe continued and it was often Leopold who was entrusted with the task of pursuing it. He attended the great meeting of princes held under the aegis of Napoleon at Erfurt in 1808 and passed his apprenticeship in dynastic politics.

Coburg's courting of Napoleon had its price: the Coburgers had to supply troops to France for the war in Spain, for the suppression of the rising by their fellow Germans in the Tyrol, and for the campaign in Russia. Many Coburg soldiers met their deaths on distant battlefields, but the duchy got no additional territory out of Napoleon. At least

Ernst changed sides in time when the fortunes of war turned. Not that his subjects were any more delighted by the presence of Allied troops and their demands than they had been by the French. Later it was the German nationalist myth that the German nation had found its identity in rising against Napoleon and France, but the truth was much more chequered. At any rate Ernst was reputed to be on friendly terms with Metternich, who was now the most powerful man in Europe. At the Congress of Vienna Coburg obtained a small additional territory of about twelve square miles, far to the west, near the Saar, the principality of Lichtenberg. It was little more than a consolation prize and was sold to Prussia in 1834. Leopold claimed, in letters to his niece Queen Victoria half a century later, that Coburg was short-changed at Vienna and that he could have got more for Coburg if the Tsar had exerted himself on his behalf. Leopold was also critical of his brother because he did not sufficiently cultivate the Tsar of Russia during the Congress. It cannot have helped that the Prussians had become hostile to Coburg because Duke Ernst had opposed their plans for the complete absorption of the kingdom of Saxony. As it was, Prussia got a large chunk of it.

There were, however, still prizes to be had in the European royal marriage market even for poverty-stricken princely families. There was a network of relationships between the ruling houses of Mecklenburg, Brunswick, Hesse, Anhalt, the Thuringian duchies and other, mainly Protestant families. Some of these ties linked them to the rulers of more considerable powers. The Duke of Saxe-Gotha-Altenburg, who through his aunt was related to the House of Hanover and therefore to the British royal family, was given the Garter in 1792. George III's queen, Charlotte, came from Mecklenburg-Strelitz, the smaller of the two Mecklenburg duchies. Catherine the Great of Russia was a Princess of Anhalt-Zerbst, who reached her eminence by arranging the murder of her husband, Tsar Peter III.

The Coburgs became successful in the marriage market without resorting to such extreme measures. It was Albert's grandmother Augusta who started the Coburg ascent into the first league of European royalty. She came from another small Thuringian territory, Reuss-Ebersdorf, the rulers of which were only counts and therefore not equal in rank to the Coburgs. She became the second wife of Franz

Friedrich Anton. Beggars could not be choosers and Augusta turned out to be a fortunate addition to the Coburg family. She stands out as their first really talented marriage broker. She needed to be, for she had four daughters and three sons to bring to the altar, though when her eldest son Ernst, then Duke of Coburg and future father of Albert, got married in 1816 she wrote in her diary: 'Many an experience of my long life makes my breast contract whenever the nuptial bond is being tied.'[1]

Augusta, who lived from 1757 to 1831, was by all accounts an estimable lady. Her grandchild and goddaughter Queen Victoria described her as a remarkable woman, almost masculine in strength and energy, yet also of great goodness of heart and with an exceptional love of nature. There was a strong Pietist element in her family background and she had very strict moral principles. In 1795 Catherine the Great, in search of a bride for her grandson Grand Duke Constantine, brother of the future Tsars Alexander I and Nicholas I, invited three of Augusta's daughters to St Petersburg. Juliana, the youngest, then only fifteen, was chosen. The marriage was not happy and was eventually dissolved, but the ties to the Russian Court were to prove useful in the turbulent times to come.

Of Augusta's three other daughters the eldest, Sophie, married an Austrian general, Count Mensdorff-Pouilly, and their son Alexander became a diplomat. In 1864, at a crucial moment in the history of the Habsburg Empire, he was the Austrian Foreign Minister who had to deal with Bismarck, then the formidable Prussian Prime Minister. The second daughter, Antoinette, married Duke Alexander of Württemberg, which created another link with St Petersburg; Alexander's sister, the Dowager Tsarina Maria Feodorovna, was the mother of Tsars Alexander I and Nicholas I. Alexander and Antoinette of Württemberg spent many of the years of Napoleon's dominance in Russia. The youngest daughter, Victoria, generally known as Victoire, handed on her name to her daughter by her second marriage to the Duke of Kent and thus gave it to a whole period of history.

Of Augusta's three sons the eldest, Ernst, was the hereditary prince of Coburg and father of Albert. The second son, Ferdinand, married the wealthy Hungarian heiress Countess Antoinette Kohary, who acquired the rank of princess. It was this branch of the family, Coburg-Kohary, that was in the 1830s to provide a King of Portugal and later in the nineteenth century a King of Bulgaria. Augusta's youngest son and her favourite, Leopold, born in 1790, rivalled his mother as a marriage broker. Even though his marriage to Charlotte, the heiress to the British throne, had ended so tragically, he became King of the Belgians in 1831 after refusing the throne of Greece. More than anyone he was responsible for the marriage of his niece Victoria with his nephew Albert and he remained hugely influential in the life of this pair. The Coburg-Kohary branch were Roman Catholics and Leopold became a Catholic when he got the Belgian throne. Not surprisingly this pragmatic approach to religion by the Coburgs added to the suspicion of Albert when he came to England to marry Victoria.

Leopold landed in Brussels only because he was the least objectionable among the potential candidates for the Belgian throne. The Belgians, after winning their independence from the Netherlands in 1830, decided somewhat reluctantly to become a constitutional monarchy rather than a republic. The great powers assembled in conference in London were willing to recognise Belgium's independence, but to have a republic into the bargain would have been too much. They then had to find someone to fill the vacant throne. The Bonapartist candidate would not have been acceptable to Louis-Philippe, just arrived on the throne of France; Louis-Philippe's son was not acceptable to the other great powers, including Britain; nor was an Austrian archduke. Saxe-Coburg-Gotha was the line of least resistance.

When the territorial bargaining at the Congress of Vienna had turned out disappointingly for Coburg, Ernst's thoughts again turned to marriage. It had already proved its worth as a means of survival and advancement for his family and dukedom, even if unnecessary as a means of sexual satisfaction. His more ambitious designs, for example a long-standing plan to marry a Russian grand duchess, had come to nothing. The scandal around his affair with Pauline Panam had become notorious all over Europe and *La Belle Grecque* made every effort to keep it alive and extract what advantage she could from it. The scandal reduced Ernst's chances in the royal marriage market below what his good looks and self-confident demeanour would otherwise have deserved. Nevertheless he still managed to turn his assets to advantage. In 1817 he married Louise of Saxe-Gotha-Altenburg, the wealthiest of the Thuringian principalities. He was thirty-three, she was sixteen. Louise had been born in December 1800 and her mother, a Princess of

Mecklenburg, had died shortly after her birth. Louise turned out to be the last offspring of the Saxe-Gotha-Altenburg branch and one day would have a claim to the territories. By marrying her Ernst put himself in a strong position to take over part of the Altenburg territory when the male line of that branch of the Ernestine dynasty came to an end, as it was expected to do in the not too distant future. This would produce another instalment of musical chairs among the Thuringian duchies. Gotha was a more considerable town than Coburg and a cultural centre of some note. Since 1763 it was the place of publication of the *Almanac de Gotha*, which had become the bible of European aristocracy.

Louise was brought up by a stepmother, her father's second wife. She was Princess Caroline Amelia of Hesse-Cassel and, along with Augusta of Saxe-Coburg, another formidable and much loved matriarch among Victoria and Albert's immediate forebears. She died aged seventy-seven, just when the revolutions of 1848 were shaking all the dynasties of Europe. Her stepdaughter Louise was an attractive, happy and romantically inclined young girl, naïve, starry-eyed and unburdened by too much concern for the world's troubles. She went into the marriage with Ernst of Coburg with all colours flying. She described the early months of her life as Duchess of Coburg in frequent, breathlessly enthusiastic letters to a friend of her youth left behind in Gotha, Augusta von Studnitz. There was a moment of anxiety when Louise was brought face to face with the portrait of the ill-fated Duchess Anna, who had been divorced and incarcerated by her husband, Duke Johann Casimir, two centuries earlier. Could his descendant, Louise's husband Ernst, behave in like manner? 'I grasped the Duke's arm and looked if in his beautiful brown eyes there was any resemblance to his fearsome ancestor', Louise wrote to her friend Augusta.[2] Her older husband probably found Louise boring, but within weeks of their marriage on 31 July 1817 she was pregnant. Augusta, her mother-in-law, made fearful by Princess Charlotte's death in childbirth in the same November, prayed that the young Duchess, suddenly transported from carefree girlhood into prospective motherhood, would survive the ordeal. 'Almighty', she prayed, 'you gave me a new daughter this year, preserve her in this painful time through which she must pass in a few months.' Louise's first son, the future Duke Ernst II of Saxe-Coburg-Gotha, was born on 21 June 1818. After little over a year, on 26 August 1819, there followed a second son, Albert, the future Prince Consort. His mother was still only eighteen. His father, the Duke, resumed his amorous exploits after, and perhaps even before, his wife had thus borne him two male heirs in swift succession. On the other hand, motherhood slowed Louise only temporarily and, when she had done her duty in that respect, her husband's neglect made her look elsewhere for amusement.

She must by this time have been aware of Ernst's involvement with Pauline Panam. *La Belle Grecque* constantly threatened to tell all and her son by Ernst went around calling himself Prince of Coburg. Panam appealed to Metternich and to her brother-out-of-law the Grand Duke Constantine. Her other brother-out-of-law Leopold tried to buy her off. Panam's memoirs, a blatant attempt at blackmail, appeared in French and English in 1823 and even Ernst's fellow-Thuringian Duke Carl August of Saxe-Weimar and his chief minister Goethe were unwilling to suppress the book. Carl August wrote about Ernst's scandalous behaviour: 'Coburg's private history deserves that the Ernestine family get together to bury the hero of this drama in the dungeon of a fortress. It is terrible that certain people can go unpunished, because the Holy Alliance protects them. One would not invite a private person, besmirched with such a history, to any dinner table.' When it came to the Last Judgement, the demagogues would be able to find excuses for their misdeeds, but were not the princes themselves 'the true Jacobins', he asked.[3]

If Louise felt that her husband's infidelities made her free to engage in her own, she was mistaken. Sauce for the gander was not sauce for the goose and the double standard was still firmly entrenched. How far her various flirtations went is impossible to tell. Much later the anti-Semitic rumour was put into circulation that Albert, who looked and behaved so very differently from his elder brother Ernst, was really the son of Baron von Mayern, a chamberlain of Jewish origin in the Coburg ducal household. This seems unlikely, for Louise had probably not yet begun to stray when she became pregnant with her second child at the end of 1818. A few years later she undoubtedly got seriously involved with a young officer, Alexander von Hanstein, whom she eventually married after her divorce from Ernst. Initially, in 1824, there was only a separation, for Ernst had to step carefully if he was to secure his share of the Saxe-Gotha-Altenburg territories, the original reason for his marriage to Louise. Ernst in his letter to Louise proposing the separation painted himself as the wronged husband with sickening hypocrisy.

It was a view not shared by his subjects, who gathered at the castle of Rosenau to give her a rousing send-off. By the time she reached Coburg a large crowd had collected and to calm them the Duke had to appear with Louise on the balcony of the Ehrenburg. Ernst complained about these goings-on to Metternich and appealed to the solidarity of the Holy Alliance against revolutionary agitation. The Austrian Chancellor, who knew a thing or two about marital shenanigans in high places, remained unmoved. The Coburgers may well have remembered the treatment that Ernst's ancestor Johann Casimir had meted out to his Duchess and felt that Louise was similarly hard done by. Nevertheless the separation went ahead and Louise was exiled to the small principality of Lichtenberg, which Coburg had acquired at the Congress of Vienna. In 1826 the eccentric and enfeebled Duke of Saxe-Gotha-Altenburg died childless. In the resulting redistribution of the Ernestine territories, chaired by the King of Saxony, Coburg obtained Gotha, giving up the much less important Saalfeld. Ernst now ruled Gotha in personal union with Coburg and the duchy became known as Saxe-Coburg-Gotha. Now it was safe to divorce Louise. She married Hanstein, who in the meantime had been made Count Poelzig. After leaving Coburg in 1824 she never saw her children again. She died of cancer in 1831, aged only thirty.

There was only one occasion in later life when his mother impinged on Albert and it was bizarre. In 1846 his attention was drawn to the neglected state of his mother's grave. Then his brother, now Duke of Coburg, told him that the church in the Palatinate where she was buried was about to collapse and that the villagers wanted to rebury her coffin in the churchyard. The choice was either to leave the matter to her second husband, Count Poelzig, who had meanwhile remarried, or do something about it. Two officials were despatched from Coburg to receive a container holding her mortal remains. They then interred it at dead of night in the ducal vault in Coburg. They had to swear that they never left the container during its transfer. Count Poelzig was expressly forbidden to be present and Louise, who would have preferred to be buried near him, came to rest in the bosom of the Coburg family.

3

Albert

It is hard to imagine a more dysfunctional family background than that experienced by Albert as a child. Louise, although she described in glowing terms the beauty and charm of her babies, especially Albert, was not an attentive mother. In her last extant letter to her friend Augusta she wrote: 'Most painful of all was parting from my children. They have the whooping cough and say "Mama cries, because she must go, since we are ill". The poor little mice, God bless them.'[1] Albert was scarcely five when she left for good. Duke Ernst was, needless to say, a distant father, though he had the boys round to breakfast fairly often and devoted considerable efforts to having them well brought up and educated. In 1831 Ernst married again: his niece, the daughter of his elder sister Antoinette of Württemberg, who was fifteen years his junior. She hardly inspired affection in her two stepsons, but in his letters to her Albert adopted the dutiful tone that also marked his correspondence with his father. Few of these circumstances of a childhood dire and deprived in its most vital relationships emerge at all clearly from the largely hagiographical account of the Prince Consort's life later written at the command of his widow. Biography in the pre-Freudian age did not dwell on such unpleasant and damaging facts.

Contradictory remarks by the Prince in later life are recorded. On the one hand, the Queen says that he talked with love and sorrow of his mother, was deeply moved when reading about her illness and death, and spoke of his childhood as the happiest time of his life. Perhaps one would expect such an account from Victoria. On the other hand, Vicky, Albert's eldest and favourite child, later the Empress Frederick of Germany, reported him as saying that he could not bear to remember his childhood: that he was so unhappy and miserable and wished himself removed from this world. Perhaps there is no contradiction between these two accounts and both shed light on

Albert's personality. His inability to relax in public and tendency to suppress his feelings, paired with the need for strong affection and closeness with his family, show how much he needed the anchor in life of which he was deprived in his childhood. His inability to relate to women outside his immediate circle and his pervasive fear of scandal and sexual licence were very obviously the consequence of his early experiences. It is puzzling that his brother Ernst shared almost none of these characteristics, even though the two were hardly ever apart until they left university.

Even before Louise disappeared from the lives of her two sons, their education was in 1823 entrusted to a twenty-five-year-old tutor, Christoph Florschütz. He had up to then been employed by the Duke's elder sister, Sophie, Countess Mensdorff-Pouilly, for her sons Arthur and Alexander, later the Austrian Foreign Minister. The Duke may well have wanted to remove his boys from the influence of their mother at a time when the marriage was on the rocks. Florschütz was recommended by Dr Christian Stockmar, by this time the *éminence grise* of the House of Coburg, and shared some of his outlook. Stockmar, later ennobled, came from an affluent family, who owned a small estate. They had come to Saxony in the wake of Gustavus Adolphus, the Swedish King, during the Thirty Years' War. Stockmar, who was born in Coburg in 1787, studied medicine, but the turbulence of the revolutionary period had prevented him from carrying his studies as far as he would have wished. He entered the medical practice of his uncle in Coburg and soon acquired an excellent reputation. The old Field Marshal Frederick Josias was a patient and Stockmar was thus known to the ducal family. When Leopold moved to England in 1816 to marry Princess Charlotte he offered Stockmar the position of his court physician, which the latter accepted. Henceforth he was inextricably linked to Leopold as an indispensable adviser and go-between. Charlotte called him 'Stocky'. Stockmar knew exactly how to exercise influence across broad swathes of the European dynastic scene without exposing himself to attention and attack. He was, in terms of the first half of the nineteenth century, a liberal, whose ideal was the establishment of constitutional government more or less along the English model. He was also a German patriot, who passionately desired a more unified constitutional Germany, capable of moving out of the stultifying repression imposed by Austria under Metternich. He placed his hope in Prussia, but it rarely came up to scratch under Frederick William III or Frederick William IV.

One can hardly avoid the conclusion that Stockmar was busy sawing off the branch on which he was sitting. His influence came from a small principality, monarchically governed, which was just the kind of set-up that would have to be transcended if his ideals were to be realised. What Stockmar regarded as constitutional monarchy was, however, hardly what most of English public opinion perceived it to be in the middle of the nineteenth century. He was by nature authoritarian and was acutely uncomfortable with the hurly-burly of parliamentary politics, the clash of parties and the unrestrained criticism of a free press. This discomfort also afflicted those who relied on his advice. The extent to which Albert came to depend on his counsel can hardly be overestimated. The position which Albert carved for himself in England, not least with the help of Stockmar, gave both of them the chance to operate on the grander scale denied to them in their native country. Stockmar was a great moraliser and his innumerable admonitory letters and memoranda sound a note alien to the modern ear, but most of the royal personages to whom they were addressed found them quite acceptable. Florschütz, in charge of Princes Ernst and Albert for some fifteen years, was a lesser and slightly younger edition of Stockmar. He had the position of counsellor in Coburg and was therefore referred to as *Rath*. He was not one to step out of line.

The education which Ernst and Albert received under the tutelage of Florschütz was wide-ranging. Besides the usual classroom subjects, it included a good deal of travel round the courts of Europe and a stay of ten months in Brussels in 1836 and 1837. Their Uncle Leopold kept an eye on them, although they lived in a separate house with Florschütz and a retired colonel as major domo. In addition to their normal subjects, language, history and so on, their uncle had them instructed by a famous mathematician and physicist. Belgium was one of the most advanced countries in Europe and the Princes got a first-hand impression of the workings of a constitutional monarchy at the head of an open society, though Leopold ran a much more authoritarian system than would have been tolerated across the Channel. In April 1837 the Princes with their household moved to the University of Bonn.

The choice was not easy and much advice was taken. Berlin was too Prussian and also too full of distractions; Vienna was too multi-ethnic. Bonn, although in Prussian territory since 1815, was at least in the Catholic Rhineland.

The Princes attended lectures by August Wilhelm Schlegel, well known for his translation of Shakespeare, which has become a German classic; by Fichte, the son of the famous philosopher; and by Bethmann-Hollweg, the grandfather of the German Chancellor in 1914. One can categorise Fichte and Bethmann Hollweg, teachers of law, as conservative reformers. Ernst and Albert were also brought up against current political issues in Germany. In Hanover the reactionary King, Victoria's uncle the Duke of Cumberland, had suspended the relatively liberal constitution brought in when William IV was still King of Hanover. Seven liberal professors at Göttingen protested against this suspension, were deprived of their chairs and became heroes to all liberals. On the Princes' doorstep at Bonn, there was the arrest by the Prussian authorities of the Catholic Archbishop of Cologne, because of his opposition to mixed marriages between Protestants and Catholics. Most German students at this time were passionately opposed to the repressive policies of the Holy Alliance and the German Confederation led by Austria under Metternich. Initially the Princes faced some hostility from their fellow students, because of their privileged status, but soon they were perceived to be in solidarity with their peers. Occasionally their father became alarmed that they were becoming infected with liberalism, but such reactionary alarm received no encouragement from their uncle in Brussels, who was paying a part of their expenses.

After Bonn the two Princes had, for the first time in their lives, to go their separate ways. Ernst had to be prepared for his future as reigning duke. Albert went on the grand tour of Italy, accompanied by Stockmar. Significantly Sir Francis Seymour, later Lord Hertford, joined the party in Florence, to polish up the Prince's English. It was probably during this tour, which began in December 1838, that Albert's dependency on Stockmar was really established. Youthful exuberance was none too evident in Albert's make-up and Stockmar impressed upon him more than ever the seriousness of life. Albert was not deeply interested in politics, rarely read the newspapers, something that disturbed Stockmar, but as a second son he did not expect to play a political role. He was, however, passionately interested in art and his Italian tour added much to his knowledge. He was a gifted amateur musician and his compositions, while giving no evidence of genius, can still be enjoyed. There were, however, few career prospects for a minor German prince other than marriage.

During his Italian tour Albert must have been aware of plans that he might marry his cousin Victoria, the Queen of England. In the 1820s it had become increasingly likely that Alexandrina Victoria, the child in Kensington Palace, would eventually inherit the British Crown. Even before the young Princess reached the age of puberty speculation was rife about a future husband for her. Some of it was plainly absurd, for instance that she would marry her cousin George, son of the widely abominated Duke of Cumberland and future King of Hanover. Even more absurd was the rumour that appeared at one time in the French press that she might marry her uncle Leopold, nearly thirty years her senior, a marriage expressly forbidden by the Church of England's Table of Kindred and Affinity. Leaving aside such outlandish suggestions, there were plenty of available princes in the Protestant royal families of Europe, and even a connection with the Orleanist branch of the French royal house could not be excluded. The thought of another Coburg connection was, however, never far from the minds of Victoria's mother and her brother Leopold. It was Leopold himself, who through his marriage to Princess Charlotte, the previous heiress to the British Crown, had begun the connection, only to see it tragically ended by Charlotte's death in childbirth. It had revived with his sister's marriage to the Duke of Kent and the birth of Victoria.

On his return from Italy, in June 1839, aged nearly twenty, Albert was well-educated and cultivated, a good deal more so than his slightly older cousin who had already been Queen of England for two years. But Albert was entirely educated as a German, whereas the Queen shared many of the attitudes and instincts of her subjects. Leopold and Stockmar had to step very gingerly in pursuing the project of a marriage between Albert and Victoria. In 1836 Albert had first met Victoria, then seventeen and the heiress presumptive to the British Crown, when he and his brother spent four weeks at Windsor. Victoria took pleasure in the company of her cousins, found Albert especially pleasing in appearance and character, but that is as far as it went. Albert's enthusiasm for his cousin was even more restrained. He must have sensed that the pleasure-seeking young girl was hardly a soulmate. She loved balls and entertainments, while Albert could scarcely stay awake. William IV was furious that the Coburg Princes had been invited at all and had also invited the Prince of Orange, son of the prince who had once been intended for Charlotte before Leopold married her. One Coburg connection, the Duchess of Kent, was more than enough for the King. Once he met him, however, he found Albert a very pleasant young man. After the Coburg Princes left Victoria wrote to her dear Uncle Leopold thanking him profusely 'for the prospect of great happiness you have contributed to give me, in the person of dear Albert', but marriage was hardly on the cards at this stage. There was no follow-up to the 1836 visit. Once Victoria was on the throne, marriage was, at least in the short run, far from her mind and she much disliked any sign of match-making.

Nevertheless, Leopold in Brussels was pushing on his plans for the marriage with Victoria and had a long talk about it with Albert during a visit by the Prince in Brussels in April 1838. It is difficult to be certain whether this was the first time that Albert heard about the plan of a marriage with his cousin Victoria, or whether he was aware of it before. His uncle Leopold made no bones about the uncertainties and difficulties that the project might entail for his nephew. If eventually the marriage failed to take place, Albert would have been left a very minor German prince with no prospects. At this time Leopold may well have been disenchanted with his position at the head of a minor kingdom. Greville reports his brother writing to him from Brussels in May 1838: 'Leopold is deadly sick of his Belgian crown, and impatient to abdicate, thinking that it is a better thing to be an English Prince, with £50,000 a year, than to be monarch of a troublesome vulgar little kingdom which all its neighbours regard with an evil or a covetous eye.'[2] What Leopold might no longer be able to achieve for himself he could instead hope to obtain vicariously through his nephew Albert.

It was only in the autumn of 1839 that a fresh move could be made, when Victoria's enjoyment of her role had been soured somewhat by the crises swirling round her earlier in the year. On 12 July she had still written in her diary that too many of her relations had already paid visits. She told Melbourne that Ernst and Albert were coming, but that she took no pleasure in seeing Albert and did not want to be pressed for a decision. These reservations flew quickly out of the window when she saw him. When he appeared pale after a stormy Channel crossing at the bottom of the staircase at which she was waiting to receive him, she fell in love. Within five days of his arrival she had decided to become engaged. Even Melbourne, who had much to lose by the Queen's marriage, had advised against delay. No man could propose to the Queen of England, so normal procedures had to be reversed. A note from her summoned him to her closet. A squeeze of the hand on going to bed the night before had assured her of his positive response. The conversation, in German, was at first self-conscious, but soon, as she wrote in her journal, they embraced over and over again.

> Oh! to *feel* I was, and am loved by such an *Angel* as Albert was *too great a delight to describe!* He is *perfection*; perfection in every way – in beauty – in everything! I told him I was quite unworthy of him and kissed his dear hand – he said he would be very happy '*das Leben mit dir zu zubringen*' and was so kind and seemed so happy, that I really felt it was the happiest brightest moment of my life, which made up for all I had suffered and endured. Oh! *how* I adore and love him, I cannot say!![3]

Albert, buttoned up as he was, reciprocated in more restrained mode, but even he wrote to her in German after their engagement: 'Dear little one, I love you so much that I can't say how'.[4] He dedicated the rest of his life to her with single-minded devotion. It was genuine enough, but Albert's whole persona was so shot through with duty and conscience that these motivations could never be shut out. It was his duty as a member of the Coburg family to marry Victoria, the biggest prize on the royal marriage market, and it was his duty to fall in love with her and all of this he duly did. He did not expect a bed of roses. The Duchess of Bedford thought at the time 'she is excessively in love with him', he 'not a bit with her'. It was not true, but Albert was a very different character from the emotional and impulsive young girl to whom he had now committed himself.

The difficulties of his position became apparent straightaway. There had been no Consort of a Queen Regnant since Queen Anne and her husband Prince George of Denmark. The arrival of yet another Prince from a small German state, to be maintained by the British taxpayer in the state to which royal personages were accustomed, was hardly

likely to be greeted with enthusiasm. The size of his civil list caused
predictable controversy. The vote of £50,000 to Leopold on his marriage to Charlotte, which he had only given up when he moved to
Brussels in 1831, still rankled, and a motion to give Albert the same
amount was defeated in the Commons. He got only £30,000. The Royal
Dukes, especially Cumberland, the King of Hanover, fought bitterly
and for the time being successfully against conceding Albert official
precedence. Nothing agitated royalty and courtiers more than questions
of precedence. Victoria had to use her royal discretion to give her
husband a place at her side, but her wish to make him King Consort
met with total resistance. 'For God's sake, let's hear no more of it,
ma'am', said Melbourne, 'for if you once get the English people in the
way of making kings, you will get them in the way of unmaking them.'[5]
So he remained a Prince of Saxe-Coburg-Gotha. There was no great
sympathy for the Coburgs, who could consider themselves lucky to
have got as much as they did, but there was even less for the hated
Cumberland, now the reactionary King Ernst of Hanover. Greville, a
Whig, thought the Tories were making a great mistake in taking sides
with the King of Hanover.

Much against his will, Albert had Melbourne's private secretary,
George Anson, foisted upon him as his own secretary and as such his
closest and most important adviser in his role as the Queen's husband.
Anson was of necessity a Whig, a member of the Lichfield clan and part
of Melbourne's inner circle. Stockmar was telling Albert that the court
had to become more politically neutral if a repetition of the Bedchamber crisis was to be avoided and taking over the Whig Prime Minister's
confidential secretary was hardly the way to do it. Victoria was still a
strong Whig partisan and put down to the wicked Tories all the failures
to grant her beloved Albert what was due to him. Albert had in fact
become a political football and the Tories were through him taking their
revenge on the Queen for the way she had treated them. Furious as she
was about the ignominy heaped upon her chosen, a certain tetchiness
crept into the correspondence between the betrothed couple. Albert
asked her to take pity on him:

> Think of my position, dearest Victoria: I am leaving my homeland with all
> friends, all old habits, all trusted beings, and am going to a country in which

everything is new and strange to me, people, language, customs, life styles, position! Apart from you, most dearest beloved, I have no one in whom I can confide; am I not allowed to have my confidants for those two or three persons who will deal with my private affairs?[6]

Uncharacteristically Victoria baulked at having to tell Albert directly that he had to accept Anson as his secretary. Much depended on Melbourne, but the Prime Minister was not inclined to overexert himself on behalf of a man who was soon to supersede him in the counsels of the Queen.

The marriage ceremony itself, on Monday 10 February 1840, occasioned a great deal of controversy and evoked much criticism and satire. The Queen was still so incensed with the behaviour of the Tories towards Albert she did not want to invite any of them to the service in the Chapel Royal. She was with difficulty persuaded to invite the Duke of Wellington, for had she failed to do so there would have been rioting. Satire homed in on the fact that the usual roles were reversed in that the Queen had had to propose to her husband and that she had had to announce her intentions to her Privy Council:

> But Queens have self-possession which defies
> Eve'n blushing cheeks and tear-besprinkled eyes.
> Down comes our maiden monarch in full state
> To tell her nobles of her happy state
>
> Paints her anticipations with a smile,
> Heedless of Melbourne leering all the while,
> Hopes the consummation may be soon,
> And prays with rapture for the honeymoon.[7]

Contrary to Albert's expectations and to the customs of the time, Victoria allowed only a few days for the honeymoon and it was to be spent at Windsor. She had to be back in London, so she claimed, when Parliament was sitting. As it was, the couple were up early on the Tuesday morning after the wedding. 'Strange that a bridal night should be so short', wrote Greville in his diary, 'and I told Lady Palmerston that this was not the way to provide us with a Prince of Wales.' They need not have worried. The Queen was a virgin on her wedding night, and Albert may well have been, but Victoria was ecstatic the next morning. In a scribbled note to Melbourne she called it a 'most gratifying and bewildering night'. The fecundity of the royal couple soon became the butt of jokes.

To begin with there can have been few in his new country who did not believe that it was a piece of great and scarcely deserved good fortune for an obscure German prince to have gained the hand of the Queen of the greatest, wealthiest and most powerful empire on earth. From his point of view he had successfully done what he owed to himself and to his family, as Leopold, Stockmar and others never tired of telling him, but he was sacrificing a lot. The deprivations of his childhood had made him more than normally dependent upon his wider family and his surroundings, the landscape he loved and the homes like Rosenau, to which he was deeply attached. Now he was being translated to a much grander environment, but it was an alien or even a positively hostile one. Those with whom he came into immediate contact were the members of the British aristocracy who populated the Court, the political sphere and Society. They had little time for him and he had little respect for them, at least until personal acquaintance persuaded both sides otherwise. Many of them came from families much grander and wealthier than his. They could hardly forget that some of their ancestors had installed another minor German prince on the British throne for their own convenience. Albert was also so very German, pedantic, humourless, and not afraid of showing that he was interested in things of the mind and that he valued education. He regarded them as idle dilettantes. His high but isolated position reinforced his natural reserve. He was afraid that any unpremeditated remark of his would make the rounds and be used against him. Albert's arrival was no more popular among the people at large, where it often reinforced an existing anti-monarchism. A satire of 1840, *The German Bridegroom*, had it thus:

> He comes the bridegroom of Victoria's choice,
> The nominee of Lehzen's vulgar voice;
> He comes to take 'for better or for worse'
> England's fat Queen and England's fatter purse.[8]

When Albert arrived Melbourne's influence was still undiminished and it did not occur to the Queen that her husband, intensely as she loved him, had any political role to play. Most of those around her and in the country at large were of the same opinion. She was pleased that he helped her with the blotting paper when she signed documents, but when he asked her anything about politics she became evasive and changed the subject, not least because she wanted to avoid any dis-agreement with him. She had become very possessive of him and did not want to share him with men who might talk politics to him.

Within two months of the wedding it was confirmed that Victoria was pregnant, much to her disgust. She hated the reproductive aspect of the female role. When she found herself pregnant it may well have been the first occasion when she vented her spleen upon him, as she was to do many times later on. But now she needed his help and gradually he managed to find a role, most importantly in politics, but also in many other spheres. At the request of the Queen, Albert was given his own key to the red boxes in which Cabinet papers were conveyed. It was not long before he appeared at the side of the Queen at ministerial audiences and she used 'we' where previously she had said 'I'.

Albert's first major political move was that he prepared the way, in the spring of 1841, for a smooth take-over of government by the Tories. It had become obvious by then that an election could not be delayed for very long and that it would end the reign of the Whigs. If an even more serious repetition of the Bedchamber Crisis was to be avoided, Peel, the Tory leader, had to be informed that he would not face the obstacles from the Queen that he had encountered two years earlier. All this was discreetly done, without Victoria, who was again pregnant, being informed. Albert was greatly helped by Anson, his private secretary, who had become totally loyal to him. In the private sphere another milestone was passed when in January 1842 Albert managed to secure the dismissal of Lehzen. She had fought with bitter determination to retain her infl-uence over the Queen and the royal household, and she was also a fierce Whig partisan. She controlled the Queen's private finances. It was said that when a minister had audience of the Queen she disappeared through a door and re-entered as soon as the minister was gone. Albert lost his usual reticence in talking about her – she was 'a domestic dragon spitting fire'. When she got jaundice, he called her 'the yellow lady'.

Vicky, the couple's first child, was born on 21 November 1840. When she was just over a year old, she became very ill, Albert blamed Lehzen, who also supervised the nursery, for the way she was being treated and there was a terrible explosion between him and Victoria. The Queen was still suffering from post-natal depression after the birth, within less than a year of his elder sister, of Albert Edward, the Prince of Wales, and became hysterical. Albert and Victoria communicated with each other only in writing for several days and Stockmar had to become the peace-maker. At this time Stockmar had private apartments both at Windsor and in Buckingham Palace. Victoria recovered her composure and saw that she had to choose between Albert and Lehzen. When such explo-sions occurred between the Queen and the Prince, as they did not infrequently over the years, they always ended in mutual contrition. These outbursts were alarming, not only to the Prince, for they reminded people around the Court of similar eruptions by George III and George IV. There were fears that Victoria might succumb to mad-ness, like her grandfather. The Baroness was sent packing by Albert, while the Queen looked the other way. When Victoria was told that Lehzen would for reasons of health leave in two months' time she exploded once more, but soon saw reason and avoided a personal farewell. Lehzen lived for nearly another thirty years in her native Hanover, where she was visited once or twice by the Queen.

With both Melbourne and Lehzen gone, Albert was to a considerable extent able to mould the Queen in his own image. She had been a gay young girl who enjoyed being Queen as well as queen of the ball, but no longer. The role of the monarch at the head of London Society was, because of the couple's growing young family, limited to essentials. In her single days Victoria had not allowed politics to preoccupy her unduly, but now the royal couple together exercised all the considerable political prerogatives of the Crown with meticulous attention. It was a new mix not entirely to the liking of the aristocratic political establish-ment, particularly the Whigs. They would rather have had a monarch providing lots of balls and levees, while leaving politics to them. It was not just the doing of Albert, for Albert and Victoria's was a genuine partnership. He was meticulous in doing everything in her name, and she had to correct his English. She had an instinctive feel for what was acceptable to the British public, while he never really came to terms with many aspects of the British, or English, national character.

Charles Greville, whose intimate knowledge of what went on began to atrophy when Peel's Tory Government took office August 1841, was not fully aware how far Albert had become identified with the Queen when the ministerial crisis of December 1845 occurred, which eventually led to Peel's downfall. Greville then wrote in his diary:

> The Prince is become so identified with the Queen that they are one person, and as he likes business, it is obvious that while she has the title he is really discharging the functions of the Sovereign. He is King to all intents and purposes. I am not surprised at this, but certainly was not aware that it had taken such definite shape.[9]

The balance of power in a marriage is always difficult to assess from the outside and is always shifting. This was, moreover, a most unusual marriage in reversing the normal order of things between husband and wife in nineteenth-century households. The Queen was the public figure on whom a great weight of real and symbolic expectation rested and in this respect the Prince was, at any rate to begin with, an interloper. Victoria was, moreover, a very strong, self-willed character, quite unable to compromise on the emotions and prejudices that governed her. When her notorious temper flared up even Albert could do little but beat at least a temporary retreat. But in the daily life of the royal family the Prince was expected to fulfil the normal role of a Victorian husband as the master of the house. The conflict with Lehzen arose from the fact that she challenged him in that particular role and ultimately she could not win. He did what he could to establish his masculine role. 'Do not think I lead a submissive life', he wrote to his brother in the early months of marriage, 'On the contrary, here, where the lawful position of the man is so [great], I have formed a prize life for myself [the German *Preisleben* means an excellent life].'[10] Once, when he was at a Royal Academy dinner, Victoria sent him a succession of messengers commanding his immediate return to the Palace, but he remained at the dinner for the rest of the evening. Assertions of her authority as the Sovereign even in her relations with her husband occurred from time to time, but in general the Queen expected him to be the master in the house. Her letters and journals are full of talk about the weak and dependent state of women, including herself, and the need of a man to lean upon. Intellectually he was very clearly her master. She was no fool, but she had nothing like as broad an education as he had had and above all she lacked the great and wide-ranging intellectual energy that was his hallmark. One could hardly expect it of her, when she was giving birth to seven children in the first ten years of their marriage and was at the mercy of her hormones. Contraception, rudimentary in any case, was frowned upon for religious reasons. The Queen, like most upper-class women, used wet nurses, when breast-feeding, as is now known, would have reduced fertility.

Albert's one great weakness, that he was an alien, became gradually less of handicap as he began to learn a great deal about his new country. From his exceptional vantage point he gained an insight into the mysteries of government and a knowledge of how to pull the levers to make things happen. Nevertheless, the country was not entirely pleased when it gradually woke up to the fact that it had virtually acquired a new King and it had not entirely come to terms with it even after twenty years. There never ceased to be, in many eyes, something illegitimate about the fact that a Coburger and German could hold such a position. Newspapers, pamphlets, printed images, which could now be produced in large editions relatively cheaply, made public figures familiar to an ever larger number of people. They constituted the national public sphere and nothing appeared in it as frequently as the Queen and her family. It was this national sphere, and not least the dominant place of the monarchy within it, that gave a new dimension to the cohesion of the nation. The existence of an international dynastic brotherhood, of which Albert was clearly a member, did not fit easily into these developments. Albert was thus both a relic of the past and a harbinger of the future. In the globalised societies of the twenty-first century there are many whose identities are not tied to one nationality, just as there were in the Europe of the *ancien régime*. Albert, so close to the throne and yet an alien, always remained a subject of suspicion and an irritant. But, as so often happens in England, once the nation grew accustomed to him as a fixture, he gained increasing acceptance and growing respect, especially from those who came into direct contact with him.

4

Queen and Consort

The accession of Victoria in 1837 had marked a sea change in the role of
the monarchy. The tawdry sleaziness of the Hanoverian kings seemed to
have been relegated to the past. But it was neither politically nor socially
a really new beginning. The key role played by Melbourne, an archetypal
figure of the old regime, showed clearly that there was a great deal of
continuity. His short-lived resignation in 1839 illustrated that, if there
had to be a change in political habits, the need was not yet recognised.
The real change of gear came with Victoria's marriage and the arrival of
Albert as her partner in steering the ship of monarchy. When she was
pregnant, it became clear that the Queen needed the assistance of her
husband in the transaction of business. In spite of her reluctance to dis-
cuss politics with her husband, Melbourne wisely encouraged her to let
Albert see the Foreign Office despatches submitted to her. He probably
calculated that it was better to divert Albert's energies from domestic
affairs and that, when he, Melbourne, eventually ceased to be Prime
Minister, his successor might find the Prince's influence an obstacle.

In any case the resultant increase in correspondence would be for
Palmerston, his Foreign Secretary and also his brother-in-law, to deal
with. Indeed quite a different tone immediately entered into the communications between the Queen and Palmerston. Previously the Queen
had written to Palmerston like a young girl accepting the superior wisdom of an elderly uncle, occasionally asking almost apologetically for an
explanation of something she did not quite understand. Sometimes she
was equally apologetic when she could not deal with papers quite as
promptly as was expected. Now, with Albert in the driving seat, there
were lengthy and substantial memoranda, putting a definite point of
view, which sometimes questioned the minister's policy. Now there
were no apologies, only an insistence to be informed and to be heard.
Albert and Palmerston were both moderate liberals, who believed that

continental Europe had to move gradually to constitutional government, more or less on the British model, if further violent upheavals
were to be avoided. Agreement on such general fundamentals was, however, more than counterbalanced by sharp differences on many specific
issues and a great contrast in temperament and character. Palmerston
was in his late fifties, Albert in his early twenties. The older man had
been a Regency buck in his youth and would by now have been regarded
as an elderly roué, had he not been so pivotal a personality for his
period. His free and easy ways could never be Albert's. The Foreign
Secretary had for many years determined the policy of a superpower.
He thought in terms of national interest and the balance of power on a
continental scale. Albert had only recently left a diminutive German
state where the only guiding principle was how to survive in very stormy
waters. Palmerston remained undisturbed if his policy of encouraging
moves towards constitutional government forced rulers in Germany or
Italy to change course or toppled them. As a prominent figure in British
politics, Palmerston had every incentive to court the liberal middle
classes and even the radicals. Albert, on the other hand, was acutely
sensitive to anything that might end the independent existence of his
beloved Coburg or endanger the thrones of his numerous relatives
round Europe.

On the Continent Palmerston had, during his almost uninterrupted
tenure of the Foreign Office from 1830 to 1841, acquired the reputation
of actively encouraging revolution and making the position of rulers
committed to the status quo increasingly difficult. Metternich, the
Austrian Chancellor, symbolised stability to some, repression to others;
Palmerston was feared as a revolutionary by those committed to the
established order and applauded as a harbinger of liberty by those desir-
ing its overthrow. There was a saying in Germany that 'if the Devil has
a son, his name is surely Palmerston'. Such was the fear and hatred
inspired by Palmerston's moderate encouragement of constitutionalism
in Courts where fear of revolution swamped all other considerations.
These sentiments were very familiar to the British royal couple from
their many relatives, particularly in Germany. The expectation of their
extended family on the Continent was that the powerful English Queen,
with Albert at her side, would do something to stop British policy from
giving aid and comfort to those bent on overthrowing their thrones.

From his copious output on foreign policy, it soon becomes apparent that Albert was only too aware how fine a line British policy-makers had to tread. Metternich's Austria was maintaining a position both in Italy and Germany that was very brittle and Albert was not alone in coming to feel that Palmerston was making Vienna's task almost impossible. Others in the foreign service, for example William Lamb, Melbourne's brother and Palmerston's brother-in-law, who during many crucial years was the British Ambassador in Vienna, felt the same. Support for moderate liberalism and constitutionalism might be the best way of avoiding a revolutionary explosion, but it was by its very nature likely to undermine the status quo as settled in 1815 at the Congress of Vienna.

The major issue of the moment, in 1840, was the tension that had arisen with France over Mehemet Ali, the ruler of Egypt. As the Egyptian Viceroy Mehemet was in conflict with his nominal sovereign, the Sultan. Palmerston's policy was designed to thwart French designs to make Egypt a satellite, without giving Russia too much influence at Constantinople. Over Mehemet Ali Britain and France were pitted against each other, when for most of the 1830s they had been ideological allies as the two liberal great powers of Europe. The management of this crisis is generally considered one of Palmerston's more successful ventures, but he was now as suspect in France as he was in the reactionary Courts of Europe. Albert and Victoria had, through King Leopold's wife, close links with the Court of Louis-Philippe, the French King. The British royal couple was clearly afraid that too blatant a setback for France would encourage the war party in Paris and plunge that country into another wave of revolution. If France was too severely thwarted, so the argument went, then the revolutionary temper would rise again among the French people, the Orleanist monarchy of Louis-Philippe might be overthrown, and all Europe would regret it.

All this was alarming to Albert and to his Coburg and other relations. He was much influenced by the strong anti-French feeling in Germany, where it was feared that another French invasion on the Rhine would be precipitated. For all the liberal and German patriotic sentiments inculcated in him by Stockmar and by his education, fear of revolution was deeply engrained in the minds of a minor princely family like the Coburgs. A kind of 'not rocking the boat' mentality became very characteristic of the royal couple's attitude to European politics.

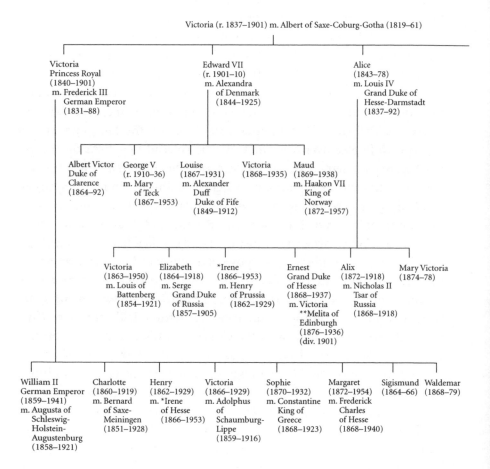

Victoria (r. 1837–1901) m. Albert of Saxe-Coburg-Gotha (1819–61)

Victoria
Princess Royal
(1840–1901)
m. Frederick III
German Emperor
(1831–88)

Edward VII
(r. 1901–10)
m. Alexandra
of Denmark
(1844–1925)

Alice
(1843–78)
m. Louis IV
Grand Duke of
Hesse-Darmstadt
(1837–92)

Albert Victor
Duke of
Clarence
(1864–92)

George V
(r. 1910–36)
m. Mary
of Teck
(1867–1953)

Louise
(1867–1931)
m. Alexander
Duff
Duke of Fife
(1849–1912)

Victoria
(1868–1935)

Maud
(1869–1938)
m. Haakon VII
King of
Norway
(1872–1957)

Victoria
(1863–1950)
m. Louis of
Battenberg
(1854–1921)

Elizabeth
(1864–1918)
m. Serge
Grand Duke
of Russia
(1857–1905)

*Irene
(1866–1953)
m. Henry
of Prussia
(1862–1929)

Ernest
Grand Duke
of Hesse
(1868–1937)
m. Victoria
**Melita of
Edinburgh
(1876–1936)
(div. 1901)

Alix
(1872–1918)
m. Nicholas II
Tsar of
Russia
(1868–1918)

Mary Victoria
(1874–78)

William II
German Emperor
(1859–1941)
m. Augusta of
Schleswig-
Holstein-
Augustenburg
(1858–1921)

Charlotte
(1860–1919)
m. Bernard
of Saxe-
Meiningen
(1851–1928)

Henry
(1862–1929)
m. *Irene
of Hesse
(1866–1953)

Victoria
(1866–1929)
m. Adolphus
of
Schaumburg-
Lippe
(1859–1916)

Sophie
(1870–1932)
m. Constantine
King of
Greece
(1868–1923)

Margaret
(1872–1954)
m. Frederick
Charles
of Hesse
(1868–1940)

Sigismund
(1864–66)

Waldemar
(1868–79)

Victoria and Albert's family tree.

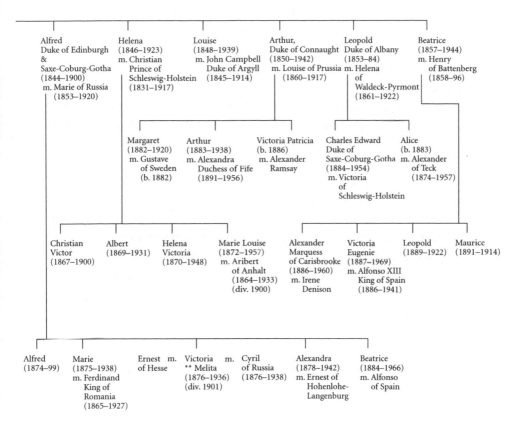

Alfred
Duke of Edinburgh
&
Saxe-Coburg-Gotha
(1844–1900)
m. Marie of Russia
(1853–1920)

Helena
(1846–1923)
m. Christian
Prince of
Schleswig-Holstein
(1831–1917)

Louise
(1848–1939)
m. John Campbell
Duke of Argyll
(1845–1914)

Arthur,
Duke of Connaught
(1850–1942)
m. Louise of Prussia
(1860–1917)

Leopold
Duke of Albany
(1853–84)
m. Helena
of
Waldeck-Pyrmont
(1861–1922)

Beatrice
(1857–1944)
m. Henry
of Battenberg
(1858–96)

Margaret
(1882–1920)
m. Gustave
of Sweden
(b. 1882)

Arthur
(1883–1938)
m. Alexandra
Duchess of Fife
(1891–1956)

Victoria Patricia
(b. 1886)
m. Alexander
Ramsay

Charles Edward
Duke of
Saxe-Coburg-Gotha
(1884–1954)
m. Victoria
of
Schleswig-Holstein

Alice
(b. 1883)
m. Alexander
of Teck
(1874–1957)

Christian
Victor
(1867–1900)

Albert
(1869–1931)

Helena
Victoria
(1870–1948)

Marie Louise
(1872–1957)
m. Aribert
of Anhalt
(1864–1933)
(div. 1900)

Alexander
Marquess
of Carisbrooke
(1886–1960)
m. Irene
Denison

Victoria
Eugenie
(1887–1969)
m. Alfonso XIII
King of Spain
(1886–1941)

Leopold
(1889–1922)

Maurice
(1891–1914)

Alfred
(1874–99)

Marie
(1875–1938)
m. Ferdinand
King of
Romania
(1865–1927)

Ernest m.
of Hesse

Victoria m.
** Melita
(1876–1936)
(div. 1901)

Cyril
of Russia
(1876–1938)

Alexandra
(1878–1942)
m. Ernest of
Hohenlohe-
Langenburg

Beatrice
(1884–1966)
m. Alfonso
of Spain

Highly experienced as he was, Palmerston was aware of the thought processes and influences at work with Albert. He felt, however, that they stemmed, not from a British standpoint, but from the Prince's background in a small German court, which had family members strategically placed throughout Europe. To British minds principalities like Coburg were reactionary anachronisms. The Foreign Secretary was not best pleased when compelled to write long letters in reply to the Queen justifying his policy, when he knew perfectly well that Albert had guided her hand in the first place. It was not exactly what a member of the Whig aristocracy expected from the monarchy. Albert probably overestimated his influence when quite early on he wrote to his father that Melbourne seldom answered his letters but that he 'often had the satisfaction of seeing him act entirely in accordance with what I have said'.

This first phase of Albert's encounter with Palmerston as Foreign Secretary lasted scarcely a year. Peel became Prime Minister in August 1841 after winning a general election. Palmerston, along with the Melbourne Cabinet, left office. Previous general elections had usually been seen as appeals by the King's minister for support in the House of Commons and did not end in a clear-cut defeat of the sitting administration. In 1841 the sitting ministry was clearly repudiated by what was by now a considerably more representative electorate and the accession of the Opposition, in this case the Tories, was inescapable. The Whigs still used the Queen's name in the election of 1841, as they had done in 1837. Victoria gave some countenance to this by making a round of Whig country houses, this time in the company of Albert, who clearly disliked the exercise and was regarded as stiff and awkward by most of his hosts. When Peel kissed hands at his accession audience with the Queen, heavily pregnant with her second child, the future Edward VII, the atmosphere was still frigid, but there were was no repeat of the Bedchamber Crisis.

Melbourne had the Queen's personal interests sufficiently at heart to help make the transition smooth. To Peel he conveyed the message that he must explain to her clearly what he intended and not let her hear it through anybody but himself. 'The Queen is not conceited; she is aware that there are many things she cannot understand, and she likes to have them explained to her elementarily, not at length and detail, but shortly and clearly; neither does she like long audiences ...', is what he told Greville to be passed on to Peel.[1] It was not long before Victoria regarded Peel as the best of men and the greatest of Prime Ministers, for Peel and Albert were soulmates. They had the same serious approach to life, they were outsiders in an environment in which they were nevertheless central figures, and they shared many interests outside politics. Their political orientation was very similar – both could be called liberal conservatives. Neither of them was happy with the cut and thrust of party politics and parliamentary conflict. The Prince, as a pupil of Stockmar, disliked adversarial politics and never became fully reconciled to the tumult and shouting inseparable from elections, party politics and a free press. Both he and Peel preferred a more governmental, even authoritarian approach. With Peel, Albert did not come up against any of the supercilious superiority that members of the Whig high aristocracy displayed towards him as a minor German prince. Past slights that the Prince had suffered from the Tories when he first came upon the scene, their way of getting at the Whig Queen, were never mentioned again.

Almost immediately Albert also had to take his share in the public functions of the monarchy, which were now so much more important than they had been under previous monarchs. His first venture was a speech he made to an anti-slave trade meeting on 1 June 1840. Having learnt it by heart, he then rehearsed it to his wife and was, according to his own and Victoria's account, very nervous before delivering it. He was very pleased with the reception he got, as he told his father in a letter, 'for it is always difficult to have to speak in a foreign language before five or six thousand eager listeners'. His progress in speaking English was slowed by the fact that he and Victoria spoke German between themselves. They sometimes did so in company when they did not wish to be overheard, something distinctly unpopular among those who had dealings with the Court.

The after-effects of the 1832 Reform Bill had turned the parliamentary monarchy into a constitutional one. Much later, in the 1860s, Walter Bagehot, editor of the *Economist* and a leading pundit, devised what is often still quoted as the classical definition of the functions of a constitutional monarch. He said it was the function of the British constitutional monarch 'to be consulted, to encourage and to warn'.

This leads too easily to the assumption that a constitutional monarch cannot really do very much. Bagehot also drew a distinction between the ceremonial and the substantive functions of the monarchy – he used the terms 'dignified' as against 'efficient'. He was an intellectual liberal who believed that politics had to be a rational exercise. He had to admit with regret that the public was more interested in royal marriages than in Cabinet discussions, but hoped that with the spread of education and enlightenment this would change. For what might appropriately be called the reign of Albert and Victoria, Bagehot is an inadequate guide. Albert, primed by Stockmar and Leopold, practised a very high view of monarchy. In 1854, when the Prince was in hot water over the Crimean War, the Baron addressed a long letter to his pupil. He warned him against the Whig view of a constitutional, neutered monarchy:

> if the English Crown permit a Whig ministry to follow this rule [of a politically inactive sovereign] in practice, you must not wonder if ... you find the majority of the people impressed with the belief, *that the King, in the view of the law, is nothing but a mandarin figure, which has to nod its head in assent, or shake it in denial, as his Minister pleases.*[2]

Throughout their partnership of twenty years Albert and Victoria were never content to be mandarin figures. Bagehot's distinction between the 'efficient' and the 'dignified' functions of the monarchy was also misconceived. It implied that the 'efficient' or substantive functions were declining, while only the 'dignified', or ceremonial, ones remained. In fact, just when Albert and Victoria were beginning their partnership, the ceremonial functions, the role of the monarch as the symbol of the nation, were entering a new and vital phase. The spread of newspapers, the invention of photography and other developments made the Queen and her family known to her subjects as never before.

In politics the monarchy remained a kind of fifth wheel on the coach, which perhaps could not determine the direction in which the coach was heading but yet continuously affected its running. Beyond this, the Crown had a special role to play in foreign policy, which was still closely affected by relations with other Courts. It was in this area that the Prince was initially most active, but his ideas were not yet fully formed for a role that was itself new to him. He was pulled in contradictory directions. There were the liberal ideas that had come to him through Stockmar, Florschütz and his education in Brussels and Bonn. They had particular application to Germany, where the Prince shared the patriotic desire for greater unity and the expectations that were placed in Prussia. All this was counterbalanced by the dependence of Coburg and of his father as the Duke on the status quo maintained by Austria under Metternich.

The Earl of Aberdeen was Peel's Foreign Secretary from 1841 to 1846 and became as much a favourite with the royal couple as Sir Robert himself. Aberdeen was much more a man of the *ancien régime* than Palmerston, less willing to be swayed by public opinion or by nationalism. Even he was not totally immune from the complaints of the Queen that she was not sufficiently fully and promptly informed of the despatches going out from the Foreign Office, complaints that became a constant refrain after the arrival of Albert at her side. Nonetheless the years of the Peel government passed in relative tranquillity as far as relations between Court and Cabinet were concerned. A conspicuous event in foreign affairs, with Court and Cabinet working in perfect harmony, was the visit of Victoria and Albert in August 1843 to the Court of Louis-Philippe at Château d'Eu, near Tréport, a small private domain belonging to the French King. The *arriviste* Orleanist dynasty was none too popular with other European royal houses, a feeling reinforced by the fact that in the 1830s France with Britain formed a liberal bloc opposed to the Holy Alliance of Austria, Russia and Prussia. This alignment had been temporarily interrupted by the Mehemet Ali crisis. The royal couple's visit to Château d'Eu was therefore a way of restoring the previous cordial relations. The term 'Entente Cordiale' was first coined by Aberdeen on this occasion.

The links between the House of Coburg and the Orleanists were many and close. As Duke of Orleans Louis-Philippe had been a friend of Victoria's father, the Duke of Kent. Uncle Leopold had married Louise, the French King's daughter, in 1832. It was a way of securing his new kingdom of Belgium, under attack from the Dutch at its birth. Leopold needed French support, but he could not allow France too much influence in Brussels, something that would not be tolerated in London. He used his family ties in his delicate balancing act. Queen Louise of the Belgians, twenty years younger than her husband, and her children were great favourites with Victoria and Albert. Louis-Philippe's second son,

the Duc de Nemour, had married, in 1840, a cousin of Victoria and
Albert, Victoire of Saxe-Coburg-Kohary. Two more daughters of the
French King were to marry Coburg cousins of the British royal couple.
Victoria was ecstatic about her stay at Château d'Eu. 'I felt as though it
were a dream that I was at Eu, and that my favourite air-castle of so
many years was at length realised ... They are all so kind and delight-
ful, so united that it does one's heart good to see it, and I feel at home
with them all ...'[3]

Although the visit to Eu was not a full-scale state visit, as it would
have been to Paris, Aberdeen as Foreign Secretary had accompanied the
royal family to France. One important matter of policy was agreed at Eu,
the question of the Spanish marriages, namely whom the Spanish
Queen, Isabella II, then aged thirteen, and her younger sister would
marry. This problem formed the latest chapter in the long-running saga
of Anglo-French rivalry in the Iberian peninsula. In the 1830s both Spain
and Portugal were racked by civil war. In Spain it was a fight between
the more progressive supporters of Queen Isabella and her moderately
liberal mother, Maria Christina of Naples, acting as Regent for her
daughter, and the more conservative supporters of Don Carlos, the
Queen's uncle. In Portugal the followers of another child Queen,
Maria da Gloria, were at loggerheads with her uncle Dom Miguel, again
a conflict between more progressive and more conservative elements.

In 1834 the so-called Quadruple Alliance between Britain, France, the
Spanish Government of Isabella and the Portuguese Government of
Maria da Gloria had been concluded, a considerable success for Palmerston, then Foreign Secretary. It fitted into the alignment of the two
liberal powers, Britain and France, against the conservative powers of
the Holy Alliance, Austria, Russia and Prussia. In the 1820s Britain had
drawn away from the Holy Alliance, especially when George Canning
became Foreign Secretary in 1822. Canning was Palmerston's mentor.
The overthrow of the Bourbon monarchy in 1830 had also distanced
France from the Holy Alliance. It was by no means the end of the story,
for the rivalry between France and Britain in the Iberian peninsula was
not easily conjured away. In 1836 Albert and Victoria's cousin, Ferdinand of Saxe-Coburg-Kohary, had married the Portuguese Queen and
had become King-Consort of Portugal. He and his wife had become
embroiled with a more extreme progressive faction and had removed

them in a coup d'état. In Spain the civil war between Isabelinos and Carlists had split British public opinion almost as much as the Spanish Civil War a hundred years later and had led to the intervention of a foreign legion led by a British officer. Louis-Philippe, ageing and intent on strengthening his dynasty, would have liked his son, the Duc d'Aumale, to marry Isabella of Spain. This could hardly be acceptable to Britain; in fact, it could be claimed that it ran counter to the Treaty of Utrecht, which had ended the War of the Spanish Succession in 1713. There was a British candidate for the hand of Isabella, Leopold of Saxe-Coburg-Kohary, another cousin of Victoria and Albert. This would have put a Coburg prince on the thrones of both Spain and Portugal. During the visit to Eu there was an agreement between Aberdeen and Guizot, the French Foreign Minister and at this point a powerful figure in French politics, that France would not support Aumale for Isabella's hand, while Britain would not support Leopold. All this was to lay up trouble for the future. Altogether the visit was not perhaps as idyllic as Victoria painted it in her enthusiasm. Palmerston claimed that the French King had pinched the key to the Queen's boxes from under her pillow while she was asleep and had thus been able to see her secret correspondence. He was, however, out of office, not an unbiased observer and critical of the pro-French turn in British foreign policy. In Paris he was regarded with great suspicion.

Two years after the visit to Eu Victoria and Albert went on another foreign progress, to Coburg, in time to celebrate Albert's twenty-sixth birthday in August 1845. It was less an occasion for diplomacy than a family celebration, but the journey of the English Queen to Germany could not but evoke great public enthusiasm amid much pomp and circumstance. On the way to Thuringia the royal couple stopped off at Cologne and Bonn, visited Albert's student quarters there, and went down the Rhine by boat and were entertained at various points by the King of Prussia. Metternich and the famous Prussian savant Alexander von Humboldt, much revered by Albert, came to meet them. At Coburg it was a great family reunion: Uncle Leopold and his Queen had come from Brussels, the Duchess of Kent, Victoria's mother, from London. Ernst, Albert's brother, only recently succeeded to the dukedom, pulled out all the stops. No other minor German prince could have boasted such an array of important guests.

Victoria, who was even more enthusiastic about it all than she had been at Eu, wrote copiously about it in her journal and drew many sketches. She was delighted by the friendly, homely atmosphere and by seeing her beloved Albert's hearth and home, where some of her own roots also lay. On the way home they visited the Wartburg, where Luther had been incarcerated, were entertained by the King of Bavaria, Ludwig I, and paid another short visit to Louis-Philippe at Château d'Eu. There was, however, some criticism in the British press of the goings-on at Coburg. A *grande battue*, an immense massacre of animals was a feature of all such visits. Large numbers of wild boars and other animals were driven by beaters into small enclosures where they could be dispatched without difficulty by the male members of the royal party, while the ladies watched. At home this was felt to be slaughter and not sport and the attendance of the Queen was considered inappropriate when she was patron of the Society for the Prevention of Cruelty to Animals.

In domestic affairs the 'Hungry Forties' were difficult years. In 1842 the Chartist movement erupted into violence. The Anti-Corn Law League was a predominantly middle-class movement and its violence was verbal rather than physical, but equally indicative of serious class tensions. Its campaign for free trade in corn was not only an attack on the landowning classes, but on the very basis of the aristocratic principle. The rhetoric of its principal apostle, Richard Cobden, blamed aristocracies for war, for the origin of their privileges lay in the feudal period and their capacity as warriors. Fighting was a pastime they had never given up. Cobden claimed that the abolition of aristocracy, along with freedom of trade, would usher in an era of international concord and peace. The monarchy, at the apex of the social pyramid, was inevitably drawn into these conflicts of classes and ideologies.

It now fell to Victoria and Albert, a young couple scarcely into their twenties, to play out their role at the head of the nation in these largely uncharted waters. In June 1840, and again in May 1841, the Queen, pregnant on both occasions, was the target of assassination attempts. On both occasions the royal couple were fired on with pistols, while driving in open carriages. On the first occasion the assassin, a young waiter, who fortunately was neither a good marksman nor had great presence of mind, fired a second time, but Albert had drawn Victoria down into the carriage, out of view. In May 1841 the gunman, 'a little, swarthy, ill-looking rascal', as Albert described him, was not caught. Nevertheless the royal couple drove out again the following day, accompanied by their equerries, who it was hoped, would draw the assassin's fire. 'I must expose the lives of my gentlemen, but I will not those of my ladies', said the Queen.[4] A few plain clothes policemen were concealed around the Palace. John Francis, the ill-looking rascal, did make a second attempt and was close enough for the Queen to hear the hammer of his pistol. He missed again and this time was caught. He fainted in the dock when condemned to death, but the sentence was commuted. Only two months later, in July 1841, there was another attack, albeit with a pistol which turned out to be loaded mainly with tobacco and loose paper. These attempts were the work of pathetic loners and the composure of Victoria and her husband in the face of such dangers enhanced the couple's popularity. Security for public figures was by modern standards rudimentary. But such incidents indicated that the person of the Queen occupied a central place in the national consciousness in times when that consciousness was seriously disturbed and dislocated by rapid change and great social hardship. The visit to Château d'Eu was the first high-profile foreign visit by a British monarch for a long time and the newspapers published daily reports of the comings and goings, dinners and picnics. In the *Illustrated London News* these were accompanied by a large number of pictures, drawn by artists, of the arrival of the royal yacht, the Queen stepping ashore, entering a carriage with the French King and on a walk in the country on his arm.

It was an example of a package of highly publicised appearances by the royal couple throughout their home territory the like of which had not been seen before. The arrival of the railways made a royal progress of this kind much more feasible and stops at railway stations made Victoria and Albert visible to unprecedented numbers of their subjects. Big civic visits became the order of the day and cities like Manchester, Liverpool and Birmingham tried to outdo each other in laying on lavish ceremonies. There were royal carriage processions through heavily decorated streets, watched by hundreds of thousands. It was a great day for the Mayor and the Corporation and the Mayor might be rewarded for his efforts with a knighthood. 'We proceeded to the Council Room, where we stood on a throne and received the addresses of the

Mayor and Corporation, to which I read an answer, and then knighted the Mayor, Mr Bent, a very good man', the Queen noted in her diary during a visit to Liverpool in October 1851. 'The order and behaviour of the people, who were not placed behind any barriers, were the most complete we have seen in our many progresses through capitals and cities – London, Glasgow, Dublin, Edinburgh, &c., for there never was a running crowd, nobody moved, and therefore everybody saw well, and there was no squeezing ...'

The royal couple might end up spending the night at the nearby country mansion of an aristocratic grandee connected with the city. During this visit to Liverpool they stayed at Worsley Park, the seat of Lord Ellesmere. The monarchy was becoming populist and it was unbending to the municipal middle classes in a way unimaginable in earlier reigns. It might even happen that the Mayor would entertain the royal visitor at his own country mansion. In May 1857 Albert went on his own to open the Manchester Art Treasures Exhibition, in which he had taken a great interest. He stayed with Mr Watts, the Mayor, at his residence, Abney Hall. The following month the royal couple together paid another visit to Manchester and to the Arts Exhibition. They were accompanied by, among others, Vicky, the Princess Royal, and her fiancé, Prince Frederick William of Prussia, their engagement having recently been made public. It was another enthusiastic reception and the Queen noted Prussian flags among the triumphal arches and flags. On this occasion the Mayor was knighted, although only a neighbouring aristocratic country mansion was large enough to house so big a royal party.

The monarchy was thus visible to the population at large as never before, while behind the scenes the royal couple was far busier than previous monarchs in participating in the daily work of government, often down to the minutiae. In practice it was largely the work of Albert, using the name of his wife, for she was often otherwise engaged. Their fertility was at its peak in the early 1840s, Victoria giving birth to four children between November 1840 and August 1844. Exactly what was Albert's part in the political work of the monarchy was known only in the narrow world of court and politics, but the general picture reached a much wider audience. It found an echo in innumerable cartoons, popular satires and ballads, for whom the frequent appearance of royal babies also offered endless opportunities for satire. It was a confused situation for the public, high or low, radical or aristocratic, monarchist or republican, to come to terms with. The aristocracy, Whig or Tory, had often shown contempt for the royal family, particularly for the reprobate sons of George III, and, even as they conformed to Court etiquette by bowing and scraping, felt superior to them. But aristocracy and monarchy were bound together and if the monarch was too obviously unable to play his allotted role, it was alarming. By the same token many radicals were republicans, because those who wanted major changes in the social order could not leave one of its major pillars untouched. Outright republicanism was a minority creed and even Chartist leaders like Feargus O'Connor scorned it as a distraction from more important tasks. More common was the constitutionalism advanced in much reformist rhetoric, for example by prominent anti-establishment figures such as William Cobbett and Orator Hunt, and from a different perspective in the novels of Disraeli. This was the argument that the people had their rights enshrined in a mythical past order headed by a benign monarch and that these rights had been filched from them by the privileged classes in their pervasive greed. What was often called 'Old Corruption' was never far away and always threatened to undermine the constitutional rights of the people. Thus many positive and negative responses clustered round the person of the Queen, but now she was no longer alone and had a husband.

A woman on the throne had already confused the gender roles, and, now that she was a wife, the question was who wore the trousers. As a popular satirist put it:

> She's lovely, she is rich
> But they tell me when I marry her
> That she will wear the *britsch*.[5]

When it dawned on the public that in practice the Prince was rather more the master in the marriage than in constitutional theory he was meant to be, it caused anxiety. Unease deepened when that husband was and remained an alien who never became completely acclimatised, a fact only too evident the moment he opened his mouth. It was no wonder that doubts about his true allegiance were never laid to rest. Was he still the Coburger and German that he said he would always remain when he left home in 1840? Or was he rooted, his passion for a more united and liberal Germany notwithstanding, in a pre-national European consciousness, that was in process of being rendered obsolete by a strident national consciousness? It was a question that would become increasingly difficult for all members of Europe's interconnected royalty.

Coburg was certainly never far from his mind. As soon as he had made his move to England a ceaseless and mostly unedifying correspondence with his brother began. Ernst was a careless spender and whenever he visited England left unpaid bills which did the Coburg reputation no good. He expected Albert to give him access to his sister-in-law's copious purse, but the usual response he got was, not surprisingly, unenthusiastic: 'I can well believe that your travels have produced this excess, especially as you make such tremendous purchases because you cannot resist anything you find attractive. Naturally I am very willing to assist you in the way you ask, but I must know what amount ... I only know so much, that if I were to proceed in this manner, I would soon land in the Queen's Bench'. Even more embarrassing were Ernst's affairs with women. While serving as an officer in Dresden he had got a serving maid pregnant, who then blackmailed him. While in London, Ernst had experienced the symptoms of venereal disease. 'If you want me to be of any use to you in future, I must demand the fullest truth and honesty, for if I am to defend you and one laughs at me for being ignorant of the facts, my help would be useless', wrote Albert to his brother.[6] It spilt over into Albert's relations with his father, until 1844 the reigning Duke. The father had wanted his successor to marry a Russian grand duchess. In the circumstances Albert strongly advised against marriage for the time being: 'To marry would be as immoral as dangerous and pernicious for you. In the worst case you would deprive your wife of health and honour.' In any case such an ambitious marriage would force a minor German prince into the slipstream of Russian policy. Albert was becoming a liberal-constitutional English counterbalance to the long-standing connections of the House of Coburg with the autocratic Russian Romanovs.

In the event Ernst junior made do with a Princess of Baden, but Ernst senior was also disappointed that his second son did not do more to advance the concerns of Coburg. For years the Duke had wished to be elevated from a Serene Highness to a Royal Highness, something that was finally achieved in 1844. Then he wanted to become Prince of Crete, something hardly on the cards, and he had other, sometimes far-fetched items on his wish list. Albert could only pour cold water on his pretensions. In November 1840 he wrote to his brother:

> Papa ... accused me of putting myself on the same footing as Uncle Leopold. This is without foundation, for such a thing never occurs to me. It is true that my position is very similar to his [Leopold's], in that we cannot sacrifice important interests to every whim from Coburg. If he wishes to find in Russia the support for his House which he thinks he cannot find in me, he will be badly advised and soon will have to succumb to the yoke of Russian whims.[7]

Ernst senior wrote to his elder son that he regarded it as Albert's duty, since he now had a rich wife, to give him an annual salary. When this letter was passed to Albert he complained: 'The principles, which he expresses, hurt me in the depth of my soul. Always money and for ever money!' Albert's letters to his brother were a constant stream of moralising homilies, and in them the Prince showed himself once more as a most adept disciple of Stockmar. 'You well know the events and scandals that had always happened in Coburg Castle and in the town, and just this knowledge has made you indifferent to morality', he wrote in May 1840.

Such letters must have become intensely irritating to their recipient. Ernst's behaviour was, however, not only disturbing to his brother in his innermost being. It threatened to counteract the strenuous efforts Albert was making to cleanse the English Court of all trace of scandal and immorality. These strains and stresses did not alter the fact that Albert remained deeply attached to Coburg, his family, and to his father and brother, in spite of all their moral failings. When Ernst senior died, in January 1844, the mourning was not only the usual wallowing in death characteristic of the period but a real and painful feeling that a vital link had been lost. Four years before, when Ernst had left to return to Coburg after attending Albert and Victoria's wedding, Albert was in tears and so overcome that he had to retire to his room. It was some consolation that Ernst had left a will that provided, in case of a failure of the main male line, that the succession should pass to the son of the second son. When Ernst II succeeded as Duke in 1844 relations between the brothers became rather less difficult.

The Queen's uncle, the reactionary Duke of Cumberland, was now King Ernst August of Hanover. He was another German ruler, a rather more important one than the Duke of Coburg, to cause the royal couple a lot of trouble. One of Albert's great merits in the eyes of the British public was that, by providing so many heirs to the Crown, he had put paid to any possibility of succession by the Cumberland line. This only increased the determination of the King of Hanover to make a nuisance of himself. He insisted on taking his seat in the House of Lords. He was always trying to challenge the precedence of Albert. In 1843, at the wedding of his niece, the daughter of the Duke of Cambridge, he tried to push Albert out of the way at the signing of the register. He then claimed that the Queen's jewellery was really his property and that he would not leave the country until it had been handed over to him. Trying to be conciliatory, the Queen submitted his claim to a panel of three judges, who eventually, in 1857, reported in his favour. By that time Victoria, who initially had little jewellery of her own, had acquired plenty from elsewhere. Before leaving during his visit in 1843 Ernst August wanted Albert to accompany him on a walk through the streets of London. When the Prince complained that this would expose them to unwelcome attention from the crowd, the King said, for all to hear: 'Oh, never mind that, I was more unpopular than you are now, and used to walk about with perfect impunity.' Ernst August was in fact one of the more unpopular German rulers and a principal source of the many complaints from Albert and Victoria's relations about Palmerston's alleged encouragement of revolution.

When Albert first appeared at Victoria's side there was a widespread expectation that he would and should be unobtrusive and insignificant. Melbourne remarked to Anson: 'The Prince is indolent and it would be better if he was more so, for in his position we want no activity.' It was a judgement wide of the mark and Anson knew better: 'If you require a cypher in the difficult position of consort of the Queen you ought not to have selected the Prince; having got him you must make the most of him, and when he sees the power of being useful to the Queen he will act.'[8] Soon he was acting in a great many directions, not only as her political secretary and effective mastermind. He became master of the house in the fullest sense, in that he reshaped the management of the royal palaces. He also created private residences for his growing family at Osborne and Balmoral, to which they could escape from the goldfish bowl that the monarchy had become.

The wasteful and archaic administration of the royal palaces meant that every day servants took away hundreds of candles that had not been lit and sold them, or drew supplies for tasks that were never performed; three different departments were responsible for the most essential daily tasks, such as lighting fires or cleaning windows or replacing them when they were broken, and to get anything done to make life comfortable was an uphill struggle. The three great officers of state responsible for the royal palaces, the Lord Chamberlain, the Lord Steward and the Master of the Horse, did not live in and therefore the servants answering to them could more or less do as they pleased. Those working for the Lord Chamberlain would on no account undertake any tasks deemed to be in the Lord Steward's department.

Meanwhile the wind blew in through broken windowpanes. When a seventeen-year-old boy intruder, Edmund Jones, was found in Buckingham Palace, sitting upon the throne, seeing the Queen and hearing the Princess Royal 'squall', claiming that he had done so on repeated intrusions into the palace, the incident played into Albert's hands and enabled him to make a start in getting a grip on these chaotic arrangements. Stockmar wrote one of his meticulous memoranda, setting out how it might all be rationalised, but to clean out these Augean Stables was never going to make Albert popular. He also took a close interest in the rich royal collections of paintings, prints, books and documents, much of which he found in a neglected state. With the help of archivists and experts, some of them imported from Germany, he brought order into what is now regarded as a repository of unrivalled historic importance.

Albert took on a growing number of chairmanships, for example the Royal Society of Arts, which was later to serve him as the launching pad for the Great Exhibition, the Fine Arts Commission, which supervised the rebuilding of the Palace of Westminster after the great fire of 1834, the London Library, Trinity House and many more. He never treated such positions as purely honorific, but on the contrary was active in exercising his role. He set up a model farm at Windsor and exhibited pigs and beef cattle at agricultural shows. He worked hard at developing the Osborne estate, where he was free from civil service supervision.

He roused great enthusiasm when at the annual meeting of the Royal Agricultural Society in 1848, he talked of 'we agriculturalists assembled together', but his popularity received a real boost from riding to hounds with considerable dash, as he did at Chatsworth and Belvoir. The Prince's burgeoning portfolio of non-political interests and activities helped to divert attention from his political role and the criticism this was bound to attract.

Before her marriage Victoria did not like the company of men who might show up the narrowness of her education and knowledge of the world, though the risk was mitigated by the fact that it was only she who could initiate a conversation. In the face of the Queen's reluctance, Albert tried to widen the circle of those who were received and entertained at Court to artists, literary men and scientists. The composer Mendelssohn made a famous visit to Buckingham Palace in 1842, during which not only Mendelssohn himself but both the Queen and her husband played and sang. Music and sketching were interests that Victoria and Albert shared. The Queen and the Prince paid public visits to Oxford and Cambridge when Albert was given honorary degrees. The connection with Cambridge led to his election, against considerable opposition, as Chancellor of the University in 1847, which gave him the chance to play a very active role in the reform of both ancient universities in the 1850s. Albert was a field-marshal in the British Army, something that provided a field day for the cartoonists, especially when he designed a shako cap in the Hungarian style for the Household Cavalry. His input into military affairs, especially at times of crisis, like the Crimean War and the Indian Mutiny, was formidable. Wisely, one may think, he declined to succeed the Duke of Wellington as Commander-in-Chief in 1850. By that time he had learnt that, whatever he did and however beneficial his interventions, he always came under fire. He was either a pedantic meddler or a laughing stock and recognition came much more grudgingly.

Whatever the criticism, the monarchy that Victoria and Albert and their growing family now offered to the public exerted a powerful fascination for a population whose ability to participate in such a spectacle had also grown by leaps and bounds. Even anti-monarchists who would rather have had it otherwise could not escape the pull which a royalty almost bourgeois in character exercised upon the imagination of most sections of society. Almost the only class exempt from this fascination was ironically the high aristocracy, who turned up their noses at such a vulgar exhibition, and particularly at the prudery and pedantry of Albert. *Reynolds's Newspaper* was an anti-monarchist radical popular paper. It started publishing in 1850 and five years later had a circulation of 100,000. Its editor, George Reynolds, had published in the 1840s a number of books, under titles like *The Mysteries of London*, which purported to give a voyeuristic look at what went on in the family life of Albert and Victoria. The story line was modelled on the boy intruder Edmund Jones. It was a mixture of scandalous tittle-tattle and sympathy for the Queen and her family, who would be 'just like us' if they were not hemmed in by absurd and anachronistic etiquette, or spoiled by excessive pomp and wealth. It is an early example of the ambivalent media attention given to royalty that has remained a feature of the symbiotic relationship between media and monarchy down to our day. Outright republicanism was a minority creed, but this was largely because it was believed that the monarchy was now so limited in its powers that politically it was indistinguishable from a republic. Had the monarchical activism that Albert practised in the name of the Queen been more fully recognised republicanism might have gathered more support. As it was, criticism of the monarchy focused mostly on incidentals, such as the cost, wealth and extravagance of the Court at a time of widespread and degrading poverty.

The fall of Peel ushered in a new phase in the political activities of the royal couple. Albert had become almost as closely identified with Peel as Victoria had with Melbourne before her marriage. This identification came more into the open than ever when in January 1846 Peel nailed his colours to the mast and proposed the total repeal of the Corn Laws in the House of Commons. Albert appeared in the Visitors' Gallery of the House to lend his support. Fierce passions had been aroused and Lord George Bentinck, previously renowned only for his prowess on the Turf, emerged, with Disraeli, as the spokesman of the landed interest. In his speech on the twelfth night of debate Lord George said:

> If so humble an individual as myself might be permitted to whisper a word in the ear of that illustrious and Royal personage, who, as he stands nearest, so he is justly dearest to Her who sits upon the Throne, I would take leave to say that I cannot but think he listened to ill advice when ... he allowed

himself to be seduced by the first Minister of the Crown to come down to this House to usher in, to give *éclat*, and as it were, by reflection from the Queen, to give the semblance of a personal sanction of Her Majesty to a measure, which, be it for good or for evil, a great majority, at least of the landed aristocracy of England, Scotland, and of Ireland, imagine fraught with deep injury, if not ruin to them ...[9]

It was almost a return to the false situation in which the Tories had found themselves in the days before Victoria's marriage, when they had to attack her as a Whig Queen. Now those members of the Tory party who considered themselves the true protagonists of the creed seemed to find themselves abandoned by the throne in favour of the liberal apostasy committed by Peel and his Cabinet. Albert never appeared in the House again.

5

Controversy and Conflict

The return to government of the Whigs under Lord John Russell in July 1846 ushered in a period of more intense and controversial political involvement by Victoria and Albert. It brought Palmerston back to the Foreign Office. In some ways he had a stronger claim to the premiership than the diminutive Johnny Russell, but his Whig credentials were less strong. There was continuing unease about Palmerston's personality and style in his own party and political circles generally, fully shared by the royal couple. His popularity in the country at large, however, was such that Russell could not have formed a government without him, nor could he risk his resignation in the many clashes that occurred in the next few years. When Pam was finally dismissed, five years later, the fall of Russell followed in short order. This stark reality limited what Albert could do to control him. The days were in any case far distant when Victoria had been a Whig Queen. Albert did not like the way the Whigs treated government almost like a family affair, yet quarrelled between themselves about the allocation of offices and the details of policy. He did not find Lord John Russell a good man of business and indeed he was not. Yet Victoria and Albert were now convinced free traders and the only way by which the free trade policy could be maintained for the moment was through a Whig government sustained by Peel and his friends.

Almost immediately the problems in the Iberian peninsula, the Spanish marriages and the civil war in Portugal, bounced back to cause tension between Palmerston and the Court. One of the first despatches Palmerston wrote on returning to his desk in the Foreign Office was to Henry Bulwer, the British Minister in Madrid, about the marriage of Queen Isabella:

> The British Government is not prepared to give active support to the pretensions of any of the Princes who are now Candidates for the Queen of

Spain's hand, and does not feel itself called upon to make objection to any
of them ... unless there should be a probability that the choice would fall
upon some Prince so directly belonging to the Reigning Family of some Powerful Foreign State, that he would be likely to connect the Policy of the
Country of his adoption with the Policy of the Country of his birth, in a
manner that would be injurious to the Balance of Power ... [1]

It meant a continuation of Aberdeen's previous policy of no special
support of the Coburg candidacy but objection to having a son of
Louis-Philippe on the Spanish throne. Palmerston then enumerated the
candidates whom he still thought in the running, including Leopold of
Saxe-Coburg-Kohary. Contrary to his usual practice, he showed this
despatch to the French Chargé d'Affaires in London. It put the cat among
the pigeons, because Guizot, the French Prime Minister, made out that
this revived the Coburg candidature and that he was therefore released
from the agreement made with Aberdeen at Eu about the Spanish marriages. In September the virtual simultaneous marriages were announced
of the Spanish Queen with the Spanish Prince Francisco, known to be
impotent, and of her sister, the Infanta, with the Duke of Montpensier,
son of Louis-Philippe. The possibility of a French Orleanist prince on the
Spanish throne moved back into the frame. No account was taken of the
notoriously active libido of Spain's pubescent Queen.

There was outrage in London and for once the royal couple and
Palmerston were on the same side. Victoria was infuriated by a letter
from the French Queen Marie-Amélie announcing the marriage of her
son to the Spanish Infanta as if it was simply a family matter without any
political implications, and moreover in breach of the pledges apparently
given at Eu. Victoria complained bitterly to her uncle in Brussels about
the breach of faith within the immediate family circle, and Albert was
even more angry. He wrote to Aberdeen, now out of office, in October
1846: 'The Spanish marriage affair is running its course, and every stage
through which it goes produces new disgust in our minds. The King and,
more even, Guizot, stop at no lie, at no trick to consummate the affair.'
In everything they wrote Victoria and Albert emphasised that they had
done nothing to forward the Coburg candidature and had discouraged
rather than encouraged it. 'This is *too* bad, for *we* were so honest as
almost to prevent Leo's marriage (which *might* have been, and which
Lord Palmerston, as matters now stand, regrets much did not take

place) ...', the Queen wrote to her uncle in Brussels. It was just the kind of situation in which the Queen felt even more emotionally involved than her husband. The royal couple would have been less than human, however, if the prospect of a Coburger both on the Spanish and Portuguese thrones had not given them pleasure. Although they fully backed Palmerston on this occasion, an undercurrent of unease about his manner of doing business still runs through the royal correspondence. 'No doubt if Lord Aberdeen had been at his post what has happened would *not* have taken place, and suspicion of Lord Palmerston *has* been the cause of the *unjustifiable* conduct of the French Government', the Queen wrote to her uncle Leopold. The affair of the Spanish marriages took the shine off the Entente Cordiale and made it more difficult for Britain and France to act together in subsequent crises. Some commentators saw a direct link between the Anglo-French breach and the fall of the French monarchy less than eighteen months later. The dynastic links between the British royal family and the House of Orleans did not therefore preclude rivalry; and in the Iberian peninsula the dynastic competition coincided with the national rivalry between Britain and France.

There was greater disagreement between the royal couple and the Foreign Secretary over Portugal than over Spain. A Coburg prince on the throne of Spain might have been to the advantage of Britain and the cause of liberalism, but the Coburg King of Portugal did not always help the British national interest or behave as a liberal. He and his wife could bend the ears of their British royal cousins and thereby interfere with Palmerston's policy. A government installed by the Queen, Maria da Gloria, and Ferdinand, her Coburg husband, was defeated in elections in 1845. Ferdinand and Maria then suspended the constitution. The radical opposition in Portugal, the Septembrists, unleashed a civil war and British radicals supported them. Palmerston would probably have liked to do the same, but Albert and Victoria's concern for their cousin in Lisbon and his wife limited his ability to do so. Albert and Victoria were bombarded by complaints from their cousins, whose physical security was threatened, claiming that Palmerston was giving too much encouragement to the Septembrists and that this was making their position impossible. Ferdinand had brought with him a German adviser named Dietz. He was a kind of Portuguese Stockmar, but much less liberal, and even Albert thought he was a bad influence.

Then the *Morning Chronicle*, generally regarded as Pam's mouthpiece, attacked the Portuguese Court as reactionary and aroused the suspicion of the British royal couple. Palmerston, who begged 'to assure your Majesty that he has no power of exercising any detailed control over the language and opinions of that paper', wrote: 'A newspaper like the *Chronicle* looks to an extensive circulation ... and the Government has nothing in its power to offer which could at all compensate for a diminution of circulation.'[2] Colonel Wylde, an equerry to Prince Albert, was sent to broker a compromise with the Septembrists, but failed. Ferdinand of Saxe-Coburg-Kohary, Victoria's uncle and father of the King of Portugal, sent another Coburg cousin, Count Alexander Mensdorff-Pouilly, the future Austrian Foreign Minister and then a young man of thirty-three, to Lisbon. 'This is rather too great a number of councillors', admitted the Queen to Palmerston.

In March 1847 the Septembrists surrendered to a British naval force, but Maria da Gloria had to restore the constitution. It was as much as Palmerston could achieve and a considerable success for him. It still left him open to attacks from Radicals like Joseph Hume in the Commons, who wanted a decisive result in favour of the Septembrists. The air was full of rumours that the Foreign Secretary had been hamstrung by Coburg influences from the Court. Greville wrote in April 1847: 'Our Court continues to take the same interest in the Lisbon Coburgs, and would willingly interfere in their favour with more vigour if the Ministers would consent to do so. Palmerston's defects prove rather useful in his intercourse with the Court. To their wishes or remonstrances he expresses the greatest deference, and then goes on his own course without paying the least attention to what they have been saying to him.' Albert fully realised how the Portuguese imbroglio would strike the public. He wrote to Stockmar before a big Commons debate on Portugal in June:

> The public will set down the business as a Coburg family affair, and especially in connection with the fact that Sir Hamilton Seymour [the British envoy to Portugal] went direct from Brussels to Lisbon, that Wylde is in my service, that we have received Dietz at Court here, and say that Ministers have taken the step unwillingly etc. Nous verrons![3]

The situation was not without danger to Russell's weak government, for the Protectionists could combine with the Radicals dissatisfied with Portuguese policy and force a premature general election, which was in any case due in 1847. In the debate Palmerston had to keep his head down and did not speak, but the government survived.

The survival owed something to an intervention by Sir Robert Peel, highly praised by Albert. Peel's chief political object at this time was to prevent a return of the Protectionists to power and a reversal of free trade. After the debate Albert wrote to Stockmar: 'The chief attacks have been directed against poor Wylde, "that firebrand!" as Hume called him. The debate was, moreover, distinguished by boundless one-sidedness and adhesion to the Junta [the Septembrists].' Not unnaturally the Radicals suspected that Wylde, acting for Albert and Victoria, had been sent to Portugal to save the skins of Maria da Gloria and her Coburg consort. In another debate the following month Palmerston was able to explain himself more fully: 'Our object has been neither to serve the Portuguese Crown nor to oppress the Portuguese people.' The departure of the Septembrists by grace of the Royal Navy was in fact not just undertaken at the behest of Albert, as the Radicals tended to believe. Palmerston could not have supported them more than he did in face of the opposition of the other powers, Spain and France, and he got the best compromise he could.

Tensions also arose between the Foreign Secretary and the Court over Greece, somewhat similar though less acute than those over Portugal. Here the King was Otto of Bavaria, who had ascended the Greek throne at the age of seventeen in 1830. He was the son of Ludwig I of Bavaria, regarded as one of the more liberal German rulers. The Bavarian Wittelsbachs were Catholics, frequently intermarried with the Habsburgs, but also immediate neighbours of Coburg. Otto disappointed liberal hopes and governed as an absolute monarch, and also made himself unpopular by building expensive palaces, though it was also said that the Greeks liked their King to cut a figure. Greece was a difficult country to govern, racked by uprisings and coups, and torn between three great powers, Britain, France and Russia. Nevertheless Uncle Leopold always retained some nostalgia for the romantic throne he had to forego in Athens in favour of the prosaic one in Brussels. Albert could not really defend Otto: 'I must disclaim all intention of being or ever becoming King Otho's champion, whose total incapacity to govern with or without a constitution, is but too evident to me ...', he wrote to Palmerston in December 1847, when they were locked in controversy over the affairs of Greece.[4] But Otto was a German prince and enjoyed the support of other German rulers, including not only the King of Bavaria but also the King of Prussia. With the Prussian King, Frederick William IV, who was married to a Bavarian Princess, Albert's relations were particularly close. Palmerston did not like direct communications between foreign sovereigns and the British royal couple and it was said that he sometimes opened such letters when they arrived in the Foreign Office in the diplomatic bag. In general Albert did not withhold such letters from ministers and sometimes translated them himself, but for particularly confidential letters he used his librarian, Dr Praetor, as a private courier. This may well have been the case with the King of Prussia. Albert and Victoria, as well as the Prussian King, had a running complaint against Sir Edmund Lyons, the British Minister in Athens and a former naval officer, who in their view was putting Otto under too much pressure and favouring the constitutional party too openly.[5] Palmerston stuck to his view that Otto and his chosen ministers were governing against the desires of the Greek people for more freedom and that this would ultimately lead to disaster. Lyons and his chief were also anxious to counter French influence in Athens, which was built on the encouragement of the absolutist elements.

Europe was in ferment in 1847 even before revolution plunged it into upheaval the following year. The problems of Portugal and Greece, civil war in Switzerland, the annexation by the Austrians of Cracow, the only surviving remnant of an independent Poland, all of these were preludes to even greater turmoil to come. This gave Albert plenty to worry about and to direct a steady stream of letters and memoranda at his wife's ministers. How much difference his interventions really made is debateable but at the very least they required a deferentially phrased if non-committal reply. It was not in Albert's nature to remain on the sidelines and it was said that he was so busy that he often passed through the corridors of Buckingham Palace and Windsor Castle almost at a running pace while reading through sheaves of paper.

The future of Italy and Germany were the really big European problems. In the autumn of 1847 Palmerston decided to send a member of the Cabinet, Lord Minto, Lord Privy Seal and father-in-law of the Prime

Minister, to Italy, gently to encourage the various Italian governments towards reform and to express the British Government's interest in such moves. The Pope, Pius IX, generally known as Pio Nono, had been elected in 1846 and had embarked upon a modest reform programme. What happened to him in the year of revolution, 1848, thoroughly cured him of any such liberal tendencies and for the rest of his long pontificate he became a bulwark of defiant anti-liberalism. Minto was to encourage the Pope in his reformist policy and also enlist his help in persuading the Irish priesthood to give British policy in Ireland a chance. The Minto mission drew a long memorandum from the Prince, composed at Ardverikie in Scotland. It was before the royal couple's love affair with Scotland had led to the purchase of Balmoral. In the memorandum he put his finger on the risks surrounding the Minto mission:

> The progress of Liberal institutions and the establishment of Constitutional Government in Italy is (and not without justice) considered by Austria as an affair of life and death to herself and will therefore be opposed by her almost at any risk, and with all her might. We must not conceal from ourselves, that sending a mission to Rome with the avowed or apparent object of supporting and encouraging the Pope in those measures of political reform which Austria has reason to dread so much is *a most hostile step* towards our old and natural ally.[6]

Albert proposed that the British Government should inform other European governments that Britain had no intention of interfering in Italy in any way, but that if the Italians introduced reforms of their own free will no other country had a right to stop them. No doubt Russell and Palmerston knew full well what they were doing in sending Minto to Italy and did not need the Prince to tell them. Albert's dilemma about Austria and his ambivalent feelings towards her went deep. Pam was never slow to break a few eggs and the royal couple did not want to rock the boat too much. Later Albert advanced an intriguing explanation for the Minto mission, namely that it arose out of Minto's wish to be with his daughter, Lady John Russell's sister, who was about to be confined at Turin, and did not want to pay for the journey.

Germany was, however, the country the affairs of which touched Albert and Victoria most closely and from which their numerous family relations were constantly beating a way to their door. The German situation was moved a step forward in February 1847, when Frederick

William IV of Prussia summoned a United Diet, which raised hopes that there might be a real advance towards constitutionalism. There was, however, for the time being nothing in the affairs of Germany that needed to lead to any immediate disagreement between Palmerston and the Court. The Foreign Secretary had for long been keen on a more liberal course in Germany and saw no danger to British interests in the goal of greater German unity. On the contrary, most British policy-makers felt that a stronger Germany would be a beneficial counterbalance to France and Russia. There was slight unease about the customs union, the Zollverein, founded under the aegis of Prussia in 1834. Its protectionist thrust, which is inherent in the notion of a customs union, ran counter to British free trade principles and was seen as posing a potential threat to British commercial interests in Germany. At one time, when Hanover was still under the British Crown before 1837, an attempt was made to block the further spread of the Zollverein. Soon, however, the industrial development helped by the Zollverein, for example vigorous railway building, was perceived to be beneficial to British trade. The political consequences of the Zollverein were generally welcomed in London. The strengthening of Prussia in Germany, her possible detachment from the Holy Alliance and the decline of Austrian influence were viewed favourably.

All this was not far removed from how Albert saw the German situation. While at Ardverikie in September 1847, the Prince had produced a long memorandum on Germany as well as on Italy. While the latter was rendered immediately relevant by the Minto mission, the former was more of an academic exercise. Palmerston, the minister in attendance for part of the royal couple's stay at Ardverikie, was no doubt pleased to see the Prince's energies diverted to a subject on which they could for the moment and for the most part agree. In replying to Albert's memorandum Palmerston was, however, still worried by the effect of the Zollverein's prohibitory duties on British trade and thought that every effort should be made to persuade those north German states and cities, for example Hamburg, which had not joined the Zollverein, to refrain from doing so.

Albert's memorandum on Germany was one of a series which he produced over the next year or so, by which time the Continent was engulfed in revolution, in which he sketched a new constitution for

1. The marriage of Albert and Victoria, 1840, by George Hayter (detail).

2. Coburg.

3. Rosenau.

4. Duke Ernst I of Coburg.

5. Duchess Louise of Coburg.

6. Leopold I, King of the Belgians.

7. Duke Ernst II of Coburg.

8. Queen Victoria holding a portrait of Prince Albert, 1854, photograph by B. E. Duppa. (*Royal Archives*)

9. Prince Albert, 1854, photograph by B. E. Duppa. (*Royal Archives*)

10. The Great Exhibition, 1851.

11. Osborne House, Isle of Wight.

12. Albert and Victoria with their children, 1857. Left to right, Alice, Arthur, Prince Albert, the Prince of Wales, Leopold, Louise, Queen Victoria with Beatrice, Alfred, Victoria and Helena. (*Royal Archives*)

13. The royal family at the marriage of the Princess Royal, 1858.

Germany. All of these lengthy documents show how intensively the Prince concerned himself with events in Germany, but they also show up the painful dilemmas he faced. He wanted a root and branch reform of the Confederation, which had become the vehicle for Metternich's repressive policy and which had completely lost the confidence of all liberally minded Germans. Institutions which gave the country the unity it craved and needed were absolutely necessary. But how, in these circumstances, was something to be preserved of the position of the separate rulers, especially the smaller ones, like the Dukes of Coburg?

Then there was the Austrian situation, a multi-ethnic, mostly non-German empire still holding the presidency of the German Confederation. Its relationship to a future Germany was a conundrum almost impossible to resolve, especially for someone like Albert whose family owed a lot to Austria. Only a few years earlier his father, Duke Ernst I, then still alive, took it for granted that Austria was Coburg's friend, Prussia her enemy. When in November 1841 Albert and Victoria had decided to ask the King of Prussia Frederick William IV to be godfather to their first-born son Albert Edward, Albert's father protested:

> Why you pick out the King of Prussia for this honour, forgive me when I say so openly, that I find it completely inappropriate ... Prussia is the *hereditary enemy of our House* ... which has swallowed half of our territorial inheritance and is ready every day to appropriate the rest; in this the present King has shown himself more than *unhelpful, highly arrogant* and *unjust* ... If it is still possible I ask you to undo the affair, which must make the worst impression in Germany, especially in Saxony.[7]

In his reply Albert, now no longer just a Coburg Prince but the husband of the Queen of England, made it clear that such a matter, the baptism of the Prince of Wales, could not be simply regarded as a Coburg family affair, but was a concern of the British nation.

If Prussia was now to take the lead in Germany, the character of its present ruler, Frederick William IV, would become a major problem. Albert was, in spite of his father's reservations, close to the Prussian King, but very clearly aware of his limitations. When Frederick William had opened the United Diet in February 1847, Albert had written to Stockmar: 'Those who know and love the King recognise him and his views and feelings in every word, and will be grateful to him for the frankness with which he expresses himself; but if we put ourselves into the position of a cold critical public, our heart sinks. What confusion of ideas!'[8] Albert recognised that the King had qualities that were in many ways attractive, but which fatally undermined his ability to deal with the practicalities of politics. This was to become appallingly obvious in the following year of revolution.

When Stockmar heard of the Prince's Ardverikie memorandum on Germany, without actually seeing it, he switched into warning mode. His apprehension was aroused by Albert telling him how much he owed to recent conversations with Victoria's half-brother Prince Charles of Leiningen. Clearly Stockmar felt that Prince Charles would see matters from the perspective of the ruling dynasties. Leiningen was an influential figure in Bavaria and in the year of revolution would be briefly Prime Minister of the Reich under the provisional constitution drawn up under the aegis of the Frankfurt Parliament. Along with Albert, his brother Duke Ernst of Coburg, King Leopold, Stockmar and Bunsen, the Prussian envoy in London, they formed the core of the so-called Coburg Circle. They tried to nudge German affairs in the direction of greater unity and constitutionalism under Prussia, while preserving a role for the separate dynasties. 'You left the Fatherland eight years since, and when you were very young', wrote the good Baron, '. . . Prince Charles could furnish you with only very limited, and probably very one-sided results ... In dealing with the German question, your Royal Highness can scarcely look at it from any other point of view than that of a German Prince.' In his long-winded analysis of the German situation, the Baron then put forward what had become the stock argument of German nationalism, namely that the view that German cultural grandeur 'was mainly due to the Fatherland being split up under separate rulers' had been rendered obsolete by the brutal invasion of Napoleon and by the united will of the people in repulsing it. The division of the country had been the cause of its weakness and of the 'spirit of servility'. 'It is not to be denied that public opinion among the middle classes in Germany is now anti-dynastic', he finally wrote.[9] It may have been true, but it would undermine the very order on which the Baron had built up his own life and influence. The Prince took it in good part, as he did all the homilies emanating from his mentor.

It all came rather close to the bone before the year 1848 was more than a few weeks old. There were plenty of reasons for the explosion which now shook Europe to its foundations and why France was again the country that triggered it. The conservative order restored in 1815 was breaking down in many places. Even back in 1830, the previous occasion when France had erupted into revolution, the powers of the Holy Alliance had not been able to save the Bourbon monarchy. Louis-Philippe's more liberal, less legitimist regime was ushered in. By the 1840s it had become the preserve of the richer middle classes and was no longer able to appeal to other important sections of French society. A widening of the franchise had become a key issue, but Guizot, the leading figure of the period, refused to contemplate it. Alexis de Tocqueville, most perceptive of nineteenth-century social commentators, said that the middle classes were exploiting the country rather than governing it and that government in France had become like a business operation, where everything was decided on the basis of financial advantage. Yet France was also the country of early socialism, developed into an ideology by writers like St-Simon, Fourier and Proudhon. Some of their ideas had percolated to the proletariat in Paris. Boredom played a part in the collapse of the bourgeois monarchy, headed by a king usually drawn pear-shaped by the cartoonists. Embourgeoisement enhanced the popularity of the monarchy in Britain, but in France there was still nostalgia for the glories of Napoleon. Elsewhere in Europe the mid-forties were years of economic depression, aggravating the miseries of the artisan classes threatened by early industrialism. Given the political grievances of the articulate classes and the economic suffering of the poor, it is not surprising that the revolution in Paris acted as a trigger for revolution over much of Europe.

When on 22 February 1848 a reform banquet was banned in Paris the masses took to the streets. Louis-Philippe was unable or unwilling to crush the uprising by force and within days the French royal family was in precipitate and piecemeal flight across the Channel in humiliating circumstances. In spite of the recent rift between the two Courts, caused by the affair of the Spanish marriages, it was a harrowing experience for Albert and Victoria, who was about to be delivered of her sixth child, Princess Louise, born on 18 March 1848. Desperate letters arrived from the Queen of the Belgians, the French King's daughter. It cannot have been easy for Victoria to write to her uncle Leopold on 1 March, before any of the Orleans family had arrived and the whereabouts of the French King and Queen were still unknown:

> We do everything we can for the poor dear Family, who are indeed most dreadfully to be pitied; but you will naturally understand that we cannot *make cause commune* with them, and cannot take a hostile position opposite to the new state of things in France; we leave them alone, but if a Government which has the approbation of the country be formed, we shall feel it necessary to recognise it.

A few days later Palmerston sent the Queen a letter from the British Consul at Le Havre, which described graphically the cloak-and-dagger methods by which the French King, with his whiskers shaven off, was spirited on board a steamer leaving Honfleur for Le Havre, and thence on the packet for Newhaven. Arrangements were made for the French royal family to be accommodated at Claremont, Leopold's English home. £1000 out of secret service moneys was made available by Palmerston to the deposed King, disguised as a payment from a well-wisher. Victoria took a great personal interest in Louis-Philippe and his family and admired their fortitude in their misfortune. After her confinement on 18 March, just as thrones were toppling all over Europe, she told her uncle:

> Thank God, I am *particularly strong* and *well* in *every possible respect*, which is a blessing in these *awful, sad, heart-breaking* times. From the first I heard all that passed and my only thoughts and talk were – Politics; but I never was calmer and quieter and less nervous. *Great* events make me quiet and calm, and little trifles fidget me and irritate my nerves. But I feel grown old and serious, and the future is very dark ... *Germany* makes me so sad; on the other hand, Belgium is a real pride and happiness.

The thought that the tide of revolution might sweep across the Channel can never have been far from the minds of the Queen and her husband in those days. Another important royal refugee arrived in London on 27 March, the Prince of Prussia, heir to his brother Frederick William IV and later William I, German Emperor after 1871. The revolutionary crowds in Berlin had taken particular exception to him, as he was thought to have given orders for the troops to fire, and he was known as the 'Grapeshot Prince'. It was perhaps not quite deserved, but neither was the liberal reputation he long enjoyed with Albert and Victoria. He probably owed it to his wife, Princess Augusta, a grand-daughter of the Duke of Saxe-Weimar, for whom Goethe had worked as chief minister. Augusta grew particularly close to Victoria and she became an inveterate enemy of Bismarck. The Prince of Prussia was to have been godfather to Princess Louise, but Palmerston advised against it. The Prince stayed with Bunsen, the Prussian envoy, in his embassy, and was given diplomatic status, to make him seem less of a refugee. The most high-profile non-royal fugitive among those who made for the safety of London was Metternich himself, who had to flee Vienna under cover of darkness on 13 March, as the system which he had for so long upheld throughout Europe came crashing down. He eventually bought a house in Richmond. Guizot and his mistress, Princess Lieven, who had arrived in February, installed themselves in Kensington. In years gone by the Princess had been one among Palmerston's many mistresses, which perhaps explains her and her current lover's resentment of the Foreign Secretary.

Albert, probably more than the pregnant Queen, was occasionally, during the stormy days of February and March, in doubt if the safety of London would hold. There was plenty to alarm him. The continental revolutions gave a fillip to radical agitation in many major British cities and there was a good deal of disorder. This came on top of the financial panic of 1847, when Peel's Bank Charter Act had had to be suspended. The Irish situation continued to weigh heavily on the minds of the political establishment. The crunch point came on 10 April, when the last monster Chartist demonstration was scheduled. Everywhere special constables were called up, one among whom was the exiled Louis Napoleon, the Emperor Napoleon's nephew, later Napoleon III. In London Wellington was in charge. The royal couple was advised to leave London and on 8 April Waterloo Station was closed to the public as they left for Osborne. The Queen had a reputation for personal bravery, acquired by her conduct during the numerous attempts on her life, and with her sixth confinement only three weeks behind her few were inclined to criticise her for having bolted, though Albert was slightly more prone to attract such criticism. Anyhow, the great Chartist rally on Kennington Common, followed by a march on the Houses of Parliament to present a petition, proved a damp squib and attracted only ridicule. There was to be no revolution in Britain and national self-confidence rose by leaps and bounds.

So did Palmerston's. Events seem to have been borne out everything he had said and done for years. Metternich and Guizot, his personal enemies, had been brought low and had almost to throw themselves on his mercy. Reactionary rulers like Ernst August of Hanover, the old Duke of Cumberland, blamed him personally for 'throwing fire and flame throughout Europe'. By the same token he became more than ever a hero for British radicals, his reputation as a radical-liberal sympathiser inflated far beyond what his real position warranted. As one dramatic event followed upon another, history as it were speeding up its normal pace, relations between the royal couple and the Foreign Secretary became more and more acerbic. The Queen and her husband thrashed around with increasing desperation trying to control the Foreign Secretary, but neither they nor the Prime Minister and the Cabinet could get the better of so popular a minister. Russell and his colleagues did not most of the time want to do so nor could they afford to. If Pam resigned, the days of the Russell government would be numbered. This was an outcome the royal couple could hardly wish for. It would bring them up against the Tories, for them a political and personal nightmare, not least because of 'that horrid Mr D'Israeli' who had been so beastly to dear Sir Robert Peel, as the Queen saw it.

The steady drip of complaint and remonstrance from the Court, mostly the work of Albert, did sometimes have an inhibiting effect on the impetuous Foreign Secretary, but he had no intention of letting them cramp his style too much. For the Queen he had some emotional loyalty, having been close to her ever since she came to the throne as a young girl, but for Albert his feelings were much more ambivalent. Albert believed in constitutionalism and Palmerston hated revolution, but such common views on generalities did not lessen their specific disagreements. They started with the situation in France, the eventual cause of Palmerston's dismissal. The Foreign Secretary and the British ambassador in Paris, Lord Normanby, were keen to get on terms with the republican government that emerged after the fall of the monarchy. Albert and Victoria were more suspicious and feared French designs in Italy. As already foreshadowed at the time of the Minto Mission, Italy became a serious cause for disagreement. Palmerston genuinely sympathised with Italian aspirations for unity, even if this meant displacing the various Austrian satellite princes, while Albert and Victoria were fearful of undermining the Austrian position in the peninsula. Albert found it disturbing and inconsistent that Pam encouraged the King of Piedmont to put himself at the disposal of the Italian desire to expel the Austrians, while he opposed the Prussian drive to expel the Danes from Schleswig, a cause as dear to German nationalists as the recovery of Lombardy was to Italian patriots. For the Foreign Secretary the weakening of the Danish position in a highly sensitive strategic area was against the British national interest.

The situation in Germany remained closest to Albert's heart. In August 1847 he had already advised his brother, the Duke of Coburg, to take reforms in hand in his small territory before they were forced on him. Ernst did not need much prodding and had begun the process of constitutional change before 1848. He took it further in 1848 and subsequent years. The Duchy of Coburg stayed relatively quiet during the year of revolution, but the pressure to give a more unified shape to Germany would profoundly affect petty princes like the ruler of Saxe-Coburg-Gotha. Prince Albert went into overdrive, producing constitutional schemes for the new Germany, of which he sent copies to all and sundry, kings and princes, and last but not least Palmerston.[10] The confederation would become a federal state, with a diet consisting of two chambers, one composed of representatives from the estates of the separate states, then an upper house consisting of the ruling princes. There would be a federal ministry responsible to the diet, consisting of a foreign, a defence and a trade minister. The princes in the Upper House would elect an emperor. Albert was not quite sure whether this emperor should be elected for life or a term of years. The latter option would have made him less powerful and more amenable to control by his fellow sovereigns. Albert's chief concern was clearly to preserve a role for the separate princes and to prevent their being swallowed up by a powerful Prussian emperor. Initially Albert hoped that Austria could remain part of such a more unified Germany, but as events unfolded these hopes faded.

Albert and Palmerston did not find much to disagree about when it came to German constitutional arrangements, which were in any case in a state of constant flux. Events had produced something not too far removed from what Albert envisaged in his many memoranda. The revolution had forced the rulers throughout Germany to allow the holding of elections to an all-German Parliament, which met in Frankfurt. It was this Frankfurt Parliament that had the task of drafting a constitution for a unified Germany. It had to make a nation out of nearly forty separate countries and at the same time give the new nation a liberal constitution. To realise two such great goals simultaneously proved too much. It was a further complication that the revolutionaries were divided between moderates, whose aim was limited to replacing absolute rule with constitutional government, and radicals, who wanted to go the whole hog to democracy. After a year or so the revolution ended in failure, through the revival of the power of the separate rulers, especially of the two major ones, the Emperor of Austria and the King of Prussia. Their armies turned out to be more decisive than the talking shop in Frankfurt.

The fate of Schleswig-Holstein was another major issue the Frankfurt Parliament was meant to resolve. The complexities of this affair made Palmerston say at one point that only three persons had ever understood them, one was now dead, the other had gone mad and the third was himself, and he had forgotten them. The essence of what was at stake was simple enough. It was a clash between German and Danish nationalism. Northern Schleswig had a majority of Danish speakers, elsewhere the two duchies were German. The Frankfurt Parliament as the representative of German national aspirations had to wrest the duchies from Danish control and Prussian troops were to be its agents in this endeavour. It was, however, not in the British national interest to allow a weakening of the Danish monarchy, which was the guardian of a strategically important area controlling access to the Baltic. While Victoria and Albert had sympathy for the German case and for the Prussian Court, Palmerston's main concern was the British national interest. When in September 1848 the Prussians signed an armistice with Danes, without having recovered the duchies, there was outrage in Germany and rioting in the streets of Frankfurt. Over Schleswig-Holstein Prussia had thus failed to stand up for the German cause and the Frankfurt Parliament, having no forces of its own, was revealed to be no more than a talking shop. The failure to wrest Schleswig-Holstein from the Danes was a mortal blow for the revolution and the claw-back of real power by the German princes began.

Albert and Stockmar were deeply disappointed that the dream of

German unity was fading, but the Prince's reaction also shows the ambivalence of his position. He still felt that what remained of the loyalty of the people to their princes must be respected. In a letter to Palmerston in October 1848, he blamed the collapse of public order on the lack of such loyalty among those populations that had been shunted around between different sovereignties in the Napoleonic era. States like Baden and Württemberg had absorbed, by grace of the French Emperor, large tracts of territory previously split into a number of smaller principalities. The loyalty of their inhabitants was to their original local princes, who had now been deprived of their territorial control; the technical term was *mediatised*. The same was true of the new provinces on the Rhine which Prussia had acquired at the Congress of Vienna. Albert wrote: 'one would have thought that the Central Power would feel the advantage of respecting the little that remains. I believe it has been the idea of some politicians at Frankfurt to buy the consent of the various kingdoms to the omnipotence of the Central power by sacrificing to them the smaller states. At Coburg-Gotha the Court has hitherto cost nothing to the people ...' A few weeks earlier Victoria had written in similar vein to her uncle Leopold:

> I do not think the fate of the Minor Princes in Germany is so completely decided as Charles [her half-brother Charles of Leiningen, at that moment the Prime Minister of the short-lived Frankfurt executive] ... is *so* anxious to make one believe. There is only a question of taking certain powers and rights, and not at all of getting rid of them; and I think you will see that the *Ausführung* [execution] of the Unity will be an impossibility, at least in the sense they propose at Frankfurt. The Archduke John [the Austrian archduke who was the head of the Frankfurt executive as *Reichsverweser*, Vicar of the Empire] has spoken very reassuringly both to Ernest and the Duke of Meiningen, and the attachment in many of those smaller principalities is still extremely great, and I am sure they will never consent to being *ausgewischt* [wiped out]. Coburg, for instance, on the occasion of the suppression of a very small riot, showed the greatest attachment and devotion to Ernest; at Gotha, the feeling of independence is very great, and at Strelitz, on the occasion of Augusta's confinement [Augusta of Cambridge, Victoria's cousin, Grand Duchess of Mecklenburg-Strelitz], with a son, the enthusiasm and rejoicing was universal. All this enthusiasm cannot be entirely despised.

Victoria was here simply making the views of her husband her own.

The mantra of the royal couple, in face of all upheavals, was that the ordinary people of Germany still retained their traditional loyalty to their princes. To Albert, for all his wish for a more united and liberal Germany, the continued existence of Coburg was ultimately non-negotiable. It is unlikely that Palmerston lost much sleep over what was happening at Coburg-Gotha, but in fact the power of the Frankfurt Parliament was ebbing away even faster than Albert thought.

In September 1848 the Court was staying at the recently acquired Balmoral Castle. Lord John Russell was in attendance. The Queen had a long talk with the Prime Minister, suggesting that Palmerston be moved from the Foreign Office, perhaps to change places with Lord Clarendon, the Lord Lieutenant of Ireland. The Queen, no doubt briefed by her husband, was treading here on dangerous ground, for there was no chance that Pam would accept such a move. Lord John Russell defended his colleague stoutly, but in the next three years he was often to find himself in this situation, between a rock and a hard place. Every now and then it looked as if Palmerston had stuck his neck out too far. In the autumn of 1848, after being specifically asked by the War Office for his advice, he had authorised the release of surplus arms back to the manufacturer, who then sold them to the Sicilian rebels who were fighting the reactionary Bourbon King of Naples, King 'Bomba'. It was an occasion when Pam eventually gave way to the view of his Cabinet colleagues that an apology should be sent to Naples. It was this kind of incident that made Albert and Victoria's relations all over Europe feel that the British Foreign Secretary was fanning the flames of revolution.

The flames were everywhere dying anyway and the sovereigns were recovering their strength. Austria, in particular, was regaining her strength and was on the way to being able to restore the pre-revolutionary situation in Germany. Perhaps because these developments were viewed with mixed feelings by the royal couple, as well as by the Foreign Minister, the removal of Palmerston from the Foreign Office was not for the moment raised again. Plenty of niggling complaints continued, about Palmerston's failure to submit despatches or of altering their wording, and about diplomatic appointments. Substantial issues like Schleswig-Holstein continued to fester and were the cause of renewed fighting on the ground. Ernst, Albert's brother, the Duke of Saxe-Coburg, fought against Denmark in these renewed hostilities as a Saxon general. In April 1849 he won a victory against an attempted Danish landing at Eckernförde and became a popular figure throughout Germany. Palmerston embarked upon mediation and eventually a conference in London agreed on a settlement that broadly restored the Danish position. It was an outcome which was due in large measure to the pressure of the Great Powers, especially Britain, and which caused great bitterness among German nationalists. Albert shared these feelings and he and the Queen made them known, but to little avail. When all was settled in August 1850, when tensions ran again high between the royal couple and Palmerston, Albert wrote to Stockmar:

> The fixed idea here is that Germany's only object is to incorporate them [the duchies of Schleswig and Holstein] with herself and draw them from the English into the Prussian commercial system. Denmark will then become a State too small to maintain a separate independence, and so the division of European territory and the balance of power will be disturbed. I grant that this is a tenable view ... but assuredly this affords no ground for doing violence to law, honour, to equity, and morality ... Schleswig is entitled to union with Holstein; Holstein belongs to Germany and the Augustenburgs [the dynasty favoured by German sentiment] are the heirs.[11]

It was clearly a case where Albert and, under his influence, the Queen were torn between what they felt and what their position dictated.

Palmerston had from time to time used gunboat diplomacy to enforce the rights of British subjects who had been maltreated in foreign parts. He generally did so when the offending country was weak and accessible to the British navy, but it made him popular. The high-minded and the highly placed tended to disapprove, and so did the Queen and the Prince. The most conspicuous case of that kind was that of Don Pacifico, a Gibraltese Jew who held a British passport. His house in Athens had been ransacked and set on fire in an anti-Semitic riot. Sir Edmund Lyons, the British Ambassador who had been so often the cause of disagreement between the royal couple and the Foreign Secretary, took up Don Pacifico's case and was encouraged by Palmerston. When the British Mediterranean Fleet paid a visit to Athens in January 1850, Palmerston sanctioned its use to enforce Don Pacifico's claims. British naval intervention caused French and Russian protests. Relations with the French Government, now headed by Louis Napoleon as

President of the Republic, became strained. Eventually Palmerston had to retreat somewhat, but he had British public opinion, as opposed to establishment opinion, behind him.

At the end of June 1850 there was a great clash in the House of Commons over Palmerston's gunboat diplomacy in Greece. Not only the Tories but Peel and many of his followers were lined up against the government and its future was in doubt. The Radical section of the government's majority fully supported Russell and Palmerston. The Foreign Secretary spoke for four and a half hours winding up with the famous peroration: 'the Roman, in days of old, held himself free from indignity when he could say *Civis Romanus sum*; so also a British subject, in whatever a land he may be, shall feel confident that the watchful eye and the strong arm of England will protect him against injustice and wrong'. It was a great triumph. Palmerston had escaped, Houdini-like, from the net in which many members of the establishment had hoped to trap him and was more popular than ever. It was, however, the aristocratic establishment and the dynastic network, and the Queen and her husband as foremost members of it, who were the champions of cosmopolitanism and who hated and feared the chauvinism of the middle and lower classes to which Palmerston appealed.

None were more disappointed than Albert and Victoria, who had had every reason to hope the Greek affair would end Palmerston's tenure of the Foreign Office. They suffered a double blow because, within a week of Palmerston's triumph, Peel died after being thrown by his horse. Even out of office Peel had been a friend and adviser. Almost immediately they returned to the attack on Pilgerstein, as they now habitually called him. (Palmer is an archaic word for pilgrim and *Pilger* is German for pilgrim.) 'We ... have incessantly waged war ... with Pilgerstein, in which he got many an ugly poke ... as it says in the White Cat [a fairy tale]', Albert wrote to Uncle Leopold, but evidently Pilgerstein was a cat with nine lives. Within days of the Foreign Secretary's triumph and Peel's death, Albert summed up the situation thus: 'The Queen has no more confidence in Lord P. now than she had before ... Foreign governments distrust and foreign nations hate Lord P. now as much as before – Lord P. himself is not likely to change his nature in his sixty-seventh year on account of a vote, which is calculated to gratify his vanity and self esteem.'[12]

A few days later Russell was called to the Palace and Albert went further than ever before in a personal attack blackening the character of Palmerston. He brought up an incident at least ten years in the past, to explain why the Queen felt such a personal repugnance to her Foreign Secretary. In 1839 Palmerston had invaded the bedroom at Windsor Castle of one of the Queen's Ladies of the Bedchamber, then Mrs Brand, later Lady Dacre. She had screamed for help. In mitigation it was later claimed that Pam had been in the habit of sleeping with another lady in the same room. It was admittedly not easy to find the right bedroom in a castle like Windsor or in large country mansions, and Palmerston was neither the first or the last to use the situation for furtive assignations. It is unlikely that the young Queen was fully apprised of the incident at the time. It was a questionable tactic for the Prince to rake over past moral lapses and evidently Russell was not as deeply shocked as Albert had hoped. He said that the Queen must be protected from having Palmerston thrust upon her as Prime Minister, a self-interested remark, but he, Russell, also knew another lady in society upon whom Pam had tried the same thing. Russell made it clear that he could not carry on without Palmerston, but the skirmishing went on.

The Prince took Russell's remark that Palmerston should not be thrust upon the Queen as Prime Minister as an occasion for enunciating some rather dubious constitutional doctrines. In a memorandum to Russell he said he knew that the sovereign could not interfere with the government and the management of Parliament. But he then went on: 'I differ completely from that doctrine. I hold that the sovereign has an immense moral responsibility upon his shoulder with regard to his Government and the duty to watch and control it.' He went on that he knew that the sovereign in theory had a free choice in selecting any MP to be his Prime Minister, but 'in fact that amounted to no choice at all' because 'the circumstances of the time always indicated who was to succeed'. Therefore the sovereign should take his share in 'the preparatory arrangement of party organisation', so that he should only have those presented to him whom 'he had before recognized as eligible'. It was pure Stockmar.[13]

In August 1850 Palmerston had an interview with the Prince, which, according to the latter's account, found the minister in contrite mood.

It was natural that there should be differences on policy, said the Foreign Secretary, but the suggestion 'that he wanted in respect to the Queen, whom he had every reason to respect as his sovereign and as a woman whose virtues he admired and to whom he was bound by every tie of duty and gratitude, was an imputation on his honour as a gentleman' and appears to have reduced him to tears and Albert to having pity on him. They were not just crocodile tears, for before her marriage Palmerston had a close and avuncular relationship with the young girl on the throne. He had instructed her on many aspects of her office and of protocol, how to write to foreign sovereigns, how to place foreign dignitaries at the dinner table, and the Queen had been grateful for such instruction. Relations had cooled when Palmerston married his long-time mistress Lady Cowper in 1839. Probably Pam still had personal feelings for the Queen, but they hardly extended to her husband. He had a lively sense of the limits of royal power and on matters of policy could hardly fail to be suspicious of the Coburg Prince who stood so close to the British throne.

At the end of this hour-long conversation between the Prince and Palmerston they turned again to the situation in Schleswig-Holstein and the way the London Protocol had settled this in favour of Denmark and the interests of Austria, Russia and not least Britain, and to the detriment of German national sentiment. Such a subject always brought out what Palmerston cannot but have seen as the divided loyalties of the Queen's husband. In Germany matters were indeed hastening towards a restoration of the pre-revolutionary status quo. The Confederation of 1815 was restored and with it the position of Austria, which held the permanent presidency of the diet in Frankfurt. Prussia had to eat humble pie. With the Convention of Olmütz in December 1850 she had to give up all attempts to form a German league of states under Prussian aegis. This gave rise to a good deal of mutual needling between the Palace and the Foreign Office. The Queen and the Prince had for years criticised the Foreign Secretary with the argument that he was encouraging revolution in Italy, thereby going too far in undermining Austria, whose survival was a vital British interest. Now Palmerston was at least acquiescing in the restoration, with Russian backing, of the Austrian ascendancy in Germany. Metternich's repressive old system was back in business, though without Metternich. The Queen, no doubt prompted by Albert, wrote in somewhat ironic vein to her Foreign Secretary in November 1850:

> The Queen is afraid however that all our Ministers abroad, at Berlin, Dresden, Munich, Stuttgart, Hanover etc. (with the exception of Lord Cowley at Frankfurt) are warm partisans of the despotic league against Prussia and a German constitution and for the maintenance of the old Diet under Austrian and Russian influences. Ought not Lord Palmerston to make his agents understand that their sentiments are at variance with those of the English Government?[14]

It was a reversal of roles, for the attitude of British representatives like Bulwer in Madrid and Lyons in Athens, favouring the liberal opposition, had long been a bone of contention between Pam and the royal couple. Only a few weeks earlier the warring parties had each exhibited the opposite attitude in their treatment of Austrian susceptibilities. An Austrian general, particularly associated with savage reprisals against Italian and Hungarian rebels, which included the flogging of women, visited London. His name was Haynau and the British public called him 'hyena'. When he visited a brewery in the London East End he was chased and beaten up by the draymen. Palmerston was unwilling to go against public sentiment and sent only a half-hearted apology, more or less saying that if someone of Haynau's reputation appeared openly in London that is what he must expect. The Queen felt that this was 'derogatory to the honour of the nation, as if no one could be safe in this country who was obnoxious to the public feeling'. In the ensuing tussle Russell sided with the Queen and Palmerston, after threatening resignation, finally gave in.

The presence in Britain of large numbers, perhaps as many as 15,000, of both oppressors and the oppressed from all over Europe was to cause further trouble. They were of every political colour, ranging from the reactionary Metternich to the revolutionary Mazzini. For the moment relations between the Court, Russell and Palmerston staggered on uneasily but without an explosion. In February 1851 the parliamentary position of the Russell Government had become so weak that Lord John had to resign. Relations between Whigs and Peelites had become frayed over what was called 'papal aggression'. The Pope had, in a rather grandiloquent bull, allotted territorial titles to Roman Catholic bishops

in Britain. It looked as if he was anticipating the imminent return of
England to the bosom of the Catholic Church. A storm of outraged
Protestantism swept the country and Russell pandered to the public hysteria. It was a sensitive moment, because the conversion to Rome of
some prominent figures of the Oxford Movement, including the later
Cardinal Manning, gave the impression that the Church of England was
in imminent danger not only from Rome but from treachery within.
Several prominent Peelites, including Gladstone, were High Anglicans
close to the Oxford Movement. They were appalled by the intolerance
and hysteria that rose to the surface and by Russell's encouragement of
it. Thus the great issue of the moment, papal aggression, phoney and
ridiculous as it in many ways was, divided the Peelites from the Whigs,
but free trade in corn was continuing to divide them from the Protectionist Tories. The attempt by Derby, the Tory leader, to form a
government failed and Russell returned to office.

Albert and Victoria were in the centre of the comings and goings produced by this governmental crisis. The uncertain and fragile situation
between the parties and groups in the House of Commons was giving
practical relevance to Albert and Stockmar's conception of an active
monarchy. The Prince and his mentor did not see equally clearly that
activism could put monarchy in a dangerously exposed position. Nor
were the royal couple remote from the ecclesiastical turmoil. Albert and
even Victoria, the pupil of Lehzen, were in essence Lutherans. They felt
most at home in the Scottish Presbyterian Church, something that
raised the hackle of Episcopalians. One of the barriers between Albert
and Englishness was the Church of England. He could just about understand the low, strongly Protestant end of Anglicanism and consistently
made his influence felt on behalf of Low Churchmen. He had no sympathy for or understanding of the High Church, the Oxford Movement
and Tractarians. Samuel Wilberforce was one High Churchman with
whom he was friendly and with whom he played chess. Wilberforce was
an intellectually distinguished clergyman well known for his social ability and ambition. It may well be due to Albert, however, that he made
it only as far as the diocese of Oxford and not to Lambeth Palace.

Meanwhile public attention was much occupied by preparations for
the Great Exhibition of 1851. From the summer of 1849 onwards this
project engrossed the Prince himself at least as much as his running

warfare with Palmerston. Albert was fascinated by science and technology and in these spheres he was wholeheartedly committed to modernity. The Royal Society of Arts, of which he was President, floated the idea of annual exhibitions of British manufactures, following models that had caught on in France and Belgium. Such exhibitions would show the world how uniquely advanced Britain was. British manufacturers, pragmatic and profit-minded, were slow to warm to the idea. In 1847 the Society of Arts managed to mount an exhibition, which proved unexpectedly successful with the public. This enabled Albert, two years later, to launch the much more ambitious project of an 'Industry of All Nations' exhibition, to be held in 1851. There were endless obstacles to overcome, not least the creation of a suitable venue. The exhibition was to be located in Hyde Park, but this offended many sensibilities and vested interests. Few of the wealthy and influential inhabitants of neighbouring Mayfair were very enthusiastic. It was a stroke of luck when Joseph Paxton, who had built a remarkably beautiful glass conservatory for the Duke of Devonshire at Chatsworth, came up with the design for a 'Crystal Palace'.

It required an enormous expenditure of energy on Albert's part to see the project through, but he was so closely identified with the idea of the Great Exhibition that failure could not be contemplated. Sometimes the narrow-minded opposition to the Exhibition was fed by a wider suspicion of the Prince's role. On the other hand, it was an enterprise on which a great deal of publicity was focused and that therefore helped to divert attention from the political influence of Albert, which was exerted more behind the scenes. The Exhibition became a great personal triumph for the Prince, which Palmerston fully acknowledged. It did not, however, lay to rest the conflict with the Foreign Secretary. This moved to a climax in the autumn of 1851, ending in the dismissal of Palmerston in December. The first explosion came in October, when the Hungarian rebel leader Kossuth came to London. Palmerston prepared to receive him in his private residence in Piccadilly. The Queen demanded that the reception should not take place and was backed by Russell. It took Pam only five minutes to answer the Prime Minister's request: 'that I do not choose to be dictated to as to whom I may or may not receive in my own house and that I shall use my own discretion on that matter. You will of course use yours as to the disposition of your government ...' On this occasion Palmerston backed down again, but he made up for it by receiving a radical delegation which called the Emperors of Austria and Russia 'odious and detestable assassins' and 'merciless tyrants and despots'. Albert and Victoria were deeply resentful of this manner of bypassing their objections. Russell, however, did not dare too make too much of an issue on which Palmerston had the support of radical opinion.

But soon another issue arose which led to the breach that had been so long coming. Louis Napoleon, who had been elected President of the Republic in 1848, carried out a *coup d'état*, on 2 December 1851, which made him dictator and caused some bloodshed. The following year he was to make himself Emperor. Palmerston expressed approval of the coup in a conversation with Count Walewski, the French ambassador in London, an illegitimate son of Napoleon I. The Cabinet decided that a strictly neutral stance should be adopted and Palmerston instructed Lord Normanby, the British Ambassador in Brussels, accordingly. When Normanby carried out his instructions he was told that Palmerston had already expressed his approval to Walewski. He was annoyed and his relations with Pam were not in any case very good. While Normanby protested in official despatches about the embarrassing position in which he had been placed, Lady Normanby wrote in stronger terms, setting out the whole story, to her husband's brother, Colonel Phipps, an equerry to Prince Albert. The royal couple were angry, perhaps particularly because the coup may have been intended to forestall an Orleanist restoration. On this occasion Palmerston had acted against radical opinion. Napoleon's coup, during which many on the left were imprisoned, could hardly be called an advance of constitutional or popular government. Lord John Russell at last decided to grasp the nettle. He asked for Palmerston's resignation as Foreign Secretary and offered him the post of Lord Lieutenant of Ireland and a United Kingdom peerage. The former would have retained him as a member of the Cabinet; the latter would have translated him to the House of Lords, for as an Irish peer Palmerston sat in the Commons. Palmerston refused both offers and withdrew in a huff to Broadlands, his estate in Hampshire.

Albert and Victoria could hardly believe their luck. 'Our relief was great and we felt quite excited by the news', the Queen wrote in her journal. What really tickled them was a note from Palmerston to Lord John, in which the dismissed minister rebutted the accusation of 'want of decorum and prudence' with which the Prime Minister had justified the dismissal. After all Russell had offered him the Lord Lieutenancy of Ireland, which required plenty of 'prudence and decorum', said Palmerston. 'Really very impertinent, but at the same time it serves Lord John right for his weakness in offering this post', the Queen wrote in her journal. To her uncle in Brussels she wrote: 'I have the greatest pleasure in announcing to you a piece of news ... *Lord Palmerston* is *no longer Foreign Secretary.*' Now the royal couple did not even want Clarendon, in whom they had so often confided, to take the Foreign Office. As Albert told Russell: 'we could have Lord Palmerston again in Lord Clarendon'. So Lord Granville, only in his thirties, was appointed to an office he was to hold again nearly twenty years later under his friend Gladstone.

It was a Pyrrhic victory for Lord John, who was turned out within two months, and for the Queen and her husband, who were only three years later to have Palmerston as Prime Minister. There was, however, widespread suspicion that it was really Albert who had engineered the fall of the popular minister. It was alleged that the dismissal was the result of an agreement between the Courts of Vienna and London and that it was known in Vienna before becoming public in London. The Chartist paper, the *Northern Star*, now a shadow of its former self, wrote: 'he [Palmerston] fell in consequence of a court intrigue against him, headed by one who up to this time has wisely kept himself aloof from such interference'. In July 1852 there appeared an article in the liberal *Westminster Review* entitled 'Lord Palmerston and his Policy'. Albert put a copy with his comments into the royal archives. In his comments the Prince wrote:

> There was no interest of the House of Coburg involved in any of the questions upon which we quarrelled with Lord Palmerston, neither in Greece nor Italy, Sicily, Holstein, Hungary etc. Why are Princes alone to be denied the credit of having political opinions based upon an anxiety for national interests and honour of their country and the welfare of mankind?

6

Triumph and Calumny

It was as well that the year of Palmerston's fall was also the year of the Great Exhibition. The remarkable personal triumph this 1851 exhibition was for Albert made up for the meagre results of his ceaseless endeavours to influence foreign policy. Nothing could have been more dispiriting to him than the outcome in Germany, which had engaged his mental energies more than anything else. None of what the Coburg circle had hoped to achieve had come about, and Prussia, in which they had placed high hopes, proved a broken reed. On the other hand, the Exhibition distracted public opinion from the political role of the Queen and particularly of her husband, which was so at variance with the commonly held view of constitutional monarchy. Yet the opposition to the Exhibition undoubtedly also had a political edge to it. The royal couple were known to be supporters of free trade and there were fears that, by bringing foreign firms and inventions into the country, British commercial supremacy would be undermined. A lot of the opposition was petty-minded, what the Prince called 'the panic of old women'. The foreign Prince, right next to the throne, would be bringing a lot of foreigners to the capital, where they would reignite the fires of revolution. Prominent visitors from the Continent themselves feared they might be assassinated. Property values in a fashionable part of London might be undermined by the influx of unruly mobs. There were some long-standing enemies of the Prince on the Tory benches, like Colonel Sibthorpe. He expressed the hope that 'some hailstorm, or some visitation of lightning, might descend to the ill-advised project', the Crystal Palace.

Even when Albert refused to accept the proposal of the Duke of Wellington to succeed him as Commander-in-Chief, suspicions were raised by the terms in which he justified his refusal. In describing himself as 'sole confidential adviser in politics, and only assistant in her

communications with the officers of Government' he seemed to be arro-
gating to himself a crucial role unknown to the constitution. Albert
would dearly have loved to be directly in command of the army, but
knew that would be going too far. As it was, he was constantly interfering in military affairs, far beyond the design of regimental headgear.
When Wellington died in September 1852 the question of who was to
succeed him became urgent. The appointments of Lord Hardinge as
Commander-in-Chief and of Fitzroy Somerset, now raised to the peerage as Lord Raglan, as Master-General of the Ordnance, had the full
authority of the then Prime Minister, Lord Derby. Nonetheless Albert's
involvement still aroused suspicion. Greville wrote that he had effectively 'made himself the heir' of Wellington, 'ridiculous as well as
odious'. In fact the Prince had for the moment prevented the appointment of his and the Queen's cousin George, Duke of Cambridge, though
this was to come about after the Crimean War and prove a dead weight
on the army for the next forty years. When it came to war only a year
on, the Prince would become very deeply involved in military affairs and
decisions.

Palmerston's dismissal in December 1851 unleashed a flood or
rumours which blamed the fall of 'the Minister of England', Lord
John Russell's phrase, on the Queen's German husband. Palmerston
himself was in unforgiving mood and his wife even more so. Lady
Palmerston spoke of treachery and stopped inviting Lord and Lady John
to her Saturday evening receptions, regarded as defining events for
London Society. According to Delane, the editor of *The Times*, an anti-
Palmerstonian, the fallen minister commissioned a scurrilous pamphlet
attacking Albert. It was said that he had invited to Broadlands Samuel
Phillips, a journalist with a somewhat murky reputation, and had provided him with relevant information and documents. The pamphlet was
never published, because Palmerston realised it would damage him
more than the Prince. On the reassembly of Parliament in February
1852, the Radicals raised the dismissal of Palmerston. They expected fireworks from the fallen minister and hoped that some of the fusillade
would go in the direction of the Palace. An open attack on the monarch
and her spouse was, however, not in the repertoire of a paid-up member of the aristocratic establishment like Palmerston. His speech was a
lame effort and he later claimed that Russell had, by dragging in the

Queen's name, made it impossible for him to defend himself without attacking his sovereign. It was, however, too early to write him off and less than three weeks later Russell was defeated on an amendment to a Militia Bill moved by Palmerston. Pam wrote to his brother William Temple: 'I have had my tit-for-tat with John Russell, and turned him out last Friday.'

It was, however, just this governmental instability and the absence of clear party majorities in the Commons that gave the Queen and her husband the opportunity to intervene in politics more than ever. Not that the immediate prospect filled them with anything but alarm. They had now little alternative but to turn to the leader of the Protectionist Tories, Lord Derby, to form a government, and this time Derby had no alternative but to form one. Derby's son wrote in his diary that his father found the Queen reserved, the Prince 'manifestly unfriendly'. It was the political orthodoxy, fully shared by the royal couple, that any return to a duty on corn, however minor, such as Derby might be unable to avoid, would immediately lead to riots in the streets.

Then there was the question of personalities. The Tories had so few men of any ability, other than Disraeli, that they had to bring in ancient dug-outs or men known to be of limited talent. When the deaf old Duke of Wellington asked for the names of the new ministers he kept shouting 'Who? Who?' and it became known as the 'Who, Who Ministry'. One way of shoring up the position would have been to bring back Palmerston, but it was a prospect abhorrent to the Queen and her husband. Fortunately Pam proved unwilling to embark on so fragile a vessel as the Derby minority government. Disraeli was equally repugnant to Albert and Victoria, but was now inescapable. He became Chancellor of the Exchequer and Leader of the House. When he remonstrated that he, a former bankrupt, had no experience of finance, Derby told him 'they give you the figures'.

Albert and Victoria soon changed their opinion of Disraeli. The Queen found his reports on the proceedings of the House of Commons intriguing: 'Mr Disraeli (alias Dizzy) writes very curious reports to me of the House of Commons proceedings – much in the style of his books ...', she wrote to her Uncle Leopold. Mutual respect grew between Albert and Dizzy, the latter clearly impressed by the former's

highly educated mind. It was, however, far from plain sailing. There
were the same complaints of Albert's interference in foreign policy as
there had been in Palmerston's day and of his correspondence with foreign sovereigns independent of the Foreign Office. Even ten months
later, when Derby was on the point of resigning, the Prince still harboured suspicions of Disraeli: 'he extolled his talent, his energy, but
expressed a fear that he was not in his heart favourable to the existing
order of things', as Derby reported Albert's views to his son. 'My Father
defended his colleague ... "He has better reason than anyone to be
attached to our constitutional system since he has experience how easily a man can rise". The Prince was glad to hear it, but still thought
Disraeli had democratic tendencies "and if that is the case, he may
become one of the most dangerous men in Europe".'[1] Albert clearly
could not believe that a man of Jewish origin could be anything but a
danger to the existing order.

Albert's fear of revolution remained undiminished. It was reinforced
by the presence of another Napoleon on the French throne – Louis
Napoleon assumed the imperial title in 1852. Fears that the French
might go on the rampage as they had done under his uncle were rife
and there were alarms about a possible invasion of England. At this
stage Victoria and Albert had no sympathy for Napoleon, who had
displaced the House of Orleans, with which the royal couple had so
many family ties. Napoleon's attempts to give himself royal legitimacy
by a suitable marriage were viewed with hostility at Windsor. A pro-
jected match with Princess Adelaide of Hohenlohe, the daughter of
Victoria's half-sister Feodora, caused the Queen to remark to her Premier Derby: 'You know our family [the Coburgs] have always been
accused of being ready to pick up any crown that had tumbled in the
dirt.' The Queen evidently felt that if Adelaide of Hohenlohe married
Louis Napoleon such an accusation would acquire some substance.
Derby's own family was sufficiently elevated to bring his eldest son Lord
Stanley into contention as a possible King of Greece, when the Bavarian King Otto was overthrown ten years later. Fortunately Adelaide
refused to marry the French Emperor and Victoria wrote to her mother
Feodora: 'Your dear child is *saved* from *ruin* of every possible *sort*. You
know what *he* is, what his moral character is ... how thoroughly
immoral France and French society are – hardly looking at what is

wrong as more than fashionable and natural – you know how very insecure *his* position is ...'[2]*

The Derby-Dizzy government could not last, because a general election in the summer of 1852 had not reinforced it sufficiently. The Tories
had still not ditched any thought of returning to a duty on corn con-
vincingly enough. In December the crunch came when Disraeli
introduced his budget. It was attacked with great ferocity by Gladstone,
the first major clash between these two titans. In his speech Disraeli
made the famous remark 'England does not love coalitions', for the long
desired coalition between Whigs and Peelites was at last in the making
and would displace Derby. It was widely believed that Albert had a large
hand in forming this coalition and that Aberdeen, the Peelite who
headed it, was now his confidant as Peel had been before his death. Stanley, Derby's son, recorded in his diary, after the fall of his father,
'Information from a person employed at Court, that lists of the present
Ministry were in the Prince's hands some time before our fall: in fact
that it was formed by him. The person in question also spoke much of
correspondence carried on between Albert and foreign courts, without
the knowledge of the Secretary for Foreign Affairs: this I cannot disbe-
lieve, knowing it true in some instances.'[3] The young Stanley had been
Under Secretary for Foreign Affairs in his father's ministry. Stanley also
mentions that in his father's papers there was a memorandum of a conversation he had had with Prince Albert:

> The substance of it to the effect that Palmerston had given grievous offence
> by insisting on his right to manage foreign affairs after his own fashion. The
> instances alleged were numerous, relating to Austria, the French *coup d'état*,
> and the German Powers. Palmerston had once told Albert 'that he was a
> German, and did not understand British interests'.[4]

It goes without saying that the Queen resisted Palmerston's return to
the Foreign Office when the Aberdeen Coalition was formed and he had
to make do with the Home Office. It was an arrangement that undoubtedly suited Aberdeen and his Peelite colleagues as much as it did the

---

* In due course Adelaide married Duke Frederick of Augustenburg, the
  claimant to the Duchies of Schleswig and Holstein, known to Albert and
  Victoria as Fritz Holstein. Adelaide and Fritz's daughter Augusta married
  Kaiser Wilhelm II.

Queen and her husband. The Peelites, who held half the posts in the Coalition, were exponents of a conservative foreign policy and disliked Palmerstonian chauvinism. The strength of Peelite representation in the Cabinet pleased the Prince but irked the Whigs. In the Commons the Peelites had by now a fraction of the numbers the Whigs had. This caused jealousy and tensions in the Coalition from the start.

By an unfortunate quirk of fate it fell to Aberdeen to take the nation into war. In the run-up to war the monarchy and its dynastic connections all over Europe came in for for fierce attack, most of it focused on the role of the Queen's husband. Britain and Napoleonic France were brought back into alliance, against Russia. Austria and Prussia, earlier Russia's partners in the Holy Alliance, remained neutral. This alignment sat uneasily with Albert and Victoria's family links. Their feelings were with the late Louis-Philippe's exiled family, who in turn were closely related to Uncle Leopold in Brussels. Charlotte, a daughter of Leopold, had recently married an Austrian Archduke, Maximilian.* None of this mattered as much as conspiracy theorists tried to make out and certainly did not determine the Prince's conduct. He was above all concerned to preserve the peace and prevent a war which from a later perspective appears somewhat unnecessary. His monarchical activism came to haunt him, however, for it was at odds with what was regarded by the majority as the proper role of constitutional monarchy. This discrepancy had been highlighted by the conflict with Palmerston and it was again Palmerston whose position now reignited the controversy. An increasingly bellicose public opinion demanded confrontation with Russia, the representative of tyranny and despotism. Palmerston, although not responsible for foreign policy, was seen as the one member of the Cabinet who wanted a policy of firmness, while Aberdeen and most of his colleagues were regarded as appeasers. Feelings against Russia rose to fever pitch when, at the end of November 1853, the Russians annihilated a Turkish fleet at Sinope in the Black Sea. Shortly afterwards Palmerston resigned from the Cabinet, though publicly it was over the intention to introduce another Franchise Reform Bill rather than over

---

* Maximilian became Emperor of Mexico a few years later and was shot by insurgents in 1867. There is a well-known painting of his execution by Edouard Manet.

foreign policy. Although Palmerston withdrew his resignation a few days later and returned to the Cabinet, reform having apparently been shelved, the public concluded that he had been forced out by the Court, as it was believed he had been two years earlier. This time a fierce newspaper campaign, backed by pamphlets and satires, was unleashed against Prince Albert, an easier target than the Queen herself, whose patriotism could hardly be impugned.

The attacks stretched right across the political spectrum. It was to be expected that Radicals of various shades would wade in. They had always regarded Palmerston as their man, though in reality that was hardly the full story. Undoubtedly his opposition to a further Reform Bill had played a part in his temporary retirement and that was not a motive radicals could back. It was, however, too tempting to see Palmerston's long-running fight against Court interference with foreign policy as the main issue. Some of the criticisms of Albert's view of the role of the monarch that now appeared in the press were substantial enough. The *Daily News*, a radical paper, stated: 'Above all, the nation distrusts the politics, however they may admire the taste, of a Prince who has breathed from childhood the air of courts tainted by the imaginative servility of Goethe.' A few days later it amplified this by saying that the Prince had been 'sedulously trained, at that period of his life when the mind is most accessible to lasting impressions, in the traditional maxims of those most inveterate of continental legitimists, the minor courts of Germany ... it is an unanswerable reason for insisting that he should abstain from all interference with English politics.' The *Morning Advertiser* stated that Germanic influences were 'rapidly undermining those free institutions which are the glory of Great Britain' and 'placing in imminent peril the very Throne itself'.[5] The fact that he was present at the Queen's interviews with ministers and had access to Cabinet memoranda became widely known and was regarded as unconstitutional, as he was one 'on whom rests no responsibility ... in the eye of the Constitution, a nonentity. He is simply a subject of the Crown.'

What was remarkable was that similar attacks also came from the Tory side. Here the Prince had long been regarded as a partisan of the liberal-conservative Peelites and the real author of the Aberdeen Coalition, a liberal-conservative construct dominated by Peelites. Lord

Stanley, using the pseudonym 'M.P.', wrote a letter to the Tory *Morning Herald*, giving details of Albert's involvement with government and foreign policy in particular. He had inside knowledge from his spell as Under Secretary of Foreign Affairs in his father's government in the previous year. He had confided to his diary his view that Palmerston's in–out vacillation had damaged his position seriously, but he also speculated: 'It is possible that P. himself desired to escape from an office he does not like, and from the society of uncongenial colleagues: but the more probable version is, that Lord Aberdeen and Albert jointly have contrived the affair, the latter being the prime mover, the former only his tool. This last is certainly the idea commonly received out of doors: and has led to loud and growing complaints of the secret influence exerted by the Prince Consort.' Stanley's own anonymous and public complaint was: 'It is too bad that one man, and he not an Englishman by birth, should be at once Foreign Secretary, Commander-in-Chief and Prime Minister in all administrations.' 300–400,000 copies of Stanley's 'M.P.' letter were distributed throughout the country.

The *Morning Herald* also identified Stockmar as a dangerous influence on Albert. They would have been confirmed in this opinion had they known the contents of the long letter which Stockmar wrote to the Prince on 5 January 1854. It was in response to urgent requests by Albert, later reinforced by the Queen, to come to England to support them in their trials and tribulations. Stockmar was too ill to travel. In his letter there were passages such as:

> You could not marry the Queen of England without meaning, and without being bound, to become a political soldier ... Constitutional Monarchy has since 1830 been constantly in danger of becoming a pure Ministerial Government. In theory one of the first duties of Ministers is to protect and preserve intact the traditional usages of Royal prerogative. But, if they do not fulfil their duty – what then? ... the extinction of the genuine Tories, and the growth of those politicians of the Aberdeen school, who treat the existing Constitution merely as a bridge to a Republic, it is of extreme importance, that this fiction should be *countenanced only provisionally, and that no opportunity should be let slip of vindicating the legitimate position of the Crown* ... For the most jealous and distrustful Liberalism ... must be satisfied, if *this be place no higher than a right on the part of the King to be the permanent President of his Ministerial Council* ... Thus then do I vindicate for the Sovereign

the position of a permanent Premier, who takes rank above the temporary head of the Cabinet ...[6]

Even twenty years later, in 1876, this letter raised eyebrows, when it was published in the second of the five-volume biography of the Prince, which the Queen commissioned from Sir Theodore Martin. Had it become known at the time when it was written, the furore surrounding the Prince's position would have been even greater than it was. Stockmar was plainly out of touch with a lot of what was going on and admitted as much, but the emotional dependence of Albert on him seemed undiminished. Albert's own wry comment on the storm that had gathered round his head was contained in a letter to his brother:

> The public had graciously selected me as its scapegoat to answer for its not yet having come to war, and says 'logically' that the interest of the Coburg family, which is Russian, Belgian, Orleanistic, Fusionistic [he probably meant union of German states], is preferred to the alliance with Louis Napoleon. The Emperor of Russia now governs England. He telegraphs to Gotha, to you in Brussels, Uncle Leopold to me, I whisper in Victoria's ear, she gets round old Aberdeen, and the voice of the only *English* Minister, Palmerston is not listened to – ay, he is always intrigued against, at the court, and by the Court.

Greville was convinced that these attacks were paid for by Napoleon, who was determined to undermine the Prince's influence. It was another unlikely conspiracy theory.

Some of the attacks on the Prince, even in Tory papers like the *Standard*, stopped scarcely short of calling him a traitor. Not surprisingly, given the anti-Russian war hysteria of the moment, popular opinion in the shires took this at face value and in the capital a mob collected waiting to see him and even the Queen taken to the Tower. Victoria herself was if anything even more deeply wounded by these calumnies than her husband, though she disliked the implication, in much of the comment, that she was entirely dependent on Albert. There was in fact no doubt that she could empathise better than he did with the upsurge of patriotic fervour against Russia and could at least understand the hysterical edge to it. The political establishment began to sense danger in the attacks on the monarch and her consort, and felt it was time to rein in the more absurd public manifestations of the campaign. Palmerston himself instructed Peter Borthwick, the editor of the *Morning Post*, regarded as the Palmerstonian house organ, to publish a paragraph stating that his resignation was due to a misunderstanding between himself and some of his colleagues and had not 'the remotest connection with anything on the part of the Court'.

The reassembly of Parliament at the end of January 1854 provided an opportunity for counterattack. Albert rode accompanied only by a groom through some of the roughest parts of London on the day before the state opening. The Queen was at first reluctant to open Parliament in person, but she then did so accompanied by Albert, in view of a large and friendly crowd. Some of those present, including Lord Stanley, said 'it was not so good as in the newspapers; cheers over-powered the hissing, but of this latter, where I stood, close by Whitehall chapel, there was a plentiful sprinkling …' Aberdeen, himself the victim of a ferocious smear campaign, defended the Prince vigorously, but he rejected as untimely the Queen's proposal that Albert should be given the title 'Prince Consort'. The defence of the Prince in Parliament did not satisfy some of the papers that had attacked him. The *Daily News* hoped that his talents could be sufficiently occupied outside government business. The *Morning Advertiser* was still not satisfied and said 'the creation and exercise of a great power in the State, wholly unrecognised by the Constitution' had been exposed. The Tories were anxious to make peace with the Court and shifted their attack on to Aberdeen. They knew it was impolitic for them to create a rift with the Queen. On 23 February 1854 Stanley noted in his diary that Disraeli had spoken to him of 'civilities received from the Queen and Prince, which he construed into proofs of political reconciliation'.

The Queen and the Prince were in fact deeply disappointed that their continental connections could not bring in Austria, Prussia and the German Confederation more decisively in on the side of the Western allies. Austria had an immediate interest in countering Russian designs in the Balkans and in fact the Crimean War marked the end of the conservative alliance between Russia and Austria, which had enabled the Habsburgs to recover their position after the Revolution of 1848. Austria had indeed, as her Chief Minister after the Revolution, Prince Schwarzenberg, said 'astonished the world by her ingratitude', but she did not actually go to war against Russia. This was more than anything

due to the situation in Germany, where Prussia refused to move from a
position of neutrality. On this occasion the smaller German states were
with Prussia rather than Austria, for they were afraid of being involved
in war with Europe's main anti-revolutionary power. They were more
afraid of Napoleonic France than they were of Russia. In Prussia the ruling elite was split between a pro-Western and a pro-Russian faction. The
vacillating King in the end dismissed most of the pro-Westerners,
including Bunsen, the ambassador in London. Bunsen and his wife had
enjoyed a close relationship with the Queen and her husband.

Albert had long given up on the unstable Prussian King and his last
exchanges with Frederick William IV were brought on by the hostilities
in the Crimea. In a letter in August 1854 Albert told Frederick William
in no uncertain terms of the animosity which Prussian neutrality had
aroused in England. The divisions in the Prussian establishment
extended right into the royal family, for the pro-Western faction clustered round the King's brother and heir, William, the 'Grapeshot Prince'
of 1848 and later German Emperor. It strengthened the feeling of
Victoria and Albert that the Prince and his wife Augusta were kindred
liberal spirits. It helped to pave the way for the marriage between Vicky,
the royal couple's eldest daughter, and Frederick William, William
and Augusta's heir. In 1854 the gulf between the King of Prussia and
his brother Prince William was so deep that it required the services of a
go-between to restore a semblance of normal relations. This service was
performed by none other than Otto von Bismarck, then aged thirty-nine
and the Prussian ambassador to the Frankfurt Diet. As a member of the
Prussian aristocracy, the Junkers, Bismarck had from his earliest days
lived close to the House of Hohenzollern, though he by no means always
saw eye to eye with either the King or Prince William, least of all with
the latter's wife Augusta.

War between Britain and Russia became official at the end of March
1854. It did not prove the walkover that much of British bellicose opinion had expected. The middle classes, especially, assumed that the
backward Tsarist empire and its armies recruited from an illiterate
peasantry would prove no match for technologically advanced, progressive and liberal Britain. When it took much longer, and much more
blood, sweat and tears to achieve victory, there had to be scapegoats. An
obvious one was the geriatric military leadership and the antiquated

military bureaucracy. Since both were the product of aristocracy and patronage, these features of Britain's social system came under attack, especially from middle-class Radicals. Anti-aristocratic sentiment was not directed against the monarchy, and the Queen and her husband were well in harmony with the patriotic feeling in the country.

A cordial relationship was established between Windsor and Napoleon III, which put paid to any talk of a dynastic conspiracy by the Coburg family. In September 1854 the Prince, on his own, paid a visit to the French Emperor, during which they reviewed troops encamped around Boulogne and St-Omer. They had wide-ranging and frank discussions on all current issues and, according to Albert's memorandum on the visit, there was a real meeting of minds. The Prince found the Emperor unpretentious, humorous, and for the moment the only man who had 'any hold on France'. On the other hand, Albert did not think that Napoleon was very well informed on many subjects. For example, on the question of Schleswig-Holstein he found him as ignorant as many English politicians. No doubt Albert took the opportunity to give him a lecture on the matter – 'he was glad to receive from me a general condensed history of the whole transaction'. The Prince was not impressed by the Emperor's horsemanship and disapproved of his heavy smoking. More seriously, he perceptively assessed the weakness of the Napoleonic regime: 'Having deprived the people of every active participation in the government, and having reduced them to mere passive spectators, he is bound to keep up the "spectacle", and, as at a fireworks, whenever a pause takes place between the different displays, the public immediately grows impatient ...'[7] The visit was a prelude to the French Emperor's visit to Windsor in April 1855 and to the state visit of Victoria and Albert to Paris in August 1855.

The deep personal sympathy the Queen felt for the sufferings of her troops in the Crimea and her intense concern for their welfare caught the public imagination. She always thought of herself as a soldier's daughter. There was a strong emotional charge in having a woman as the symbolic head of Britain's armed forces. Albert's constant and deep involvement in military affairs and operational decisions came in for some criticism, but perhaps less criticism than for his political interference. There had been some attacks on him when Lord Hardinge succeeded the Duke of Wellington as Commander-in-Chief and he was still often seen as the Prince's placeman. Since Hardinge was nearly seventy when the war broke out, he could also easily come to be regarded as a prime example of the gerontocracy that was thwarting Britain's war effort. Albert at thirty-five was much the youngest field-marshal in the army and his prolific output of plans and schemes about the armed forces and the conduct of operations could at least not be attributed to an ageing brain. In some quarters suspicion was so strong that nothing could assuage it. In October 1855, when Sebastopol had been taken, but not sacked, the *Morning Advertiser* attributed such pusillanimity to Albert's 'pro-Russianism'. When in the summer of that year the Prince had said in a speech at Trinity House that the war had placed free parliamentary government 'on its trial', even this was described by *Reynolds's Newspaper* as an 'anti-constitutional tirade' and 'a plain and unmistakable intimation that in this country the popular power it too ample and the royal prerogative too restricted'.

The war and the disappointments about its course spelt the end of Aberdeen's government. When this point was reached in February 1855 it was an occasion which illustrated how politically important the monarchy was when the party and personal situation in Parliament was confused and uncertain. It also showed the extent to which the Queen's hands were tied in such circumstances, for the final outcome was the emergence of Palmerston as Prime Minister, a post he was to hold, with an interruption of fifteen months, until his death more than ten years later. It was an outcome which Victoria and Albert went to considerable lengths to avoid. The failure in the Crimea required a ministerial sacrificial lamb as well as a saviour. Public opinion, roused to a pitch of hysteria, homed in on the Secretary of State for War, the Peelite Duke of Newcastle, as the most immediately guilty man, though Aberdeen himself was scarcely less in the firing line. Palmerston was seen as the saviour, even though at age seventy many in the political world regarded him as a spent force. Disraeli, badly frustrated by the course this political crisis was taking, described him thus to his friend, Lady Londonderry:

> now the inevitable man, and tho' he is really an imposter, utterly exhausted, and at best only ginger beer and not champaign, and now an old painted Pantaloon, very deaf, very blind, and with false teeth, which would fall out of his mouth when speaking, if he did not hesitate and halt so in his talk – he

is a name which the country resolves to associate with energy, wisdom, and eloquence, and will until he has tried and failed.[8]

The country turned out to be more right than Disraeli. The Queen and her husband, in their attempts to explore all possibilities before turning to the dreaded Palmerston, had first turned to Derby, as leader of the largest opposition party, to form a government. To the intense annoyance of his lieutenant, Disraeli, Derby had decided that he was unable to form a government without Palmerston, who refused to join him. Then it was the turn of Lord John Russell, still the most senior Whig, but who had by his erratic behaviour helped to bring Aberdeen down. Russell found to his consternation that his wilful conduct had so damaged his reputation that almost none of the other Whigs any longer supported him. So it was Palmerston. The situation has been compared to that in 1940, when, after the fall of Neville Chamberlain, many in the Conservative Party as well as the King would have preferred Lord Halifax to succeed him, but Churchill became the inevitable man. In 1855 the Queen was much praised for having swallowed her well-known doubts about Palmerston and it was widely felt that the course of the governmental crisis confirmed that the monarchy was genuinely a constitutional one. *The Times*, which, under its editor Delane, had usually been anti-Palmerstonian and had therefore sided with the Court and the political establishment, switched its support broadly to Palmerston. Delane was now often to be seen at Lady Palmerston's parties, something that produced from Disraeli the accusation that 'the once stern guardians of popular rights simper in the enervating atmosphere of gilded salons'. In the past Aberdeen had been close to Delane and often supplied him with information when he took over as editor at the age of twenty-three in 1841, but this friendship now no longer influenced the paper. William Howard Russell, the correspondent of *The Times* in the Crimea, had through his reports done more than anybody to arouse public anger about bureaucratic mismanagement and the sufferings of the troops. Albert was never at ease with the press, especially when it attacked authority, and called Russell a 'miserable scribbler'. Russell was in fact a charming and amusing Irishman, who struck up a personal friendship with many officers in the Crimea and was thus able to obtain authentic information.

In April 1855 the French Emperor visited Windsor. He had in the meantime married a Spanish lady, Eugénie de Montijo, a more suitable match in Victoria's eyes than a marriage to her half-niece Adelaide. Such thoughts were now laid aside and the Queen, in her impulsive way, was much taken with the Emperor and waxed enthusiastic about his charm and personal attraction. He was 'so very good natured and unassuming and natural', yet there was 'something fascinating, melancholy and engaging' about him, 'a very *extraordinary* man with great qualities ... wonderful *self-control*, great *calmness*, even *gentleness* ... as *unlike a Frenchman* as possible, being much more *German* than French in character', and more in the same vein including '*indomitable, indomitable courage, unflinching firmness of purpose, self-reliance, perseverance and great secrecy*'. 'I felt – I do not know how to express it – safe with him', she wrote.[9] Lord Clarendon, the Foreign Secretary, who had an intimate knowledge of European royalty, remarked: '*Le Coquin*! He has evidently been making love to her.'

In August 1855 Victoria and Albert, accompanied by their two eldest children, Vicky and the Prince of Wales, paid a state visit to Paris. It was a glittering occasion which set the seal on the full acceptance of Napoleon as a legitimate ruler by the British royal family. Victoria was not in the least put out by the fact that Eugénie outshone her in beauty and fashionable dress. The Queen wrote about the Empress: 'charming, lovable creature', so 'lively and talkative', and so good-looking and graceful that even Albert admired her. 'Altogether I am delighted to see how much he likes and admires her, as it is so seldom I see him do so with *any* woman.' No jealousy there and no one could outshine Victoria in dignity. This made its mark with the Parisian crowds and made up for the English Queen's lack of fashionable attire. A particularly poignant moment came when Victoria and Albert visited the Hôtel des Invalides. Napoleon I's coffin had not yet been put in its final resting place but was in a side chapel, where the Queen saw it: 'there I stood, at the arm of Napoleon III, his nephew, before the coffin of England's bitterest foe; I, the granddaughter of that King who hated him most, and who most vigorously opposed him, and this very nephew, who bears his name, being my nearest and dearest ally!' Victoria now compared this visit favourably to her earlier visits to Louis-Philippe: 'Everything is beautifully *monté*, – in the greatest style and all so *quiet*, no noise, *no hustle*, – I must say *infinitely* better and more royal and *anständig* [decent] than in the poor King's time', she wrote to her mother, the Duchess of Kent.[10]

Royal visits of this kind are always described in superlatives in most contemporary press reports and this one was no exception. A more jaundiced observer, Bismarck, the Prussian envoy to the Diet in Frankfurt, noticed little enthusiasm among the crowds for the English Queen. He was probably biased, because he belonged to that faction in the Prussian establishment that did not want their country to enter the war on the side of Britain and France. He was introduced to the British royal couple and, curiously enough, he too found Napoleon fascinating, and for the moment firmly in the saddle, but to his brother he wrote: 'He looks frightened, like the frontal view of a rat.' It was just as well that neither Napoleon nor Victoria and Albert knew that Bismarck, one of hundreds at the official receptions that marked the royal visit, would be the man of destiny preparing a future quite different from what they hoped for.

The warmth of personal relations between the British royal couple and the Bonapartes were not a full substitute for the close family relations between the House of Coburg and so many other European dynasties, nor could they have the same endurance. At this very moment a new dynastic tie was in the making, the marriage between Vicky, Albert and Victoria's eldest daughter, and Frederick William, the son of the Prince of Prussia, William, and his wife Augusta. William was the heir of his childless brother Frederick William IV of Prussia, and Frederick William would eventually inherit the Prussian throne. Such a tie between the Houses of Coburg and Hohenzollern fitted perfectly into the vision of a liberal Germany united under the aegis of Prussia so long cherished by Albert and Stockmar. It also carried the hallmark of Uncle Leopold in Brussels, who at this moment felt distinctly uneasy about the close relationship between his English niece and nephew and the Bonapartes. Vicky was fourteen in 1855, Frederick William nearly ten years older.

They had first met in London at the time of the Great Exhibition in 1851, and the possibility of a marriage may well have been in the minds of their elders even then. Frederick William and his parents had attended the opening of the Exhibition in spite of strong pressures in the Prussian Court against such a visit. Foreign royalty had picked up all the old wives' tales about what would happen, that the Crystal Palace would shatter from the salvo of guns at the opening or collapse under the weight of bird droppings. In addition they feared assassination and revolution. That permanently carping reactionary Uncle Cumberland, King of Hanover, by then distinctly senile, had written to Berlin that 'the excommunicated of all lands' were in London and 'that the Ministers will not allow the Queen and the originator of this folly, Prince Albert to be in London while the Exhibition is on'. The Prussian King reluctantly gave his permission for his brother and heir to go to London with his family.

The friendship between Augusta, Frederick William's mother, and the Queen went back to the time when Augusta paid a visit to England in 1846. Victoria had then written to her Uncle Leopold: 'I find her so clever, so amiable, so well informed, and so good; she seem to have some enemies for there are whispers of her being false; but from all that I have seen of her ... I cannot and will not believe it. Her position is a very difficult one; she is too enlightened and liberal for the Prussian Court not to have enemies; but I believe she is a friend to us and our family ...' Augusta may or may not have been false, but her husband certainly was. There were mistresses in his life, in spite of the heroic image he later acquired as German Emperor. It was well known that in his youth he would have preferred to marry Princess Radziwill, but the Hohenzollerns had very rigid notions of who was sufficiently royal to be eligible. Marital relations between William and Augusta had long ceased. Victoria was correct about the difficulty of Augusta's position in Prussia, but she and Albert convinced themselves that Augusta's husband had been weaned from his reactionary views by his experiences in 1848 and subsequently. Albert had certainly done his best to convert him, but homilies in the style of Stockmar cannot have made much of an impression on a man who was twenty-two years the Prince's senior.

William was in fact a somewhat narrow-minded soldier, honest enough within his limits, but totally dedicated to the maintenance of the Prussian military monarchy. After his return to Germany from his brief exile in London in 1848, he commanded the troops which extinguished the last embers of revolt in south-west Germany in the following year. In the revolution of 1848 the continued grip of the Prussian monarch on his armies, as of other monarchs on their troops, proved the key factor in defeating the revolution. It was a lesson William did not forget and it is enshrined in the German rhyming couplet 'Gegen Demokraten helfen nur Soldaten' (against democrats the only help is soldiers). The experience of the Crimean War, when William and Augusta appeared to be a pro-Western counterpoise to the pro-Russian orientation of the Prussian King and most of those around him may, well have confirmed Victoria and Albert in the view that the marriage project should be pursued. In the House of Hohenzollern, even more than in the House of Coburg, there was a Russian connection. William's sister Charlotte was married to Tsar Nicholas I and became in Russia the Tsarina Alexandra Feodorovna. Augusta, on the other hand, hated Russia. Her maternal grandfather was Tsar Paul, Catherine the Great's son, murdered in 1801 with the connivance of his own son and heir Alexander I. Such Russian shenanigans were miles removed from the liberal court of Weimar, where Augusta had grown up. What better than that William's heir should make an English marriage?

During the royal visit to Paris in August 1855 Vicky had accompanied her parents, come before a wider public and had herself been captivated by the splendours of the Parisian Court. The beautiful and kind Eugénie had greatly impressed the young girl. Shortly afterwards Frederick William came to England to view the girl who was envisaged as his future wife. He was accompanied by Helmuth von Moltke, who in the next decade was, as Prussian Chief of Staff, to lead the Prussian armies to victory in Bismarck's wars. The royal family was at Balmoral and the Prussian Prince may well have been impressed by the relaxed and easy-going atmosphere. It was very different from the Prussian Court, yet the British royal family was so much more important than the Hohenzollerns. Frederick William was, in spite of his soldierly bearing and education, not a strong character. He was affected by the uneasy, ideologically divided marriage of his parents. His mother had seen to it that his education inculcated in him a modicum of liberalism. With his father there was a cold relationship, but filial piety, as the future was to show, was deeply implanted, as was attachment to the military character of the Prussian monarchy. Towards Vicky his feelings immediately blossomed and were fully reciprocated. An engagement was agreed upon, though the marriage was to be delayed for two years, until after the Princess Royal had reached her seventeenth birthday. The young couple had great difficulty in finding any time alone together, for no one could have taken the need for constant chaperonage more seriously than the Queen herself.

Rumours of the engagement almost immediately got out, to a mixed reception in both countries. In Britain Prussian neutrality in the Crimean War was decidedly unpopular and the prestige of Prussia and her King was low. It confirmed the view of Prussia as the least among the European great powers. In a leading article on 3 October 1855 *The Times* called the Hohenzollerns one of many 'paltry German dynasties', who, because they had reneged on their promises of 1848, might be heading for extinction. 'What sympathy can exist between a Court supported like ours on the solid basis of popular freedom ... and a camarilla ... engaged ... in trampling out the last embers of popular government?', it asked. In Prussia the Liberals had always looked to England as their *beau idéal*, but they were in the doldrums, licking their wounds from the defeats of 1848 and 1849. None of their high aspirations for parliamentary government and German unity had been realised. The camarilla referred to by *The Times* was a narrow clique of reactionary courtiers surrounding the King. They ran a system in which personal liberties and freedom of speech were severely repressed. Bismarck's comments on the proposed marriage between Windsor and Potsdam were characteristic of opinion prevailing in these ruling circles: 'If the Princess can leave the Englishwoman at home and become a Prussian, then she may be a blessing to the country ... If our future Queen remains even only partly English, I can see our Court in danger of being surrounded by English influence.'[11] Bismarck regarded the Anglophilia of the liberals with the gravest of suspicions.

At home Palmerston did his best to deflect the widespread criticism, even among his own Cabinet colleagues, provoked by the tie to the House of Hohenzollern. Such a helpful attitude was one of many reasons why relations between Palmerston as Prime Minister and the royal couple were less fraught than they had been in previous years. Albert's close and expert intervention in military affairs met with respect rather than resistance by the Prime Minister. Nobody could fault the royal couple's efforts to maintain friendly relations with the French Emperor or now accuse them of putting the dynastic concerns of the Coburgs before the national interest. In fact the insistence on adequate peace terms, fully shared by Albert and the Queen, caused some difference of opinion with Uncle Leopold, who had never felt comfortable with the alignment of Britain and France against Russia. When the end of the war came, in the spring of 1856, the Queen conferred the Garter on Palmerston.

Shortly afterwards the Queen raised again her long-standing wish to confer a title and status upon her husband. Palmerston took the matter up, somewhat reluctantly, and long-drawn out discussions on a Prince Consort Bill took place with the Lord Chancellor, in Cabinet and between the party leaders. They proved abortive and in June 1857 the Queen, much exasperated, finally conferred, by letters patent, the title on her husband that had long been in common use. Palmerston's personal domination of the political scene reached an apogee when he won a general election in the early summer of 1857. He had asked the Queen to dissolve Parliament, in circumstances somewhat similar to the Don Pacifico affair, which had enabled him to score such a signal triumph seven years earlier. This time it was the affair of the *Arrow*, a Chinese-built boat flying the British flag, which was boarded by a Chinese war-junk and the crew carried off on a charge of piracy. The Governor of Hong Kong called in the fleet to demand satisfaction and Palmerston defended his action. The Prime Minister was attacked from all quarters, by the Tories led by Disraeli, by the Manchester Radicals led by Cobden and Bright, by Peelites like Gladstone, and even by Whigs like Lord John Russell. The election showed that Palmerston had judged the chauvinist mood of the country better than his opponents. Bright and Cobden lost their seats, Lord John Russell saw his constituency majority much reduced and Palmerston had a parliamentary majority of at least eighty-five.

The mood of the country was, however, fickle and the government was soon in trouble over the Indian Mutiny, an event which presented a massive challenge to Britain's imperial position. The news from India led to hysterical demands for vengeance fuelled by a strong dose of racism. There were fears that some European countries might take advantage of the fact that British military resources were fully stretched. For the moment the Anglo-French alliance remained intact. Napoleon III and Eugénie paid a visit to Victoria and Albert at Osborne, which showed how friendly and intimate the relations between the two couples had become. A year earlier Eugénie had given Napoleon an heir, the Prince Imperial, and in April 1857 Victoria had given birth to her last child, Beatrice. Such happy events created a further bond between two families isolated from normal life by their exalted position. In the exchange of letters after the end of the visit, normally a formality, but on this occasion marked by unusual warmth, Victoria was undoubtedly sincere when she wrote: 'In a position so isolated as ours, we can find no greater consolation, no support more sure, than the sympathy and counsel of him or her who is called to share our lot in life, and the dear Empress, with her generous impulses, is your guardian angel, as the Prince is my true friend.' There was for the moment no hint that Napoleon and the Bonapartes were upstarts in an insecure position, nor that the Anglo-French alliance might be merely an interlude in a long-running rivalry.

When scarcely a fortnight later Victoria and Albert paid a return visit to Cherbourg, there was behind the scenes a somewhat different note. The Prince, with his keen eye for military and naval matters, was taken aback by the amount of fortification building works that were going on around the French naval base. Britain was the most obvious country against which they might be directed and Albert, on his return, lost no time in making his anxieties known to the government. In the next few years fears about a French invasion at times took on a hysterical note. They produced the Volunteer Movement, an earlier version of the Home Guard. There was anxiety what the advance of technology, steam propulsion and the arrival of the iron-clad, might do to Britain's naval supremacy. Contrary to the accusations of meddling and unconstitutional conduct that had so often been flung against the Prince, Greville and Clarendon, both of them highly qualified insiders, gave Albert full credit for what he did for the country's governance in general and for its armed forces in particular. Greville quotes Clarendon as saying:

> the manner in which the Queen in her own name, but with the assistance of the Prince, exercised her functions, was exceedingly good, and well became her position and was eminently useful. She held each Minister to the discharge of his duty and his responsibility to her ... This is what none of her predecessors ever did, and it is in fact the act of Prince Albert, who is to all intents and purposes King ... All his views and notions are those of a Constitutional Sovereign, and he fulfils the duties of one, and at the same time makes the Crown an entity, and discharges the functions which properly

belong to the Sovereign. I told Clarendon that I had been told the Prince had upon many occasions rendered the most important services to the Government, and had repeatedly prevented their getting into scrapes of various sorts. He said it was perfectly true ...

In February 1858 Palmerston, whom the general election nine months earlier had seemed to put in an impregnable political position, was suddenly brought down by a storm in Anglo-French relations. One of the many plots to assassinate the French Emperor was found to have been hatched in London by an Italian conspirator, Orsini. Wild accusations flew to and fro across the Channel. Palmerston felt bound to respond by bringing in an early version of modern anti-terrorist legislation, the Conspiracy to Murder Bill. This time the Most English Minister was hoist by his own petard. He was felt to have buckled under pressure from a foreign potentate. The attack now came from the Radicals, who in the past had often cheered him. Among them was John Bright, who had got back into the House to represent Birmingham. Palmerston was infuriated that the pacifist left should now attack him on his own ground and lost his temper. Disraeli turned the occasion opportunistically but brilliantly to his own account and the government was defeated by nineteen votes. The Cabinet decided unanimously to resign.

In these mid-century Parliaments there were no clear majorities and party ties were loose. The House of Commons enjoyed a degree of supremacy which it soon lost with the arrival of tighter party discipline. The Conspiracy to Murder Bill was probably not the only reason for Palmerston's defeat. A few weeks earlier he had appointed Clanricarde Lord Privy Seal and a member of the Cabinet. Clanricarde had been involved in some notorious sexual scandals as well as in a case of child abuse. The appointment had evoked universal condemnation and Pam had suddenly become unpopular. Albert and Victoria could have been forgiven for a little *Schadenfreude* at their old enemy's downfall. In fact such signals of political instability alarmed them, even though it highlighted the function of the monarchy as the sheet anchor of the whole system. Anyway, they had no alternative but to call on Lord Derby and for the second time in six years there was a Tory Government led by Derby in the Lords and Disraeli in the Commons. Its hold on power was precarious.

On the Continent a new political crisis was in the making. Ever since

Napoleon III had come to power there had been apprehension throughout Europe that he would seek to rival his uncle's conquests. It was widely believed that, without spectacular military triumphs, his regime could not survive. Albert and Victoria shared these fears, and they had only temporarily been suppressed when the Crimean War produced an Anglo-French entente. Now the opportunity beckoned for the French Emperor to redraw the map of Europe imposed on his country after the defeat of his uncle at Waterloo. Italy and Germany were the two great European nations that had not yet achieved the political unity that the rise of nationalism made into an overriding aspiration. The Italian cause was close to Napoleon's heart and would enhance French power, while German unity was feared as a threat to French security. Napoleon would help to liberate Italy from Austrian control and at the same time get compensation for France. He might achieve her so-called natural frontiers, along the Alps, by obtaining Savoy from Piedmont, in return for helping her against Austria. A plan of this kind was discussed at a secret meeting at Plombières in July 1858 between Napoleon and Cavour, the Prime Minister of Piedmont. In May 1859 war broke out between Piedmont and France, on the one hand, and Austria, on the other. The prospect of this war became the dominant European question in the autumn and winter 1858/59. It also became a major issue in British politics.

The dilemma over the Italian question, which had faced Britain in 1848, now once more became acute. On the one hand, there was sympathy with the liberal Italian national movement, the *risorgimento*, and a desire to see the end of Austrian repression in Italy. On the other, there was the fear that the collapse of Austrian power in Italy and possibly elsewhere would be the final nail in the coffin for the settlement of 1815 and might cause a new revolutionary wave to sweep Europe. A further complication was the deep-seated fear of France under another Napoleon. Events in Italy had a direct bearing on the situation in Germany, the other country still awaiting political formation. In Germany there was also great sympathy for the Italian *risorgimento* and a feeling that if the Italians could obtain a unified state so could the Germans. On the other hand, German sentiment was almost universally behind their Austrian brothers in their fight against France. There were fears that sooner or later France might want the Rhine as her natural frontier in the East and nothing did more to arouse German nationalism than that fear.

In Britain the Conservative government in office at that moment was mainly concerned that an Austrian collapse might undermine the European balance of power and promote revolution. Suspicion of Napoleon and his ambitions ran high again. The weak Derby–Dizzy government could, however, hardly ignore the strong sympathies of the British public with the Italian *Risorgimento*. Victoria and Albert agreed with the government's broadly pro-Austrian stance and feared the Italian proclivities of Palmerston, Russell and other personalities in the Whig, Radical and Peelite opposition. They were also deeply concerned about the evolving German situation, now that the Coburg connection had been supplemented by the Hohenzollern link.

7

The Prussian Marriage

The marriage between Vicky and Frederick William was celebrated with suitable pomp in January 1858. The Queen had insisted that the wedding should take place in England. In spite of the negative comments that the engagement had provoked when it first became public, there was the usual popular enthusiasm when the wedding actually took place. Large crowds lined the route from Buckingham Palace to St James's Chapel. There were eighteen carriages, over three hundred soldiers and 220 horses. There was a plentiful display of Prussian flags entwined with the Union Jack. The Queen asked the Prince of Prussia, now Vicky's father-in-law, to call her 'Du', the German 'thou', only bestowed upon close friends and family. The parting from the young bride was a highly emotional moment for Victoria and even more for Albert. The Prince had invested in her, rather than in Bertie, the Prince of Wales, all his hopes for the future. If only female offspring had had the same rights of succession as males, and Vicky could have inherited the British crown, events would have evolved very differently. Instead she was plunged into the Prussian Court at a highly sensitive moment.

Not that she lacked advice. A correspondence started with her mother which continued for the next forty years, often several times a week. There are over four thousand letters from mother to daughter and nearly as many the other way. Victoria gave her daughter advice and admonitions on every detail of her private and sometimes her public life. Against the inclination of Vicky's husband, the son of Stockmar, Baron Ernst von Stockmar, became her private secretary. She had some English ladies-in-waiting and English physicians. It was an incursion that provoked much resentment and hostility in Prussia. Victoria was appalled when her daughter became pregnant very quickly. 'If I had a year of *happy* enjoyment *with* dear Papa, to myself – *how* thankful I should have been! But I was 3 years & ½ older; & *therefore* I was *in for it* at *once* – & furious I was', she wrote to her daughter.[1] Victoria had done little to enlighten Vicky about the facts of life, beyond giving her a book entitled *The Bridal Offering* on the morning of the wedding. When Vicky complained about the discomforts of pregnancy, the Queen returned to one of her recurrent themes, the selfishness of men and the poor lot of women: 'I *hope* Fritz is *duly shocked* at your sufferings, for those *very selfish* men would not bear for a *minute* what *we* poor *slaves* have to endure.' It was decided that the Princess could not travel to Coburg for a family reunion and in May her father visited her briefly in Berlin. Albert persuaded himself that everything was rosy in the garden in Berlin and that Frederick William and his wife were a very happy couple, as indeed they were.

In August both Victoria and Albert paid a visit to their daughter in Potsdam. Stockmar, old and ill, came to Berlin for the occasion and so did Albert's brother Ernst, the Duke of Coburg. There were visits to Frederick the Great's tomb and to his rococo palace of Sans Souci, encounters with Alexander von Humboldt, the famous explorer and scientist aged nearly ninety, and much military display. The prevalence of military uniforms at every turn did strike the English visitors as strange. Prussia was a country that had been made by the success of its armies, under rulers like Frederick the Great. It has been said that it was not a country with an army but an army with a country. Military values were pervasive throughout society and the rise of liberalism and constitutionalism was seen as a threat to these values. Since the collapse of the revolution of 1848 Prussian governments had been committed to keeping liberal aspirations at bay. It was the army, made up of peasant recruits officered by Junker aristocrats, that had saved the monarchy in 1848, and no parliament or constitution were to be allowed to interfere with royal control of the army.

Outwardly all went well during the British royal visit. The Queen in her journal professed herself, as usual, delighted with what she saw and the friendly reception, but to many in the Prussian establishment she and her husband were not welcome. They were seen as symbols of English liberal constitutionalism and of the Coburg connection, and their arrival in the heart of the repressive Prussian regime was resented. Even Victoria had to admit in her journal that the head of that regime, the Prime Minister Otto von Manteuffel, 'was most unpleasant, cross and disagreeable'. The presence of Stockmar especially aroused the ire of the Prussian Conservative Party, as he was seen as a strong champion of a liberal united Germany and the inspiration of the Coburg connection. Ernst, the Coburg Duke, had hardly endeared himself to the Prussian Court by giving refuge to various journalists and politicians who had had to flee the Prussian police. The best known of these was Gustav Freytag, a writer and journalist, who is still remembered today for some of his novels. He had become a close adviser to Ernst. The Coburg Duke was trying to use his popularity in Germany, acquired during the Danish war in 1849, to carve for himself a role much beyond that usually attaching to the ruler of a minor principality. His brother in London helped him with advice and encouragement. Unfortunately, Ernst was not the equal of Albert in intelligence and seriousness of purpose.

The birth of Vicky's baby in January was difficult. It was a breech presentation and the German doctor who was to have officiated arrived late, because a palace servant had failed to get an immediate message to him. When he did get there he probably saved the lives of both mother and baby, but got little thanks for it. Sir James Clark, the Queen's doctor, administered chloroform and there was then mutual recrimination between British and German doctors. Dr Wegner, Vicky's German physician-in-residence, was more courtier than doctor and knew well how to distance himself from hazardous events like royal confinements. He is unlikely to have conducted the kind of examination that would have spotted the breech position ahead of time. Caesarian section, the modern way of dealing with this problem, was in any case not possible in those days. The baby, the future Kaiser William II, suffered a dislocated left arm in the delivery, which left him with a disability that is generally thought to have seriously affected his personality. It disturbed his balance and made it difficult for him to sit a horse. Another theory is that there was partial oxygen starvation at birth, which caused some brain damage. In later life the Kaiser was notoriously volatile and mercurial, to an extent that seemed at times to come close to insanity. For the moment, however, there was joy at the arrival of a male heir and the bells rang out.

The political situation in Prussia was at a delicate stage. The German liberal movement, defeated in 1849, had not gone away, nor had the desire for greater unity in Germany. A new factor was rapid industrial development, particularly in Prussia's Rhineland provinces. Since 1850 Prussia had had a constitution, with an elected Parliament, a Landtag. This Parliament had very restricted powers and was elected on a very restricted franchise. The voters were divided into three classes, each paying the same amount of tax and electing the same number of deputies. Thus a handful of voters in the top class had the same power as a very large number of electors in the bottom class. It was a system that survived in Prussia until 1918 and was one of the reasons for Germany's retarded political development after unification in 1871. In the 1850s even this restrictive system was sooner or later likely to produce a challenge to the authoritarian and repressive regime built round Frederick William IV after the collapse of the revolution. The emerging commercial and industrial middle classes were bound to claim their share of power. If the drive towards reform of the German Confederation was to be resumed under Prussian leadership, Prussia would have to give itself a more liberal image. Such were the hopes of Albert and Stockmar and the many moderate liberals who thought like them.

In the autumn of 1857 the health of Frederick William IV had declined so much that his brother and heir, Prince William, had to act on his behalf. But this transfer of power was only temporary and the Conservatives surrounding the King, often called the Camarilla, fought tooth and nail against a permanent regency. In October 1858 the regency had to be made permanent and William became Prince Regent with the full powers of the Crown. This was the beginning of the so-called New Era, a move towards greater liberalisation. Manteuffel was made to resign and a more liberal ministry installed. Among the many personnel changes, Schleinitz, a man close to Augusta, became Foreign Minister; Bismarck, often spoken of as the potential strong man of conservatism, was moved from his key post in Frankfurt and sent as ambassador to St Petersburg. On paper it was promotion, but in fact he was 'being put into cold storage on the Neva'. The Prince Regent made a speech to his new ministers in which he said Prussia must make 'moral conquests' in Germany 'by taking up elements of unity'. The speech reverberated throughout Germany and was read as a signal that the new Prussian ruler would take up the torch dropped by his brother ten years before.

Albert greatly applauded these developments from afar and wrote

encouraging letters to the Prince Regent. Stockmar confirmed him in
the view that this was really the beginning of a more liberal new era. The
Prince Consort wrote to his mentor: 'What an excellent turn all political matters have taken in Berlin! Indeed one cannot sufficiently praise
the Prince! I am much gratified by his inviting his son to the delibera-
tions in Council!' In his reply Stockmar wrote about the Prince Regent
personally: 'when he expounded to me his views as to the policy of Prussia in regard to a neighbouring state, I found them so sound, so simple,
so sincere and honourable, that I kissed his hand'. A week later Albert
wrote to the Prince Regent himself:

> The position you have taken up in home and in foreign, in secular and in
> ecclesiastical, in Prussian and in German politics, seems to me thoroughly
> sound, and it gives the assurance of a happy future for Prussia and yourself.
> Neither do I think you need fear being driven into another line of action
> against your better judgment. The course the elections have taken proves tol-
> erably clearly, that the party of orderly progress and of natural development
> has nothing in common with the Democrats, and that it is upon that party
> the bulk of the people rely, and that they will have nothing to do with the
> others.[2]

In his speech the Regent had also warned 'against the stereotypical
phrase, that the government must allow itself to be driven on and on to
develop liberal ideas, which would otherwise make their way anyhow'.
The Prince Consort had clearly taken notice of that part of the speech,
but many German liberals had not.

They were all to be badly disillusioned. Soon the Prince Regent was
to find himself in conflict with the moderate liberals of whom Albert
approved so much. The nub of the conflict was the shape and control
of the army, and on that William was immovable. He regarded the army
as the real bastion of the monarchy against revolution and the instrument which had made the Hohenzollerns great. He surrounded himself
increasingly with men who were prepared to back him against the liberal
majorities in the Chamber of Deputies. These majorities, which grew
larger in election after election, demanded at least a minimum of parliamentary control of the army. During the years of repression the
Prussian government had shamelessly used every available device to
control the elections and to prevent a resurgence of liberalism. Albert
had strongly advised William to call a halt to such practices, but when

such government interference was dropped the liberals were able to show their true support among the electorate.

Within six months of William becoming Regent the Italian War broke out, which Napoleon and the Piedmontese Prime Minister Cavour had planned during their secret meeting at Plombières in July 1858. At home the minority Derby–Dizzy Cabinet had introduced a Bill for a further reform of the franchise, which it hoped might be the issue on which it could win a majority and establish itself more firmly in power. By the time the Tory Reform Bill was defeated and the Cabinet decided to ask for a dissolution, the reform issue was overshadowed by the impending war in Italy. Throughout Europe there was now fear of Napoleon III's aggressive designs and these fears were shared by the Queen and Albert. For all the friendliness of relations with Napoleon and Eugénie and their Court, such suspicions had always been there, particularly in the mind of Albert. The French Emperor in his turn suspected that the Coburg connection of Leopold, Albert and Ernst was trying to line up Prussia and the German states against him. It would not have been in their power to do so, even if they had tried. The European situation of 1859 was one of extraordinary complexity, in which all parties found themselves pulled in contradictory directions.

The immediate concern of the Queen and the Prince Consort was the change of government at home. The Tories strengthened their position in the general election of May and hoped to be able to stay in office. In fact the election precipitated a renewed rally of all the forces opposing them, Whigs, Radicals and what remained of the Peelites. A famous meeting at Willis's Rooms on 6 June 1859 can be seen as the foundation of the Liberal Party of the later Victorian age. The long-standing rivals, Palmerston and Russell, had a public reconciliation, Pam helping the much shorter Russell on to the platform. Four days later the Tory government was narrowly defeated on a confidence motion and Derby resigned. Victoria and Albert were not keen to have either Palmerston or Russell back as Prime Minister, these 'two dreadful old men', as the Queen called them. To escape having to call on them, they turned to Lord Granville, who had briefly replaced the dismissed Palmerston as Foreign Secretary in 1851, to form a government, but his attempt failed. Palmerston now became Prime Minister again and occupied the post until his death in October 1865. Lord John Russell was Foreign Secretary.

What particularly alarmed the royal couple was that these two men were professed pro-Italians. The question of Italian unity had figured largely in the general election and the public perception that the Tory government was sympathetic to Austria had damaged them with the voters. The British public was suspicious of the motives of the French Emperor in coming to the help of Piedmont against Austria, but their sympathy for the Italian *risorgimento* was greater. Twelve days after Palmerston's return to Downing Street the bloody battle of Solferino sealed the Austrian defeat in Italy. Then to everybody's surprise Napoleon and Francis Joseph, the French and Austrian Emperors, met at Villafranca on 11 July and signed an armistice which handed Lombardy to Piedmont.

One reason why Napoleon decided to call a halt was his fear that the forces of Prussia and the German Confederation might come to Austria's aid and attack him across the Rhine. In Germany as a whole sentiment was strongly in favour of helping their Austrian brothers and hostile to France, widely seen as the hereditary enemy. 'They shall not have it, the German River Rhine' was a slogan on many lips. Efforts were made to mobilise the forces of the German Confederation to protect the Rhine frontier and at the same time to help Austria by threatening France with a second front. In Prussia the situation was complicated by the long-standing rivalry with Austria. If German forces were to be mobilised, then the Prussian Regent should be their commander, asserting Prussian claims to equality with Austria in German affairs. Before the Prussians had got very far in asserting themselves, the Peace of Villafranca cut the ground from under their feet. Everybody, including Vicky's husband Frederick William, had been preparing for a war that did not come. Prussia again looked feeble, as she had done during the Crimean War. Napoleon's sudden volte-face did not suit Palmerston's book either. He had hoped for a much more decisive end to Austria's presence in the Italian peninsula. The Queen, putting her signature under a draft by her husband, could not help teasing her Prime Minister a little:

The Queen is less disappointed with the peace than Lord Palmerston appears to be, as she never could share his sanguine hopes that the *coup d'état* and the 'Empire' could be made subservient to the establishment of independent nationalities and the diffusion of liberty and constitutional government on the Continent. The Emperor follows the dictates of his personal interests and is ready to play the highest stakes for them ...[3]

It is this slightly bantering tone that now marked the relations between Palmerston and the royal couple, but sometimes the harsher note of former resentments crept back. There was plenty of opportunity for it in the further development of Italian affairs. On the whole, the course of events justified Palmerston's contention that Italian national sentiment could not be repressed nor the rulers dependent on Austria be restored. He wanted Italian liberation and unity, but did not want Italy to become the occasion for Napoleonic aggrandisement. Albert and Victoria feared the consequences of the collapse of Austrian power. When, with the help of Garibaldi, the Kingdom of the Two Sicilies fell to Piedmont, the royal couple reminded Palmerston of his previous opinion 'that it would not at all be for the interests of this country to see the south of Italy in the hands of a power so entirely under the command and mixed up with the intrigues of France as, unfortunately, Sardinia [Piedmont] now is!' Palmerston could not afford to stop Garibaldi, for his government was dependent on the support of the Radicals, to whom Garibaldi was a hero. When Garibaldi handed his conquest over to Victor Emmanuel of Sardinia, Palmerston was satisfied.

In Prussia an immediate result of the Italian war was that a strengthening of the army assumed greater importance and the Prince Regent determined to pursue reorganisation regardless of the views of the liberals in the Prussian Landtag. In December 1859 the pro-Western war minister was replaced by Roon, a member of the conservative court party, who was to play a crucial part in securing Bismarck's appointment as chief minister in September 1862. His reorganisation plans meant that the importance of the reserve army was downgraded in favour of longer-serving recruits, who, in case of another revolutionary outbreak, could be expected to stay loyal to their officers and to the King. Thus the Prussian constitutional conflict grew more acute. In the meantime the Italian example sparked a renewed of upsurge of national feeling in Germany. There were countless gymnastic festivals, rifle-club meetings and celebrations of the centenary of the birth of the poet Schiller, all with a national theme. In this movement Albert's brother Ernst, the Duke of Coburg, played a considerable role. He became known as the Rifle-Ernst (*Schützen-Ernst*). He also housed in Coburg the offices of what was the most important organisation promoting German unity under a liberal Prussia, the *Nationalverein*. It was an association of mainly middle-class notables throughout Germany, the kind of people who were also the driving force behind the liberal parties in the Prussian Parliament. The problem was that Prussia was not moving towards the kind of liberal constitutionalism that such a vision of the future required.

Albert and Victoria had given their eldest daughter, the apple of her father's eye, as the hostage of that vision. When Victoria, more than a year after the marriage, recalled their tearful parting after the wedding, she wrote to her daughter:

> that last night when we took you to your room, and you cried so much, I said to Papa 'after all, it is like taking a poor lamb to be sacrificed' ... these are the trials which we poor women must go through; no father, no man can feel this! Papa would never enter into it all! As in fact he seldom can in my very violent feelings.[4]

In acknowledging her violent feelings, which sometimes released themselves in outbursts against her husband, she displayed some self-knowledge, but of course Albert, the real author of the Prussian marriage, felt it as much as she did, only he did not show it. Victoria's outbursts were becoming more frequent at this time. When Albert would leave the room to escape them, she would follow him. He tried to reason with her and in the end she was usually contrite. She wrote in her journal that she was trying to learn to control herself. But she also wrote to Vicky: 'you say that no one is perfect except Papa. But even he has his shortcomings. He is often very difficult – in his excessive zeal and his mania for work.'

There was much about Vicky's position at the Prussian Court that was uncomfortable. Even the physical discomforts were considerable in the gloomy palaces of Berlin and Potsdam. Plumbing was rudimentary, water-closets non-existent, badly closing windows and doors let in the cold into scarcely heated rooms, and changes could only be made with the permission of the Prince Regent. The latter was notoriously uninterested in creature comforts and continued to sleep on a hard iron bedstead when he was German Emperor in his eighties. The position of

Vicky as the Englishwoman, *die Engländerin*, at the Hohenzollern Court, had the potential for even greater discomforts. Tact was not her greatest virtue and she was apt to become assertive in the face of hostility. It can hardly have helped that the liberal party openly placed their hopes in her. The famous patriotic poet Ernst Moritz Arndt, who had years before celebrated the German liberation from the yoke of the first Napoleon, now expressed the hope that with Vicky's arrival 'an English spirit may now animate us'.

On the other hand, among her husband's relations there were several to whom English liberal constitutionalism was anathema. Vicky was seen as its unwelcome personification. Her father-in-law's younger brother Charles was just such a diehard conservative. In the revolution of 1848 he, as third in line of succession, had not scrupled to try and replace his elder brother, Frederick William IV, when the latter had buckled under revolutionary pressure and William, the next in line of succession, had fled to London. Bismarck, then a thirty-two-year-old counter-revolutionary hothead, was an instrument in this intrigue and attempted to make Augusta, William's wife, party to it. It was this that had first turned Augusta into a lifelong enemy of Bismarck. To complicate matters further, Augusta's sister was Charles's wife.

Augusta might have been thought to have been a support for Vicky, both on ideological grounds and as a friend of her parents. In fact many years of alienation in a loveless marriage and an uncongenial Court had turned Augusta into a difficult and frequently absent figure. She spent much time in her palace at Koblenz and Uncle Leopold called her 'the Dragon of the Rhine'. When she first came to reside in Koblenz with her husband, William could not venture into the streets without a guard, such was the reactionary and brutal reputation he had acquired in the years of revolution. When Augusta was in Berlin she made up for her unhappy situation by engaging in a constant round of social events, at which she expected Vicky's presence, even if the latter felt unwell. Then there were the Russian relations, headed, until her death in 1860, by the Dowager Tsarina Alexandra Feodorovna, William's sister. They were not only the ideological counterpoise to the English princess; when they came to stay with a large retinue of courtiers and unhygienic, ill-mannered servants, it added to the inconvenience of Berlin Court life.

Almost as soon as she arrived in Prussia Vicky was expected by her mother to keep an eye open for a prince that might serve as a bridegroom for her younger sister Alice and a princess that might become a bride for her brother Bertie, the Prince of Wales. Bertie, so different from his sister, had become a major worry to his parents. The one thing that might keep him out of scandalous scrapes was a successful marriage. In pursuit of such matchmaking Vicky incurred much inconvenience, staying in the castles of various minor German princes, often at least as ill-appointed as the Prussian palaces. She was assisted in her search by her mother's half-sister Feodora of Hohenlohe-Langenburg. Feodora's knowledge of the situation in Germany and the goings-on in the German courts was in many ways more realistic and immediate than that of Albert and Victoria. She realised what might await Vicky in Prussia: 'The Princess is so young and inexperienced in the world and Berlin is a hotbed of envy, jealousy, intrigue and malicious knavery.'

Vicky helped to find a prince for Alice at Hesse-Darmstadt in Prince Louis, later the Grand Duke. The Queen, mindful of the very young age at which Vicky had been despatched to Berlin, delayed Alice's wedding until July 1862, by which time she was nineteen. It was the beginning of a link with Hesse that was later to be continued by marriages into the Battenberg family, a branch of the House of Hesse. Tsar Alexander II was married to Marie of Hesse, known in Russia as the Tsarina Marie Alexandrovna, sister of Alice's future father-in-law, the Reigning Grand Duke of Hesse-Darmstadt. Another brother of the Tsarina, Alexander, had in 1851 made a morganatic marriage to one of her ladies-in-waiting, Julie von Haucke. She was a Polish countess of German origin, partly descended from commoners. Seven years later, in 1858, the Grand Duke of Hesse-Darmstadt bestowed on Julie von Haucke the title Princess of Battenberg, a small town in the north of Hesse. This morganatic marriage made the Battenbergs unequal in status in the eyes of the Romanovs and Hohenzollern, but it did not bother Victoria. In fact Alexander was one of the few people whose company she enjoyed when he came to England in the 1860s.

The link between the House of Hesse and the Romanovs was carried on through the marriages of two of Alice's daughters, Elizabeth, 'Ella', and Alice, 'Alicky'. Ella married the Grand Duke Sergei, brother of

Alexander III, in 1884. Alicky married Nicholas II in 1894. All of them met violent ends. The connection between Hesse and the Romanovs helped to make the match between Victoria's second son Affie and the Grand Duchess Marie of Russia, daughter of Alexander II and Marie of Hesse. A Russian Orthodox chapel at Darmstadt bears witness to this day to the link between the grand ducal house and the Russian Court. Alice's eldest daughter Victoria married Prince Louis of Battenberg, the son of Alexander, and they became the parents of Lord Louis Mountbatten. Alice of Hesse-Darmstadt was, like her sister Vicky in Berlin, a woman of considerable stature. She nursed the casualties of the wars of 1866 and 1870 and promoted the emancipation of women. She struck up a friendship with David Friedrich Strauss, the theologian and biblical critic, a resident of Darmstadt, whose controversial work *The Life of Jesus* was translated into English by George Eliot. Strauss's reconstruction of the historical Jesus influenced Alice's religious orientation and he dedicated to her his book on Voltaire. Alice's views on women and religion often put her at loggerheads with her mother.

It proved more difficult to find a bride for Bertie. A possible Hesse-Darmstadt princess suffered, like many of her relations but not Louis, from a twitch, the teeth of a princess of Saxe-Weimar were almost black, and so on. Finally the choice fell on Princess Alexandra of Schleswig-Holstein, the daughter of Prince Christian, who was due to inherit the throne of Denmark. She was very pretty and even Albert said, when he saw her photograph, 'I would marry her at once'. Bertie was slower to warm to her in person and, when he met her in September 1861 at the cathedral of Speyer, it was not love at first sight. Vicky was a strong supporter of the match, even though she realised that it would create a political complication: 'Oh if she only was not a Dane ... I should say yes – she is *the* one a thousand times over', she wrote to her mother. The father of Alix, the future Princess of Wales, was known throughout Germany dismissively as the Protocol Prince. His eventual succession had been imposed on the two duchies of Schleswig-Holstein by the fiat of the great powers, in the interests of maintaining the Danish position.

In German eyes the Duke of Augustenburg was the legitimate heir to the two duchies. He was a close friend of Vicky and her husband, was known to them as Fritz Holstein, and was married to a daughter of

Feodora, Victoria's half-sister. The Bertie–Alix match nearly caused a breach between Albert and his brother Ernst, who had acquired his reputation in Germany by fighting the Danes over Schleswig-Holstein in 1849. Ernst had in June 1861 signed a military convention with Prussia by which his small contingent was incorporated with the Prussian army. It was a step of some importance, for it paved the way for Coburg to side with Prussia rather than Austria in the war of 1866. It was a model which was soon followed by other smaller principalities in Central Germany and, after Prussia's victory in 1866, by some of the larger German states. Attempts to settle the affairs of Europe by dynastic marriages were perhaps reaching the end of the road. It was not only that the power of royal houses to make nations, as the Habsburgs and Hohenzollern had done, was coming up against nationalism and the sovereignty of the people. As the Bertie–Alix marriage showed, personal considerations had to prevail over political ones. It was more important for Albert and Victoria to find a bride for their eldest son, to curb what they saw as his more regrettable inclinations, even if this went against the aim they had pursued by marrying their eldest daughter to the Prussian Crown Prince.

In January 1861 Frederick William IV died. Vicky was much affected by having to see him on his deathbed – she had never experienced death before. William was now King, somewhat embittered that he had had to wait until he was nearly sixty-four. The ceremonies surrounding his accession showed how much he thought of himself as a king by divine right, rather than as a head of state sworn to uphold a constitution. The Prussian constitution of 1850, adopted after the revolution of 1848 had been crushed, was hardly a liberal document, but at least it provided for a Parliament, however restricted the franchise on which it was elected and the powers which it could exercise. William would have done away with the constitution altogether, but even he realised that this might well precipitate another revolution. Yet Albert was still telling him how much the hopes of Germans rested on a liberal Prussia and on him personally. Had the promises made by the princes in 1848 been fulfilled or are the German states still police states? 'It is not for me to answer the question for I cannot say "no" to it. My hope, like that of most German patriots, rests upon Prussia – rests upon you!', wrote the Prince Consort. It was beginning to sound rather hollow.

Relations between Britain and Prussia were not at all good. *The*

Times, regarded by many on the Continent as the mouthpiece of the British government, was constantly attacking the authoritarian ways of Prussia. The Prince Consort was outraged by the damage the paper was doing, for he knew only too well how seriously it was taken in Germany. A minor incident in September 1860 gave the paper a perfect occasion for venting its dislike of what it called Prussian despotism. A British traveller, Captain Macdonald, had been forcibly removed from a train and imprisoned in a quarrel over a seat. Great offence was caused in Britain by the remarks of the judge that English travellers were 'notorious for the rudeness, impudence, and boorish arrogance of their conduct'. Palmerston demanded the dismissal of the judge and compensation for Macdonald.

At about this time Victoria and Albert again travelled to Coburg for a great family gathering. Albert was always careful not to bring too many of his relations simultaneously to London, because this would immediately have raised the suspicion of a 'Coburg conference'. Many of these relations, from Uncle Leopold and the Prussian Regent down, met Victoria and Albert on their journey and then assembled at Coburg. Victoria was again in raptures about seeing her beloved Albert on his home ground and at the friendliness of the reception. The occasion was somewhat marred by the death, shortly before their arrival, of Albert's stepmother, the Dowager Duchess of Coburg. On the other hand, the Queen was delighted by her grandson, the future Kaiser, aged twenty months, whom she now saw for the first time. 'He is a fine, fat child, with a beautiful white soft skin, very fine shoulders and limbs, and a very dear face ... He has Fritz's eyes and Vicky's mouth ... We felt so happy to see him at last!', she wrote in her journal.[5] She did not mention the damaged arm and perhaps did not notice it.

Vicky had in the meantime given birth to another child, a daughter. There was also an untoward incident when the horses of a carriage in which the Prince Consort was travelling bolted and crashed into a barrier at a railway level crossing. Albert managed to jump clear and escaped with bruises, but the coachman was seriously injured. The accident seems to have pushed the Prince Consort into intimations of mortality and into depression. Out on a walk with his brother Ernst, he burst into tears and persisted in saying that he had been here, in the landscape so precious to him from his childhood, for the last time in his life. He was a driven man, driven by his own demons, as well as by such as Stockmar and Uncle Leopold, at the age of forty-one prematurely old. Photographs of him, taken in the later 1850s, show a podgy figure with a receding hairline, the face pale and slack. He was no longer the dashing, handsome young man that had so attracted the Queen. He may have been suffering from stomach cancer – many of the symptoms of which he often complained would bear out this hypothesis.

Nothing did more to drive Albert into an early grave than the failure to mould Bertie, the Prince of Wales, in his own image. Over Bertie the Queen and her husband lost all sense of proportion. They compared him unfavourably with all young people of his age, male or female. As he grew up, his sister Vicky's evident intellectual superiority was held up to him and increased his insecurity. Then, with less reason, his cousin once removed, the young King of Portugal, Pedro V, who had succeeded his mother Maria da Gloria in 1853 at the age of sixteen, found great favour with Albert. According to Victoria, her husband loved Pedro as a son, clearly the son that Bertie was not. Pedro was a mediocre young man and hardly a success on the throne of Portugal. When Pedro died of typhoid in November 1861, it was one of many events that year that seemed to be undermining Albert's will to live. 'I do not cling to life. You do, but I don't value it', he told the Queen. 'If I knew that all my loved ones were well cared for, I would be ready to die tomorrow ... I am convinced that if I fell seriously ill, I would give up immediately and not fight for life. I do not have a tenacious will to live.' The Queen herself had surrendered to a paroxysm of grief, a kind of nervous breakdown, when her mother, the Duchess of Kent, died in March 1861. There were rumours throughout Europe that she was going mad, like her grandfather, and she herself was afraid of losing her reason. Perhaps feelings of guilt, going back to the tensions with her mother over Conroy, played a part in this. The Queen's morbid state placed an additional burden on Albert and aggravated his physical and mental malaise. He was suffering from sleeplessness and frequent loss of appetite.

As for Bertie, he had earned restrained praise from his father for his successful tour of Canada and the United States in the summer and autumn of 1860, but more praise went to the Duke of Newcastle who had accompanied the Prince. Victoria was glad to see her son go on the long journey across the Atlantic: 'He left on Monday. His voice made me so nervous, I could hardly bear it any longer', she wrote to her daughter in Berlin. His success in the New World, making the kind of public appearances he was good at, should have earned him more encouragement. He clearly blossomed without his parents bearing down on him and the Canadians and Americans were charmed.

For Victoria and Albert these successes hardly weighed in the scales against his misdemeanours on his return. A ten-week military training period had been arranged for the Prince of Wales in Ireland, with a step up in rank every fortnight. Victoria and Albert visited The Curragh in August 1861 to see him parade a company of Grenadier Guards. Then disaster, or rather the natural sexual urges of a twenty year old, struck. Bertie's fellow officers, put on their mettle by the Prince's evident ignorance of the facts of life, smuggled a young London actress, Nellie Clifden, into his bed. She was not discreet and news of the escapade soon spread round London clubs and trickled into continental newspapers. It may well be that Bertie's interest in Nellie Clifden accounts for the slow pace of his courtship of Alix, the Danish Princess intended as his bride. It was rumoured that he had brought yet another woman into Windsor Castle at night. Although only an edited version of his son's misdemeanours reached him, the Prince Consort was beside himself with worry and grief.

Bertie had meanwhile been sent to Cambridge to study, or perhaps savour the delights of student life, as far as constant surveillance permitted. Albert went there to reason with his wayward son. He was already suffering from a chill contracted on a visit to Sandhurst. It had been raining heavily there and he had returned to Windsor wet and exhausted. 'Bin recht elend' (I feel miserable) he noted in his dairy on 24 November. Yet he immediately ordered a special train to take him to Cambridge. He went for a walk with Bertie during which he extracted a promise from his son to mend his ways. They took a wrong turning, during what appears to have been an emotional encounter, on what was another wet afternoon. When Albert was back in Windsor on 26 November, it was the beginning of his final illness. Its fatal outcome, less than three weeks later, meant that in the Queen's mind Bertie had all but killed him. It is more likely that the stomach cancer, at the time virtually impossible to diagnose and certainly incurable, had undermined her husband's resistance.

Albert's last political act was to revise and soften a despatch to the US Government in the *Trent* affair. The North had taken two Southern emissaries and their wives off this British ship on their way to Britain. The incident brought Britain and the North to the brink of war. It may be a slight overstatement to say that the Prince Consort averted a war between Britain and the United States, but his revision of the draft certainly made it easier for the American government to find a way out. Seward, the US Secretary of State, was in an excitable mood. Palmerston sympathised with the South and so did much of upper- and middle-class England. The press on both sides of the Atlantic raised a storm of indignation and in Britain *The Times* and the *Morning Post*, still regarded as Palmerston's mouthpiece, led the hue and cry. Fortunately telegraphic communication across the Atlantic did not as yet exist and so tempers had time to cool. It was characteristic of Albert that even at death's door he should have tried to dampen the fires of chauvinism and it was a fitting epitaph.

Albert's revision of the *Trent* despatch was dated 1 December 1861 and at the time he told his wife that he felt almost too weak to hold the pen. He died on 14 December, officially of typhoid fever. Faulty drains at Windsor Castle were also said to be the cause. The doctors were uncertain and slow in their diagnosis of the illness and even slower to acknowledge that it might prove fatal, for they did not want unduly to alarm the patient or the Queen. On her insistence Sir James Clark, who had been her physician ever since she was a girl, still had a leading role in treating the Prince. According to Lord Clarendon, Sir James was no longer capable of looking after 'a sick cat'. It may well be, however, that Sir James and the other doctors in attendance, including William Jenner, knew only too well that there was nothing they could do, other than sedate the patient with brandy. When Victoria realised the gravity of her husband's condition, she became distraught. 'The country, oh the country. I could perhaps bear my own misery, but the poor country', she kept repeating. As she sat by his bedside and his mind was wandering, he called her *gutes Weibchen* [good little wife]; and as the end approached she whispered into his ear *es ist dein kleines Frauchen* [it is your little woman] and asked for *ein Kuss* [a kiss], and he gave it.

The funeral of Albert was fixed for 23 December, on the advice of the Prince of Wales. It was probably the first time that he had been asked

for advice on a matter of public importance. It required time to prepare
a state funeral, but it could not be allowed to overlap with Christmas.
The Queen, for a while numb with shock, was hurried off to Osborne
and was thus spared having to be present.

In life the Prince Consort had often been the target of prejudiced criticism and had always remained something of an alien in his adopted
country. All the indications are that his death, which was unexpected by
the public at large, was felt to be a real loss, and that he was widely and
genuinely mourned. Among politicians there was apprehension that the
business of monarchy would become difficult to manage. Bereft of her
husband the Queen might not be able to fulfil her duties. What was
known of the Prince of Wales hardly inspired confidence. The Queen
herself became a prime mover in the Albert memorial cult that soon
sprang up, but many of the monuments erected up and down the country owed their existence to local initiatives. The best known of these is
the Albert Memorial, in front of the Albert Hall, now resplendent again
as the 'Golden Man'. It was not unveiled until July 1872. The more private Mausoleum at Frogmore, in which Albert and eventually Victoria
were laid to rest, was completed within a year of the Prince's death. It
is built in an Italian renaissance style, modelled on the mausoleum by
Nicholas Hawksmoor at Castle Howard, much admired by the Queen.
It cost some £200,000 and the Queen paid for it out of a legacy left to
her by an eccentric miser, John Camden Nield.

What if the Prince Consort had enjoyed a more normal lifespan? At
home it is unlikely that he could have slowed the further advance of
democracy and he probably would not have wanted to. He believed the
voice of the people had to be heeded and in the mountain of comment
and advice he produced over the years this sentiment is a constant
thread. What exactly he meant by 'the people' is difficult to pin down.
He probably thought of the multitude of different manifestations, all the
way from the articulate views of the upper social classes to the outbreak
of popular rioting, as they impinged on those who had the task of governing. He certainly felt uncomfortable with much of the modernity
that was changing the nature of politics, in Britain more than anywhere
else. He could not have played the role he did if he had not thought that
this still left room for the monarchical activism he practised. In the last
years before his premature death he was as active as ever. A kind of

balance of power had evolved, even with Palmerston, with whom there had in earlier years often prevailed a stalemate frustrating to the Prince. 'We are edging our spurs into their sides', he wrote to the Prince of Prussia, when it was a question of galvanising ministers over the Indian Mutiny.

Beyond the strictly political sphere Albert had established a strong presence in many aspects of the national life, education, science, the arts, industry and agriculture. Many of his initiatives left a permanent legacy, for example the development of South Kensington as a cultural and scientific district, started with money originally derived from the Great Exhibition. He was an active collector of pictures, his interest ranging from Italian painting to the sixteenth-century German master Lucas Cranach. In the 1840s he purchased the collection of a distant Bavarian cousin who was on the verge of bankruptcy. It included pictures by Van Eyck and Rogier van der Weyden, then not fashionable. Some of these pictures and other purchases and commissions by the Prince Consort have ended up in the National Gallery and elsewhere in the national collections. The commissions went to painters like Landseer or Winterhalter, while Turner went unrecognised by the Queen and her husband. In private the artistic taste of the royal couple was not inhibited by prudery. A visitor to Osborne House sees plenty of bare flesh on display. In the Prince's bathroom there is a painting by the German artist Anton von Gegenbaur, *Omphale and Hercules.* It shows a naked young woman sitting on the thigh of the hero. Omphale, the Queen of Lydia, kept Hercules as a sex slave. In 1852 the Queen commissioned a picture from Winterhalter for her husband's birthday. Unlike Victorian painters such as Alma-Tadema and Lord Leighton, Winterhalter had, as master of the formal court portrait, no opportunity for excursions into soft porn. This time his subject was *Florinda.* The picture, which hangs in view of the couple's adjacent desks in the Queen's private sitting room at Osborne, shows a sun-lit bevy of bare-breasted maidens.

Albert knew his limitations and that, as a creative artist, whether in music or the representative arts, he was only a lowly amateur.* He knew

---

* In 1969, on the occasion of the 150th anniversary of the Prince Consort's birth, Yehudi Menuhin called his musical compositions agreeable, charming, but undemanding and of no great significance.

enough about the technical aspects of the work of composers, painters, architects and craftsmen of all kinds to make an informed judgment. He saw his task as that of a facilitator, and everything, from the drains upwards, received his thorough attention.

Foreign policy took up even more of the energies of the Prince. No clear dividing line between international relations and dynastic relations could be drawn in the nineteenth century. Earlier, in European affairs, countries were what dynasties made them. Such was the nature of the Habsburg dominions and many others. Proverbially the Habsburgs had done it mainly by marriage – 'tu, felix Austria, nube' (you happy Austria, marry). The Hohenzollerns and others had done it by a combination of marriage, inheritance and the sword. The French Revolution and the Napoleonic wars had begun to make this procedure seem outdated, but the House of Coburg provided a striking demonstration of what could still be done. This was the framework in which Albert grew up and the family duty he fulfilled. It shaped his life by his marriage to the powerful English Queen. It shaped his consciousness and provided him with a field of operations. He could be a British patriot, as well as a loyal German and Coburger, as he said when he left home. All the foreign policy issues on which he and Victoria made their influence felt were shaped and even dominated by dynastic relations. It was thus with Anglo-French relations, with affairs in the Iberian peninsula and with great power relations in general. Revolution remained the great threat to this kind of world. All too often it raised its head in a frightening manner and could never be far from the mind of Albert. It did not put an end to the monarchical world, as was feared and hoped.

Thus Albert and Victoria were able to embark upon their most fateful venture in dynastic politics. They sent their favourite child, their eldest daughter, into the hornets' nest that was the Prussian Court. The marriage was meant to advance Albert's dream of a constitutional Germany led by Prussia. He was spared the experience of seeing it go sour. We can never know whether he would have been able to realise his vision, had he lived. He would have tried to make it more difficult for Bismarck to go in so different a direction, but he could probably not have done more than fight a rearguard action. Paradoxically, Bismarck's aim was to preserve the power of the Prussian monarchy, an aim which he succeeded in realising in defiance of the spirit of the age. The constitutional yet active monarchy which Albert practised would have been more in harmony with the *Zeitgeist*. Europe might have been spared much agony and bloodshed.

8

The Widowed Queen

The death of the Prince Consort produced in Victoria what can only be called a collapse of personality. The morbid excesses of her grief have often been described. They far exceeded what was normal even in an age when wallowing in death was common. The political world had become well aware that she had become in most respects the mouthpiece of her husband. Lord Stanley, Derby's son, put it thus:

> The Queen herself has long shown indications of a nervous and excitable disposition, requiring care, lest hereditary eccentricities should develop themselves. By the testimony of those who have the best opportunity of knowing the truth, this care has been bestowed, incessantly, and judiciously, by her late husband: her letters were written by him, he was present when she received ministers, nothing small or great was done but by his advice: I have myself, when dining at the Palace shortly after taking the Indian department [in 1858], heard him, at dinner, suggest to her in German to enquire about this, that, or the other: the question never failed to follow.

He went on to write:

> I have more than once observed, when in office, the contrast between the Queen's letters on business, and the hasty notes which she would occasionally send relating to matters of slight importance ... I have no doubt, from what others have told me, of the cause of this difference. The Prince had undoubtedly a fixed determination to increase the personal power of the Crown: had he lived to add to his great industry and talent the weight which age and long experience would have given in dealing with statesmen of his own standing, he might have made himself almost as powerful as the Prime Minister of the day.[1]

Disraeli had come to much the same conclusion. He remarked to Count Vitzthum, the Saxon ambassador in London: 'This German Prince has governed England for twenty-one years with a wisdom and energy such as none of our Kings have ever shown.' Disraeli was on more doubtful ground when he went on: 'If he had outlived some of our "old stagers", he would have given us, while retaining all constitutional guarantees, the blessings of absolute government.'[2]

A monarchy so powerful could have caused problems as time went on, for it is unlikely that it could have halted the advance of democracy. The increasing participation of the masses in politics was something that neither Lord Stanley nor Disraeli could fully foresee in 1861. Nor could they foresee another problem that occurred immediately, namely the virtual disappearance of the monarchy as a public spectacle. One can sympathise with the Queen's fear of appearing in public and a more modern approach to a psychological problem such as hers might well have eased it. In the nineteenth century a great deal was subsumed under the generic heading 'nervous disposition', and both patients and doctors resorted to variations of such a diagnosis. The Queen herself now responded to pressures by talking of 'complete breakdown of her nervous system' – 'a poor weak woman shattered by grief and anxiety and by nature terribly nervous', and there were threats of insanity.

Some of the consequences were bizarre. When the Privy Council had to meet in her presence, she was in an adjoining room and signified her assent through the open door. Much of what she did was governed by what she thought her husband would have done. When she was signing papers, she often looked up at his bust. Her correspondence is full of allusions to her belief that she would meet again in an afterlife those who had departed. She dabbled in spiritualism and was superstitious about dates and coincidences. With the passage of time, Albert's opinions and possible reactions became naturally more speculative and eventually unfathomable. One constant remained: she was determined to preserve the prerogatives of the monarchy, as they had done together in the past, and to practise the active monarchism that was his legacy. Her way of doing it was, however, very different from his. He approached problems and situations by rational analysis and nearly always preferred to put analysis and conclusions on paper. Hence the mountain of memoranda he left. It was a very Germanic approach and occasionally would have worked better with a dash of English pragmatism.

In the early years after Albert's death Victoria was desolate, bereft of this guidance. Two years after he died the Schleswig-Holstein problem was coming to the boil and causing dissension in her immediate family. '*now* this year everything that interested my Angel and that *he* understood takes place, he is not *here* to help us, and to write those admirable *memoranda* which are *gospel now*', she wrote to Uncle Leopold.[3] The Queen's reactions were immediate, fuelled by strong emotions and prejudices. She was shrewd and, with her long experience, had a great deal of background knowledge. She could not have Albert's capacity for formulating policy and for being proactive in the pursuit of it. Even he would have found it increasingly difficult to exert effective influence, at home because of the advance of democracy, abroad because a coherent policy, such as the Coburg connection had on the German question, was no longer available. This does not mean the importance of the dynastic network had disappeared, but the links between ruling houses had become more diffuse and contradictory.

In the early months of 1862 the Queen buried herself behind the walls of Windsor and Osborne. She could not bring herself to go to London. The wedding of Alice, now her eldest unmarried daughter, to Louis of Hesse-Darmstadt, in July 1862, had to be held at Osborne, at great inconvenience to the guests. It was overshadowed by the brooding presence of the Queen, swathed in black. Alice, a kind and obliging girl, had largely taken care of the household after Albert's death and the Queen was extremely reluctant to release her to Darmstadt. 'A married daughter I MUST have living with me, and must *not* be left constantly looking for help, and to have to make shift for the day which is too dreadful', she wrote. She would receive ministers only in the presence of Sir Charles Phipps and General Grey, Albert's private secretaries. Grey became her private secretary and in the years to come was an important channel of communication to the political world. He thus filled a small part of the vacuum that Albert's death had opened up around the Queen. The post of the monarch's private secretary was officially recognised in 1867 and the holder of the post became, from a political point of view, the most important official in the royal household.

In September 1862 the Queen ventured abroad for the first time since Albert's death. She stopped at Laeken, Leopold's palace near Brussels, and there met for the first time Alexandra, Bertie's intended. Alix's parents, Prince and Princess Christian, the former to become King of

Denmark little over a year later, and her sister Dagmar, later the wife of Tsar Alexander III, had also come to Brussels. The Queen was again plunged into the deepest gloom by having to go through the motions connected with an official engagement on her own. In her journal she wrote: 'Marie B.[Brabant, Leopold's daughter] brought Prince and Princess Christian upstairs, leaving them with me. Now came the terribly trying moment for me. I had alone to say and do what, under other, former happy circumstances, had devolved on both of us together.'[4] She was delighted with Alix, but could never for a moment get away from her own overwhelming grief: 'she is a dear, lovely being – whose bright image seems to float – mingled with darling Papa's – before my poor eyes – dimmed with tears!', she wrote to Vicky, 'who can know what my ... life is now! ... my warm passionate loving nature so full of that passionate adoration for that Angel whom I dared to call mine. And at 42, all, all, those earthly feelings must be crushed & smothered & the never quenched flame ... burns within me & wears me out! ... this very prospect of opening happiness and married life for our poor Bertie – while I thank God for it, yet wrings my poor heart ...'[5]

The Queen moved on to Coburg and stayed at Reinhardsbrunn, the summer residence near Gotha where Albert had often been with his step-grandmother in his youth. When the news came through that Alix had accepted Bertie, not much more than a formality, there was some discussion of the political implications of the marriage with Earl Russell, who was the minister in attendance. The Queen stressed 'the importance of Bertie's marriage being in no sense considered a political one'. Schleswig-Holstein was on her mind, the problem that would soon be brought to crisis point by the accession of Alix's father to the Danish throne.

The family gathering in Gotha was also aware of another crisis, which was going on in Berlin in these very mid-September days and the resolution of which would decide the future not only of Schleswig-Holstein but of Europe and the world. A new and more left-wing liberal party had been founded in Prussia, the Progressives, and in elections held in May 1862 had won about two-fifths of the seats in the Prussian Landtag. After the lull of the summer holidays the Progressives, supported by other liberal factions, were again confronting the King over the organisation and control of the army. King William was talking of abdicating rather than giving way. Queen Victoria and her Foreign Secretary Russell thought abdication would be the best solution. On 17 September the Queen wrote in her journal at Gotha: 'Saw Russell and talked of the alarming state of affairs at Berlin, of it being far better the King should abdicate.' Three days later Vicky, who was also at Gotha, wrote to her husband, the Crown Prince, who was in Berlin:

> If the King sees that he cannot take the necessary steps to restore order and confidence in the country without going against his conscience, I consider it wise and honest to leave it to others who can take over these duties without burdening their conscience. I see no way out and consider you should make this sacrifice for the country. If you do not accept, I believe you will regret it one day.[6]

Unfortunately Frederick William did not accept and had the next quarter of a century to regret it. Filial duty got the better of him, but he was also too much of a Hohenzollern and a Prussian soldier to want to take over the Crown in these circumstances. It would fall to him sooner rather than later anyhow, for his father was now sixty-five.

In the meantime the War Minister Roon, a hardline conservative, was moving heaven and earth to prevent the King's abdication and the triumph of the liberals. His trump card was his friend Bismarck, who had been transferred from St Petersburg to Paris as Prussian ambassador. He was still hanging around waiting to be called to ministerial office, not knowing whether he would be in the Paris post long enough to move his family there. He had spent the past few weeks deliberately absenting himself from the political hurly-burly in Berlin. He was holidaying in the south of France without his family, ending up at Biarritz with the Russian Ambassador to Brussels, Prince Orlov and his wife. The twenty-two-year-old Principessa Cathy Orlov charmed him, aged forty-seven, and he fell somewhat in love. But he knew that soon he would have to return to the real world and that his boundless ambition to do great things might be about to be satisfied. He returned to Berlin, hurried on by his friend Roon. On 22 September 1862, a Monday, he had his decisive interview with the King. He persuaded him not to abdicate, if that ever was his real intention, and instead to entrust himself to Bismarck as his Prime Minister. It was a decisive moment in European and world history.

Three weeks later, with the die cast, King William visited Queen
Victoria at Coburg. The Queen wrote in her journal on 12 October:
'Heard two days ago that the King of Prussia wished to come and see
me for a few hours. He arrived at 6 and at half past 9, as soon as I was
dressed, I saw him in my room. He was very much affected, and was
most kind, evidently much moved at seeing me. He did not allude to
politics, only said, with tears in his eyes, how much he felt the weight of
his position.' He might well feel the weight, for so many in his immediate family, his wife Augusta, his son and daughter-in-law, the Crown
Prince and Vicky, his son-in-law, the liberal Grand Duke of Baden,
whom he had just visited, had all fought tooth and nail against the
appointment of Bismarck. When the possibility of Bismarck being called
into a key position was being discussed at an earlier stage, in March
1862, Augusta had burst out: 'For God's sake not this man as minister.
It is a completely false calculation to believe that a man like Bismarck
can serve our country, who will certainly risk everything and become the
terror of everybody, because he has no principles.'[7]

By the time he came to Coburg to see Victoria, there was no turning
back for the Prussian King. During his visit to his son-in-law and
daughter in Baden ten days earlier there had been so much heated argument in the Palace that passers-by in the street outside could hear the
King shouting. Bismarck was afraid the King was going to weaken and
he took the precaution of intercepting him on his way back to Berlin.
He waited for him on an up-turned wheelbarrow at a station that was
still being built about forty miles south of Berlin. When the train drew
in he found the King alone in an ill-lit first-class carriage. William was
in a gloomy mood and forecast the fate of Strafford and Charles I for
his Prime Minister and himself. Bismarck was a consummate psycho-
logist and by the time they reached Berlin he had talked his master
round and stiffened his resolve to continue the confrontation with the
Prussian parliament. In these circumstances, it is only too obvious why
William was not anxious to talk about politics to Victoria. The Queen
did not know how fateful the decision was that had just been taken and
she could not know how irrevocable it would prove to be. There were
many who did not give Bismarck more than a few months in office and
his name was execrated throughout Germany. Bismarck had just made
the speech which contained the notorious 'blood and iron' phrase,

the means which he thought would be necessary to unify Germany. At the time the historian Heinrich von Treitschke, later one of the most strident apostles of German nationalism and most fervent admirers of Bismarck, wrote: 'When I hear a shallow Junker like this Bismarck boast of the iron and blood with which he will bring Germany under his yoke, it sounds to me even more ludicrous than it is vile.'

By the following year, 1863, when the Queen again went to Coburg in the summer, those who had hoped for a liberal Prussia leading a more unified Germany were engaged in a battle with the repressive Bismarck regime more bitter than ever. The Prussian Lower House had refused to vote the budget in the form proposed by the government, but the Bismarck Cabinet simply went on taxing and spending without a budget. It argued that the Chamber's refusal to vote the budget left a gap, which the executive had to fill if the affairs of state were to be carried on. With his 'gap theory', Bismarck had gone against one of the basic rules of parliamentary government. He accompanied this with many confrontational speeches, never giving an inch to the outraged liberal deputies. In the country at large officials not fully in support of the government were moved or retired. On 1 June 1863 a repressive press ordinance was issued under which publications could be banned 'because of a continuous attitude endangering the public welfare'.

This edict precipitated an open clash between the Bismarck government and the Crown Prince. On an official visit to Danzig (Gdansk), a town where liberal support was strong, Frederick William expressed his regret that matters had reached such a pass and denied any personal involvement in the promulgation of the press edict. Before speaking out, the Crown Prince had written both to his father and Bismarck protesting against the edict. The King replied ordering his son to abide by the decisions of his government and support them in public. Vicky carried this letter to her husband on the way to joining him for the official visit to Danzig and before he made his speech. What Frederick William said was carefully phrased, stressing the King's magnanimous intentions and attacking only the Bismarck government, but it nevertheless caused an enormous row between father and son. It looked as if the King was going to have his son court-martialled and he was pressed to do so by the reactionary court party. No Hohenzollern could forget the fact that Frederick William I, the soldier king, had had his son, the later

Frederick the Great, imprisoned and had compelled him to watch the execution of his closest friend.

It did not quite come to this a century and a half on, but the Crown Prince and even more his wife found themselves subjected to great pressure. Bismarck was too wily an operator to make a martyr of a man who might soon be king, but he unleashed a witch hunt around the couple. He was particularly incensed when some of the correspondence between the Crown Prince and the King was leaked to the press, and when in London *The Times* applauded the courage of Vicky. It was the end of the young Stockmar as adviser to Vicky and her husband. The old Baron himself died in Coburg only a month later, on 9 July 1863. The ranks of the Coburg connection were thinning, but on this occasion those who were left were facing in the same direction. They were for a liberal Prussia leading Germany, but they were against the Bismarck regime, which was tainting the good name of Prussia. Bismarck, in power for less than a year, was at this stage swimming against a powerful tide of opinion everywhere and he had not yet won any of the sensational triumphs that later bolstered him. In defiance of all liberal sentiment, he had backed Russia in the suppression of the Polish revolt earlier in the year. When the British Ambassador in Berlin warned him that Europe would not tolerate such brutality he said 'Who is Europe?' It was characteristic of his coldly calculating cynicism. Equally characteristic was the vindictiveness with which he pursued those around the Crown Prince and his wife. Vicky's letters to her mother give eloquent testimony of the desperate isolation in which they found themselves:

> The Conservatives are in a state of indignation and alarm! the King very angry! We are in this critical position without a secretary, without a single person to give advice ... We are surrounded with spies, who watch all we do ... I do not mind any difficulties so long as they end well for Fritz; indeed I enjoy a pitched battle ... exceedingly. Fritz feels his courage rise in every emergency; only the thought of his father makes him feel powerless ... what a wretched time we have of it ... surrounded with people determined to put an insurmountable barrier to all we wish to do in a liberal sense ... M. de Bismarck has not even answered Fritz's letter and the King has forbidden him to give it to the rest of the Ministers![8]

At the time Augusta, the Queen of Prussia, was staying at Windsor. Queen Victoria noted in her journal on 22 June: 'the Queen [Augusta] read me a ... Memorandum, which the poor King [of Prussia] had written and given her with instructions as to what language she should hold and what she should say about his Government. It goes to show how sadly he deceives himself, his natural honesty and conscientiousness making it impossible for him to understand how dangerous is the course he is pursuing.' Augusta was naturally very unhappy about the course of events in her country. On the other hand, King Leopold was advising his niece not to give too much encouragement to any disobedience by Frederick William to his father. 'My opinion about Fritz remains unchanged; he cannot meet his father's commands with a simple refusal', he wrote to Victoria, 'Vicky wrote to you that as a freeborn Englishwoman she would not submit to certain things etc.: we have the first commandment "Honour thy father and mother", etc., which cannot be set aside *ad libitum*; and the Princess Royal in a foreign land cannot alter what is to a certain extent there the law ...'

By the time Victoria came to Coburg again, in August 1863, the Prussian King had become further entangled in the Machiavellian web of policies spun for him by his overpowering Prime Minister. Bismarck was not only fighting the liberal movement in Prussia and Germany, he was also determined to put paid to any vestiges of Austrian supremacy in Germany. Austria had tried to seize the initiative by calling a congress of German princes in Frankfurt to agree on a reform of the German Confederation. Francis Joseph, the Austrian Emperor, had sprung an invitation to this congress on William of Prussia while the latter was taking the waters at Bad Gastein, within the Austrian borders, in early August. After a tremendous battle of wills, Bismarck managed to get his master to refuse the invitation. When the German princes were actually assembled at Frankfurt, three weeks later, they sent one of their number, the King of Saxony, to William to ask him to come after all. William found it extremely difficult to refuse again. 'Thirty ruling gentlemen and a king as courier!' he kept repeating. Again Bismarck forced him to refuse. The King had crossed a Rubicon when he made this man his minister and there was no way back.

Dynasties meant little to Bismarck and even the quasi-feudal loyalty he had pledged to his own King seemed at times more than a little conditional. Ultimately, however, it would have been in the power of the King to dismiss him and for this reason Bismarck was paranoid about the hostile dynastic influences that surrounded the King. Once, when telling an Italian diplomat that he could not do something because the King would not accept it, Bismarck said 'si je pouvais coucher avec lui, comme fait la Reine, cela marcherait'. He knew only too well that the Queen no longer slept with her husband, but she was still a dangerous influence. So was the Crown Prince, propelled by his strong-willed English wife, and so was the whole Coburg connection, even without Albert and Stockmar. Nothing enraged Bismarck more than these influences, which made him aware that his own power might come up against forces beyond his control. He had been called into office to save the Prussian monarchy from the rising tides of liberalism and constitutionalism. This he achieved, but it also made him dependent on whoever, for the time being, represented that monarchy. For William it was increasingly difficult to get rid of him; by the time Bismarck had won his great triumphs it became virtually unthinkable. But William was already sixty-five when he chose Bismarck as his chief minister.

The Prussian Prime Minister was far too wily an operator to think that one could impose a preconceived plan on the unpredictable course of events. One of his favourite Latin tags was 'unda fert, nec regitur' – you cannot make a wave, you can only let it carry you. He was, however, a genius in assessing the forces at work in the situation in which he found himself, and nudging them in the direction that suited him. The diehard conservatives who had surrounded Frederick William IV and were still hovering around William I wanted simply to confront the liberals dominating the Prussian Landtag. They were prepared if necessary to risk a *coup d'état* to abolish the constitution that had set up the Landtag. Such a course was likely to lead to another revolution, as in 1848, which it might this time prove impossible to suppress. Bismarck saw that it would be possible to divert the liberals from their aim of having a greater say in government at home if their aims abroad were brought nearer to satisfaction. What they wanted, outside Prussia, was a unified Germany in which Prussia would dominate. They wanted this not only for idealistic, nationalist reasons, the greater power and glory of the German people; for them it was also an economic necessity. They were the new middle classes, businessmen and entrepreneurs, who could not operate successfully when the country was divided into dozens of separate states. Bismarck also discerned that this new middle class produced by the coming of industrialism was at bottom conservative. They could be enlisted to support a conservative order of society still dominated by a powerful monarchy. They were already being challenged by a rising industrial proletariat, and in this conflict of classes the bourgeosie would be on the side of the established order. Such insights provided Bismarck with a basis for formulating policy that proved sensationally successful in the 1860s. He has been called, not without reason, the White Revolutionary: he was a revolutionary, and therefore he frightened at times even his own master, the King; but it was a revolution from above he was making. Another of his favourite sayings was that it is better to make a revolution than to suffer it.

While Queen Victoria was at Coburg in September 1863, both the King of Prussia and the Emperor of Austria visited her. They were putting, as it were, their respective cases, following the congress of German princes at Frankfurt, which, without the participation of Prussia, proved abortive. William said that the conflict whether to accept or refuse the invitation to Frankfurt had made him 'quite ill'. Francis Joseph said it was 'not the King personally, who made great difficulties, but his Government'. The Queen did not say much to either of them, beyond giving the anodyne advice that Austria and Prussia should work together in Germany and neither should seek supremacy over the other. Bismarck and Roon had accompanied their master to Coburg, but they were not received by the Queen. Victoria came across Bismarck at one point and noted 'the horrid expression' on his face. To her he was becoming a *bête noire*.

The long-running saga of Schleswig-Holstein was about to reach a critical stage. In March 1863 the King of Denmark, Frederick VII, had issued a patent that envisaged a constitution for Denmark as a whole, including Schleswig, while Holstein, part of the German Confederation, was to retain a separate status under the Danish Crown. German national opinion was up in arms. Once more it looked as if Schleswig was to be detached from Germany and that even in Holstein the wishes of the population were not to be fully respected. In November 1863 Frederick VII died and, in accordance with the London Protocol of 1852, Christian IX, the Prince of Wales's father-in-law, ascended the Danish throne and also proclaimed himself Duke of Schleswig and of Holstein. He signed the constitution initiated by his predecessor, under which

Schleswig was incorporated into the Danish state. At the same time the Duke of Augustenburg, seen throughout Germany as the rightful ruler of the two duchies, proclaimed himself Duke of Schleswig and Holstein and was widely supported by the German-speaking population of both territories. Augustenburg was none other than Fritz Holstein, the friend of Vicky and her husband and the son-in-law of Victoria's half-sister Feodora. All of them were now firmly lined up behind Augustenburg, as was the Duke of Coburg, who had done all he could to present himself as the German ruler most in tune with German national sentiment. In Prussia it was not only the liberals who supported Augustenburg; even Bismarck's own secretary thought rather naively that it was the obvious thing to do, until instructed otherwise by his master. The King felt sorely tempted to support Augustenburg; for, like all Germans, he was sure he was the legitimate ruler of the duchies. Supporting Augustenburg would at last realign Prussia with most of German opinion and give her the 'moral conquests', which William had written into his manifesto on becoming Regent five years earlier.

Bismarck had quite different plans. The last thing he wanted was to create another medium-sized German state on Prussia's doorstep and he was hopeful that he could eventually engineer the annexation of the duchies into Prussia. It is often regarded as his diplomatic masterpiece that he managed to get Austria to go along with him. If ever there was a country suffering from imperial overstretch, it was Austria at this stage of her history. She could not give up her position in Italy, nor in the Balkans, least of all in Germany. It now looked to the Austrians that they might as well join forces with the Bismarck regime, which appeared to be a bulwark of conservatism. They could not afford to flout international agreements like the London Protocol of 1852, nor did they want to align themselves with the German liberal national movement behind the Duke of Augustenburg. So they joined the Bismarck government in going to war against the Danes, not in order to give the duchies to Augustenburg but to reverse the illegal incorporation of Schleswig into Denmark and the separation of the two 'for ever united' duchies. The fighting fell into two phases, interrupted by a conference of the powers in London in April 1864 to find a compromise. The Danes were foolish enough to reject what was on offer, for even before the conference met Prussian troops had stormed the fortifications of Düppel. The victory roused most of Germany into a frenzy of nationalist fervour. Many liberals who had execrated Bismarck were beginning to change their minds.

For the Queen of England and her family it was an agonising time. She was pro-Prussian, in her own inclinations, but even more so because this is what she thought Albert would have been. He had always regarded the London Protocol of 1852 as an injustice to Germany and had written many a letter and memorandum on the subject. But now Victoria had a Danish daughter-in-law, who was fervently on the side of her father and her countrymen. So was the Prince of Wales and most of British public opinion. Most people saw it as a flagrant example of a small country being bullied, and moreover it was a small country in the integrity of which Britain had a strategic interest. The Palmerston government had given the impression that Britain would come to the aid of the Danes, but this could only have been done with a major continental ally. For a variety of reasons Napoleon III was unwilling to intervene and Britain could not send more than twenty thousand troops to the Continent.

Suddenly Palmerston looked like an emperor without clothes and he survived in the House of Commons by only eighteen votes in July 1864. He was nearly eighty and no match for Bismarck. Some of the old acerbity crept back into the correspondence between Palmerston and the pro-Prussian Queen: 'Viscount Palmerston can quite understand your Majesty's reluctance to take any active part in measures in any conflict against Germany, but he is sure that your Majesty will never forget that you are sovereign of Great Britain ...'[9] Who would end up in the Tower first? The Queen was widely and publicly blamed for having prevented her government from coming to the aid of the Danes. Such accusations infuriated her and made her feel, without Albert, more isolated and exposed than ever. She strongly rebutted them and claimed that her sole desire was to preserve her country from being involved in an unnecessary war. Lord Clarendon, who was out of office at the time and therefore free to criticise the government, told the Queen, during a dinner at Windsor, that Britain was lucky to have escaped having to come to the assistance of the Danes. There might have been a general European war and Napoleon III would have availed himself of the opportunity to seize the Rhine provinces.

Fierce and contrary emotions flared up within the Queen's own family from the moment the Schleswig-Holstein affair reached crisis point and she became more distraught than ever. A few days after the death of the old Danish King, Frederick VII, she wrote to her Uncle Leopold, himself old and ill and with only just a year to live:

> My beloved Albert felt *very* strongly the injustice of the Protocol of '52, which was a Russian intrigue; but he also felt that, if the Danes fulfilled the stipulations, there was nothing for it but abiding by it. Now we were on the point of getting matters in a *fair* train of settlement, when this wretched King dies ... Still anything is better than a war, for where is that to end? It will give our mischievous neighbour [Napoleon III] the opportunity he has been anxiously looking out for ... Some sort of mediation or arbitration ought to be thought of, if *possible*. Fritz W. is very violent, Vicky sensible, Feodore very anxious and at times violent ... and I *miserable*, wretched, almost frantic, without my angel to stand by me, and *put* the *others* down, and in their right place!

At the end of January 1864, the eve of the Prussian-Austrian invasion of Schleswig, the Queen wrote to her daughter Vicky: 'my heart and sympathies are all German. Where I do, however, blame Germany is in their wanting the two great Powers to break their engagements, and in not being contented with all the rights of the Duchies being obtained. They have mixed up the two questions, and gone so violently mad upon the subject ...'[10]

Frederick William was in fact all girded up to fight the Danes and did so with some distinction. The King had refused to put him in command, because his insubordination at Danzig still rankled, but he held a key position on the staff of General Wrangel, who was over eighty and no longer capable of exercising command. Fritz was in the thick of the fighting at Düppel and his father became sufficiently reconciled to decorate him for his bravery. Vicky hated it all, and her position within the Hohenzollern clan, and with much of the Prussian public, was more difficult than ever. 'The family here look upon me with a certain look of virtuous indignation and raise their eyes to the skies when they mention England, as if I could help it', she wrote to her mother, '[a newspaper] says it hopes the infamous conduct of England towards Prussia, as declared in the English Press, will open the eyes of all for ever and prevent the danger arising of English and Coburg influence returning'.

In the end pride in her husband and the Prussian victory got the better of her. She rationalised the war by saying King Christian should never have set aside the legitimate claims of Fritz Holstein, the Augustenburger. At home Alix, pregnant with her first child, was passionately on the side of her Papa and was so upset that she gave birth prematurely to a son, Albert Victor, later Duke of Clarence, weighing less than four pounds, in January 1864. Dynastic connections were increasingly difficult to manage in the age of nationalism. Victoria, at the age of only forty-five, was becoming the matriarch of European monarchies and had to manage it all on her own. Alix, the Princess of Wales, remained obsessively anti-Prussian all her life and found meetings with her Hohenzollern relations very difficult.

After their final defeat in July 1864 the Danes were compelled to cede the two duchies jointly to Prussia and Austria. It took the Austrians some time to realise the full extent to which Bismarck had taken them for a ride. The conquest of Holstein and Schleswig could hardly do them much good when both territories were on Prussia's doorstep, while the Habsburg monarchy was too far away to counteract the endless series of manipulations that were now available to Bismarck. In the autumn of 1864 the Austrian Foreign Minister Rechberg was forced to resign, for he was thought in Vienna to have put too much trust in the alliance with the Bismarck government in Prussia. An attempt to reach an agreement between Vienna and Berlin, along the lines of Prussian supremacy north of the River Main and Austrian supremacy to the south, proved stillborn. Rechberg's successor was Alexander Mensdorff-Pouilly, Albert and Victoria's cousin, son of their aunt Sophie of Saxe-Coburg-Gotha.

The issue that was driving Austria and Prussia apart was the Zollverein, the German customs union. It was one of Bismarck's strongest cards. Most German states were now members of it and it was dominated by a rapidly industrializing Prussia. Austria could not join it, because she was economically too backward. States like Saxony, on the way to becoming one of Germany's major industrial regions, could not leave it, even though politically Saxony, a lot of whose territory had been taken by Prussia in 1815, was mainly aligned with Austria.

The Queen went to Coburg again in August 1865, amongst other things to unveil a statue of Albert on what would have been his birthday, 26 August. Relations between the two rival German powers had become uneasy again in the earlier months of 1865, but even Bismarck did not want a premature breach. In April 1865 the Austrians openly reversed their earlier stance and declared themselves willing to recognise the Augustenburg Duke as the rightful ruler of Schleswig-Holstein, provided Prussia did the same. The Austrians thereby got back into step with what was the overwhelming majority of German opinion, and with what was undoubtedly the feeling on the ground in the two duchies, but Prussia remained adamant in refusing to recognize the Augustenburg claim. Bismarck was more than ever in control of Prussian policy. The King felt uneasy about setting aside the Augustenburger, but Bismarck managed to convince him that the unlucky Fritz Holstein was disloyal to Prussia. In a Prussian Crown Council on 29 May 1865 the Crown Prince was the only one who spoke out in favour of Augustenburg and said that an eventual war with Austria would be a civil war. Bismarck was quite prepared to risk war with Austria, if necessary, but did not judge the time ripe yet.

The overstretched Austrians were, even more than Bismarck, under pressure to avoid war, which might precipitate revolutions that would tear the Habsburg Empire apart. Thus another agreement between Berlin and Vienna was in the making. It was called the Gastein Convention, because King William was again taking the waters at this spa in Austria, accompanied by his Prime Minister. Schleswig was to come under Prussia's control, Holstein under Austria's. It was a cynical bargain, which caused outrage in Germany and throughout Europe. The Austrians were the real losers. They had surrendered the moral high ground in Germany, which they had just tried to regain, and they deeply offended the smaller German states, most of whom were their traditional allies. Holstein was of little use to them and Bismarck could make their position there very difficult at any time of his choosing.

All this was going on as the Queen was about to go to Coburg. She was now herself worked up against the Prussians. 'Prussia seems inclined to behave as atrociously as possible, and as she *always has done!*', she wrote to Uncle Leopold while still at Osborne on 3 August 1865, 'Odious people the Prussians are, *that* I *must* say'. To similar complaints her daughter Vicky had replied: 'If you are furious at the way these unfortunate Elbe Duchies and Fritz Holstein are treated what do you think we are! ... I wish we and the nation were rid of him

[Bismarck] and all that are like him. If my letter is opened by the Post
Officials I shall be accused of high treason – but I am as loyal as anyone
as I love the King and would do anything to serve him ...'[11] So it was
all the fault of Bismarck, who had deceived the honest King.

The Queen was now 'much plagued' by telegrams from King William
proposing to come and see her at Coburg. On the day the Gastein Convention was signed, Ernst Stockmar came to see the Queen and spoke
of 'the infamous conduct of the King and Bismarck relative to
Schleswig-Holstein; how he began to doubt the King's honesty; how
painful Fritz's [the Crown Prince] position was'. Yet the Queen could
hardly refuse outright to meet the Prussian King. Eventually they met at
Darmstadt, in the castle of the father-in-law of her second daughter
Alice, in early September. 'He was very kind and friendly, but we talked
of nothing but *pluie et beau temps*, and he left again in less than half an
hour', she noted in her journal. Alexander Mensdorff, her cousin, and
one of the architects of the Gastein Convention on the Austrian side,
had come to see her a few days earlier at the Rosenau in Coburg: 'Dear
Alexander Mensdorff came and sat with me talking of the sad Schleswig-
Holstein affair. He is now Prince and Foreign Minister and *all*-powerful;
so good, wise, and honest. I spoke very strongly to him about the infamy
of the conduct of the Prussians, and he promised me that Austria would
not, indeed he said she could not, allow Prussia to annex the duchies. I
also spoke strongly in favour of poor good Fritz Holstein. Alexander
once more promised that Austria would be firm.'

The Queen might well put in a good word for Fritz Holstein, for she
had decided that his younger brother, Prince Christian, to give him
his full title, of Schleswig-Holstein-Sonderburg-Augustenburg, should
become the husband of her third daughter Helena, 'Lenchen'. He had
found favour with her when in England earlier that year. To Vicky
she described him as 'our *Hausfreund*. He comes and goes when he
likes, walks and breakfasts and dines with us, when he is here and we
are alone. He is the best creature in the world; not as clever as Fritz
[Holstein], but certainly not wanting in any way.' She wanted him for
Lenchen, now her remaining daughter other than Beatrice, who was
only eight, because she needed Lenchen to stay at home and remain
available to her mother. From this point of view an impecunious German prince with otherwise uncertain prospects would be an advantage.

The other young royal women did not always meet the requirements of the self-absorbed Queen. Affie, her second son, was now an adult, but she was no less critical of him than she was of Bertie. She had vetoed his selection as King of Greece because she felt that he was, despite his shortcomings, required at home. Since it was desirable, as the Queen was well aware, to keep a French or Russian candidate out of Greece, the Greek throne was then offered to Ernst, the Duke of Coburg, her brother-in-law. He seriously considered it, but decided it would be incompatible with retaining the duchy of Coburg. Greece went to Alix's brother William, who became George I of the Hellenes.

Even Alix herself, who had to begin with so delighted the Queen and whom she thought would be such a good influence on Bertie, was no longer quite up to the mark. Quite apart from her daughter-in-law's deafness, the Queen compared her unfavourably with Antoinette, the wife of Leopold of Hohenzollern-Sigmaringen.* 'Oh if Antoinette was in Al.'s place ! She is so much more *sympathique* and *grande dame.* Our good Al. is like a distinguished lady of society but nothing more.'[12] Prince Christian of Schleswig did not find favour with some of the other royal siblings. Bertie and Alix were against the match and so was Alice. They felt that Lenchen was being sacrificed to the loneliness of her mother. It was therefore a relief to Victoria that Vicky and Fritz approved of the match, but this was another bone of contention with the rest of the Hohenzollern clan. An Augustenburger was now virtually an enemy, and a defeated one at that: what could be more contemptible? It was a relief to the Queen that during this visit to Coburg Lenchen, who did not yet know what was in store for her, told her of her own accord that she thought Prince Christian 'amiable and pleasing and agreeable'. The marriage was celebrated the following year.

Self-absorbed the Queen might be and isolated she might feel, but, wherever she was and went, she was always the focus of attention and at the centre of great affairs. Small wonder that she felt matters needed to be arranged for her comfort and convenience. No sooner was she

---

* Hohenzollern-Sigmaringen was the Catholic South German branch of the House of Hohenzollern. In 1870 Prince Leopold's candidature for the Spanish throne was the immediate cause for the outbreak of the Franco-Prussian war.

back at Balmoral in mid-October when British politics entered a period of turbulence. On 18 October 1865 Palmerston died, two days before his eighty-first birthday. He had been 'impertinent' to her during the Schleswig-Holstein crisis, but 'Still, as Prime Minister he managed affairs at home well, and behaved to me well'.[13] Earl Russell, now aged seventy-four and a member of the House of Lords, became Prime Minister for the second time; Gladstone remained Chancellor of the Exchequer and became leader of the Commons; and Clarendon went back to the Foreign Office in Russell's place. The Queen was reasonably satisfied and wrote to Uncle Leopold that 'Lord Russell is very kind and reasonable, and anxious to do all I wish'.

Little over a month later Leopold was dead, the third and original architect of the Coburg connection to depart within four years. The Queen was worried that he could not be buried in St George's Chapel, near Princess Charlotte, his first wife, but it was hardly possible for a King of the Belgians. Victoria was more than ever bereft of those who had been nearest to her. More and more frequently there is mention in her letters of John Brown, her Scottish personal servant, and of his devotion to her. For the next few years he became the person nearest to her. As a result she became the butt of jokes, she was called Mrs Brown, and scandalous rumours abounded. No amount of remonstrance by her family, her courtiers and her ministers could dissuade her from having him around her. In July 1867 the government had for once succeeded in getting the Queen to appear in public, at a military review in Hyde Park. When the Queen insisted on having Brown in attendance, the Prime Minister Lord Derby and his Home Secretary were in a quandary, for they feared a hostile reaction from the public. Then an uncovenanted event came to their rescue. It was the execution of Maximilian, who had been sent to be Emperor of Mexico by Napoleon III and was then left in the lurch. The Hyde Park review could be cancelled without loss of face.

Palmerston had for years dominated the political scene. In his final years his presence had mainly served to keep new initiatives to a minimum and his removal was bound to set things in motion. Russell had thirty-five years earlier introduced the first Reform Bill, but all his attempts to reform the franchise further had been frustrated. Now was his last chance. Movements, such as the Reform League, had sprung up in the country to admit working-class men in larger numbers to the franchise. Gladstone had shown some sympathy towards these aims and had thereby staked out a claim to lead the Liberal party after the departure of both 'the two terrible old men'. Thus the Russell government introduced a new major Reform Bill. There were many in the Liberal party who had no desire to see the franchise widened. It was a commonly held view among liberal politicians and intellectuals that parliamentary government was essentially a system that could only be operated by elites. Only elites could deliver good government and preserve freedom. The majority of Liberals, however, certainly those on the left, felt that wider political participation could no longer be blocked, even if there was in principle no stopping place until you arrived at universal suffrage. Gladstone had put exactly that argument in May 1864, in a guarded and typically circuitous way, which nonetheless earned him a reprimand from Palmerston: 'I venture to say that every man who is not presumably incapacitated by some consideration of personal unfitness or of political danger, is morally entitled to come within the pale of the constitution.'[14]

The Reform Bill put forward by the Russell government split the Liberals and in June 1866 Russell was forced to resign. The Queen sent for Lord Derby, who for the third time in fifteen years formed a minority government, which was led in the Commons by Disraeli. These events caused considerable unrest in the country. The reform movement, which had up to then been entirely peaceful and relatively low key, was goaded into protest by what was regarded as Parliament's failure to heed the popular will. A large demonstration, on 23 July 1866, which had been refused access to Hyde Park, tore down the railings of the park and there were a good many smashed windows in Mayfair and other fashionable parts of London. The situation was aggravated by an economic downturn after many years of boom. Many were alarmed and saw the spectre of revolution, not least the Queen. She pressed the Derby government to settle the reform question as soon as possible.

While these events were going on at home, the Battle of Sadowa (or Königgrätz, as it is usually called in German) on 3 July 1866 had decided the fate of Germany. The war between Austria and Prussia, which had broken out three weeks earlier, was the culmination of the tensions over Schleswig-Holstein, which had caused the Queen and her family so much anguish over the previous year. The Gastein Convention had provided only a temporary breathing space. The Bismarck government used every possible chicanery to frustrate any support for the Duke of Augustenburg in Schleswig, which was under Prussian control. They accused the Austrians of allowing activity in support of Augustenburg, which they called revolutionary, to proliferate in Holstein, where the Austrians held sway. By early 1866 Bismarck had clearly decided on war with Austria – it seems likely that without such a war, and victory at the end of it, he would have been ousted from power. Frantic efforts were made by Vicky and her mother in March 1866 to ward off war through mediation. Some of the steps taken were at official, inter-governmental level. British mediation on its own was hardly likely to succeed, but France would not join. Bismarck had been very skilful in making Napoleon III believe that a war between the two German powers would enable him to claim compensation for France, on the Rhine or in the Low Countries. This left the possibility of a direct personal appeal to the Prussian King. Everybody within the dynastic family circle believed that William was being entirely manipulated and deceived by his wicked Prime Minister. Ernst of Coburg, who was well informed of what was going on both in Vienna and Berlin, got his wife to write to Victoria, that 'in Berlin NO ONE wishes for war – neither the King, nor the Princes, nor any other mortal, but, singly and solely, Count *Bismarck*', and asked for urgent action. The Queen responded by writing a personal letter to King William, which was pressed into his hand by the British Ambassador, Lord Augustus Loftus, just as the King and his family were boarding a special train to Potsdam.

Bismarck was roused to tremendous fury by such backstairs dynastic interference, because he felt really threatened by it. He knew how difficult it was to keep the King to a course that might mean fratricidal war against his princely confrères. He said that, in respect of the King's readiness to face war with Austria, he, Bismarck, felt like a clockmaker who was having to rewind the clock every morning. Now he was again having to confront the Coburg intrigue: Queen Augusta, the Crown Prince, Vicky, her mother, Ernst in Coburg and Alexander Mensdorff in Vienna. He inspired articles in the press attacking the Duke of Coburg. Bismarck had in place a well-developed public relations apparatus and the newspapers in Prussia were far from free. On this occasion his attack on the Coburg connection proved counter-productive. The King did not like attacks on his fellow rulers and family members and for some days relations between him and his Prime Minister became strained. Bismarck defended himself by writing to his master, with scarcely concealed allusion to the Queen and the Crown Prince, that he would have to be superhuman to remain silent when his difficult, all-consuming duties were made even more difficult by those 'for whom the success of Prussian policy, the repute of Your Majesty and the royal house should rank above all else'. It was far too late to separate the King from his over-powering minister and this was probably the last time the Coburg connection made a politically significant appearance. Duke Ernst was militarily and economically too committed to Prussia to take sides against her and the survival of his House had always depended on choosing the winning side in the nick of time. Of all the seventeen minor German states that joined the Prussian side, Coburg did so with the least delay, when only weeks earlier Ernst had still been deeply involved with the pro-Augustenburg movement.

The Battle of Sadowa was the most decisive passage of arms in Europe since Waterloo. 'Casca il mondo', the world has collapsed, said Pope Pius IX when he heard the news of the Austrian defeat. Desperate cries for help from the defeated members of her royal connections reached Queen Victoria, but she could do nothing to help them. The worst case was that of Hanover, the most important north German state to have fought against Prussia and to have been defeated, in the Battle of Langensalza a few days before Sadowa. George, the Duke of Cambridge, Commander-in-Chief of the British Army, and also next in line for the throne of Hanover, wrote to his cousin Victoria four days after Sadowa: 'It certainly never entered my head that I should live to see the day when the King of Hanover was to be driven from his Kingdom by his neighbour the King of Prussia, nor would I have believed that my old friends of the Hanoverian Army would have to lay down their arms, after making a most gallant resistance.' The Queen could only advise him 'to speak strongly to Lord Derby and Lord Stanley [Derby's son was now Foreign Secretary], and point out to them your rightful claims. I hear, however, that there is no intention of annexing Hanover.'

She was quite wrong. The territory of Hanover divided the rest of

Prussia from her important Rhine provinces and Bismarck decided on the outright annexation of the kingdom. The Prussian King, always so sensitive to royal legitimacy, made no objection. Some of the property of the Hanoverian royal family went into a secret fund at the disposal of Bismarck, the so-called Guelph Fund, which he used in future years to bribe journalists and even diplomats and finance espionage. The Queen had ambivalent feelings about King George of Hanover and did not want him in England, whither he had sent the bulk of his fortune. Affie had fallen in love with George's daughter and that was a match she certainly did not want.

The King of Saxony, a refugee in Schönbrunn Palace at Vienna, also pleaded his case to Victoria as a member of the Saxon royal house. King William was keen to annex Saxony, for it had always been on the opposite side of the fence to Prussia. Bismarck decided against annexation, but Saxony was bound to Prussia hand and foot as a member of the North German Confederation. A few months later Derby and Stanley asked the Queen's permission to close the British Embassy in Dresden, which would save £3000 a year, the peace treaty between Prussia and Saxony 'having in effect deprived the latter country of its independence in foreign affairs'. The Queen later regretted having given permission too precipitately. Hesse-Darmstadt had also fought on the losing side and the Queen received a heartrending letter from her daughter Alice at Darmstadt, written less than three weeks after Sadowa:

> The Prussians marched in this morning, their bands playing and making as great a demonstration as they could. My parents-in-law were with me at the moment, and my father-in-law [the Grand Duke of Hesse-Darmstadt] walked up and down in despair and indignation, in feeling that his home and his country were no more his own; as the Prussians pay for nothing and demand everything, the place will soon be ruined ... We must get the gracious permission of the Prussians for anything we want, we smuggle people with our things with difficulty out of the town, if we wish anything, but the Prussians watch so well, to prevent our communicating with our troops or with anywhere outside, that we are the most complete prisoners. This goes so far, we have difficulty in getting any decent meat, or the common luxuries of life, for the Prussians devour everything, and we can get nothing even from Frankfort.

At least Hesse-Darmstadt was allowed to survive, its northern part within the North German Confederation. The liberal city of Frankfurt was very badly treated by the Prussians and its mayor committed suicide.

Vicky, with all her ambivalent feelings, was on the winning side. She was proud of her husband, who had played a key role in winning the Battle of Sadowa. Nobody was more relieved than Bismarck when he saw through his field glasses that the Crown Prince's army was arriving on the battlefield. It was the moment of decision. The victory was by no means so complete that the Prussians could have gratuitously prolonged the war, which would also have risked a French intervention on the Rhine. Bismarck had to fight a bitter battle with his own King, who was raring to go on to Vienna, to get him to agree to an armistice. It was probably the most nerve-racking moment of his career and again Frederick William's intervention was decisive. He managed to talk his father round and the preliminary peace of Nikolsburg was signed. The Habsburg Empire was left intact; but, having been so long the premier German power, it now no longer had a role in Germany.

The Crown Prince was never given the credit for the military and political service he performed for his country in 1866, for he and his wife were still vilified as 'the democratic Hohenzollerns'. For Vicky this was a particularly difficult time. In April 1866, during the run-up to a war she abhorred, she gave birth to her fifth child, named Victoria after her grandmother, but known as Moretta. Two months later, just after her husband left for the war, her fourth child and third son, Sigismund, died at the age of twenty-two months. She was inconsolable and driven to the edge of reason by her grief. Her mother gave her all the epistolary support she could. When politics crept back into their correspondence Vicky wrote:

> At this sad time one *must separate* one's feelings for one's relations quite from one's *judgment* on *political necessities* ... Nothing will or can ever shake Fritz's principles of sound liberalism and justice, but you know from experience that one must proceed in the direction given by the political events that have come to pass. Those who are now in such precarious positions might have *quite well* foreseen what danger they were running into ... they *chose* to go with Austria and they now share the sad fate she confers on her Allies. Those who have taken our side or remained neutral are quite unharmed, for example Uncle Ernest ... I cannot and will not forget that I

am a Prussian, but as such I know it is very difficult to make you, or any other non-German, see how our case lies.

In September 1866 there was a great victory parade in Berlin and Vicky could not help sharing in the enthusiasm. Her Fritz rode with Moltke, Roon and Bismarck in front of the King. Uncle Ernst rode at the head of his battalion and Vicky told her mother: 'I am not accustomed to hearing so much praise of Coburg *here.*' She was glad that Ernst was not among 'many of one's friends suffering from the effects of their miscalculations'.[15]

The political scene in Prussia was utterly changed. Bismarck was the hero of the hour. He had already been made a Count a year earlier after his success in Schleswig-Holstein. Now a grateful nation gave him the money to buy an estate in Pomerania, where he had spent much of his youth and early adult years. Varzin was four hours by rail from Berlin, followed by a long carriage drive over scarcely made up roads. Bismarck spent much time there, sometimes with real or diplomatic illnesses, usually with a cipher operated by a member of his family or a clerk, but occasionally incommunicado. He was now so powerful and irreplaceable that he could absent himself from Berlin for months on end and still dominate Prussia, Germany and Europe. After 1871 he was given an even larger estate, Friedrichsruh, near Hamburg, on the Hamburg–Berlin railway line, which made access to the capital easier, but he still went often to Varzin. Once the victory parades of September 1866 were over, he suffered from nervous exhaustion and withdrew to the estates of a friend, Prince Putbus, on the island of Rügen off the Pomeranian coast. There he dictated the memoranda on which the Constitution of the North German Confederation and later of Imperial Germany was based. It was that curious halfway house, sometimes called German constitutionalism, which comprised on the one hand a parliament, the Reichstag, elected on a broad franchise of universal male suffrage, equipped with considerable legislative and budgetary powers. Against this was set the federal executive, consisting initially only of the Reich Chancellor, namely Bismarck himself. He was appointed by the King-Emperor and could not be removed by the Reichstag. This system remained in place until the collapse of the Empire in 1918.

In the debates on these proposals Bismarck was helped by the support given by the Crown Prince. Frederick William naturally had a vital interest how his now much extended country would be run. With his father now seventy, he himself would soon be running it. He would have preferred a more unitary constitution, with what remained of the separate states more or less reduced to the status of provinces. Bismarck preferred to leave most of the German princes, other than those whose territory he had annexed, *in situ*. Above all he did not want to do away with Prussia, much the largest component of the federation. Under Bismarck's proposals Prussia would anyhow have its way on any federal matter. It would be easier for the remaining South German states, Bavaria, Württemberg and Baden, to accede to the federation if their identity was preserved, even if most of their independence was gone. This system would also limit the power of the federal Reichstag. It was killing parliamentarism with parliaments, because the other parliaments, Prussian, Bavarian and so on, would continue to exist. Only Bismarck himself could operate so complex a system and being able to do so made him indispensable for a long time to come.

Frederick William and Vicky had to apply their liberal principles in a completely changed landscape. With consummate but Machiavellian skill Bismarck had divided the liberal movement. He had offered an indemnity bill, which would wipe the slate clean of the constitutional conflict that had raged with the liberals since he came to power. A large number of liberals now accepted Bismarck's olive branch, for they saw no further purpose in opposing him. He had realised, and was on his way to completing the realisation, of one of their aims, a united Germany. By cooperating with him the liberals could hope to shape this united Germany in their image. The liberals who saw it that way became known as the National Liberals and dominated the Reichstag for a decade, until 1879. During this time the laws were passed that made Germany into a unified market and laid the foundations for turning it into the industrial powerhouse of Europe. The liberals achieved their economic goals, but their political power remained limited.

Many historians have seen this as a liberal surrender and an indication of the weakness of German liberalism. It did not look like this at the time. For the Crown Prince there was still all to play for. When he inherited the throne he could insist on the implementation of a fully-fledged parliamentary regime. It was a sword of Damocles that hung continuously over Bismarck. It was contrary to all expectations that this interim period lasted twenty years. By the time Frederick William became Emperor in 1888 it was not only the fact that he was a dying man that prevented him from advancing his vision. The time had gone when it was relevant. Liberalism had been fatally weakened by the Great Depression of the 1870s, by the switch to protection and by the rise of strident nationalism. An air of resignation had enveloped the Crown Prince, Vicky and their entourage.

The war of 1866 also marked a change in the position of Britain in relation to the rest of Europe. Gone were the days when Britain was in any position to decide the fate of countries like Italy and Germany. She was still one of the great powers and, outside Europe, where her real interests lay, her influence was pervasive. In Europe the period of splendid isolation was beginning for Britain. Stanley, Foreign Secretary in the Cabinet formed by his father in July 1866, has sometimes been called the most isolationist British Foreign Secretary of the nineteenth century, but this phase really began when Palmerston proved powerless over Schleswig-Holstein. It was another reason why dynastic connections were losing their political influence.

9

The Matriarch of Monarchs

In Britain the ministers of the third Derby-Disraeli Cabinet were just settling into their offices when the Battle of Sadowa was fought. They could do little to influence the earth-shaking events that followed, but they had plenty to occupy their minds at home. The major question confronting them was what to do about parliamentary reform. When the autumn Cabinets met in November 1866, the Queen strongly put her view that the reform question should be settled as soon as possible and offered her services to mediate between the parties. The Hyde Park riots of 23 July 1866, as well as signs of unrest in other cities, had made her even more nervous than usual. In these later years of her reign divisive issues, conflicts between the parties and the two Houses of Parliament, would often, though not always, see her use her influence in favour of compromise. It was a manifestation of the monarchical tendency, evident even in the days of Albert, to avoid the boat being rocked.

Pressure from the Queen was only one factor in pushing Derby and Disraeli to the conclusion that their best option was to capitalise on the Liberal split over reform by bringing in a Reform Bill of their own. They were cautiously limbering up for what was to prove one of the most remarkable parliamentary battles of the century. It ended by the Tories putting an extension of the franchise on the statute book that was more far-reaching than that proposed by the Liberals the year before. In principle it gave the vote to most working-class men in British cities, though it took a while yet before this was realised in practice. Disraeli was seen as a master of parliamentary tactics, who had comprehensively upstaged his rival Gladstone. To the question 'why is Gladstone like a telescope?', the answer was 'because Disraeli draws him out, sees through him and shuts him up'. Disraeli had laid the foundation for the claim that he was the author of popular Conservatism, sometimes called Tory Democracy.

What was even more important was that there was now virtually no theoretical or ideological stopping place before universal male suffrage was reached. It amounted to a further sea-change in constitutional practice, which would profoundly affect the position of the monarchy. It was no accident that Bagehot's commentary on the British constitution was published in book form in 1867 and swiftly became a new orthodoxy. The received wisdom about the monarchy therefore was that it was constitutional and the Queen's political function was limited to being consulted, to encourage and to warn. The real problem was not with what Bagehot called the sovereign's 'efficient' task, but with her failure to fulfil her 'dignified' task.

In February 1868 Derby, with the reform bill on the statute book, had to resign on health grounds. He recommended Disraeli to the Queen as his successor and she accepted his recommendation. It was by no means a foregone conclusion, because Disraeli had never been popular in his party and the Reform Bill had made him many enemies. The most prominent of them was the man who was about to become the third Marquis of Salisbury. As Lord Robert Cecil, and then as Viscount Cranborne, he had long been an opponent of Disraeli's tendency 'to steal the Whigs' clothing while they were bathing'. Salisbury was an exponent of what might be called 'resistance conservatism', the argument that by bowing to prevailing progressivism the Tories were allowing the centre of political gravity to slip ever further to the left. On such grounds Cranborne, as he then was, had resigned from the Derby–Disraeli Cabinet in March 1867 over the proposed Reform Bill. He had thus set himself up as an alternative party leader to Disraeli, whose position 'at the top of the greasy pole' was in the prevailing circumstances highly precarious.

His stay there would have been very brief, had not the Queen's growing favour enabled him to postpone the impending general election by nearly ten months. The ostensible grounds for the postponement were that time was needed to prepare the new electoral registers necessitated by the widening of the franchise. Salisbury described this situation to a follower thus: 'Matters seem very critical, a woman on the throne, & a Jew adventurer who [has] found out the secret of getting round her.'[1] It was in fact the beginning of seventeen years during which the premiership alternated between Disraeli and Gladstone. The Queen's growing conservatism and aversion to radicalism, which she found increasingly difficult to distinguish from liberalism, was reinforced by her rising regard for Disraeli, 'extremely agreeable and original', and dislike of Gladstone, 'wonderfully unsympathetic'. These were relatively early expressions of her opinion of these two men and were much more forcefully put as time went on. The ten months of Disraeli's first premiership was the beginning of a relationship that has become legendary. It was genuine enough on both sides, though not without an element of tongue-in-cheek. Disraeli had now become the vizier of the greatest of Queens, a dream he had conjured up with oriental opulence in some of his novels. He could now act it out in real life. It was an approach that found her immediately responsive. 'He is full of poetry, romance & chivalry. When he knelt down to kiss my hand wh. he took in his – he said: "In loving loyalty & faith"', she wrote to Vicky, describing his accession audience as Prime Minister.[2] Disraeli, for his part, began to speak of her, in private, as 'the Faery'.

Not much of this penetrated, for the time being, into the consciousness of the general public. The growing criticism of the Queen on account of her failure to fulfil the ceremonial functions of the monarchy led in the early 1870s to the rise of the most considerable republican movement of her reign. Paradoxically, even this bout of republicanism scarcely entered the political mainstream, because it was still the general perception that Victoria was a strictly constitutional monarch. It was hardly worthwhile, even in the view of such radical elders like John Bright, to incur the burden and unpopularity of rooting for a republic when the constitutional monarchy was like a republic in all but name. Bright refused to preside over the National Republican Conference in Birmingham in 1873. The most public political intervention of the Queen did make it look as if she really was above party and did the bidding of whoever was in power. In 1869 the chief contentious political issue was the disestablishment of the Irish Church, on which the election of December 1868 had hinged. It was the first of Gladstone's attempts to solve the Irish question, though he was to find that whenever he proposed a solution the Irish changed the question. The Irish Church was an Anglican church, an 'alien church', and it had all the privileges of an established church in a predominantly Roman Catholic country, a very obvious grievance. On this occasion the Queen, who was later to become a violent opponent of Gladstone's Irish policies, played a very public mediating role, when the Liberal disestablishment bill was threatened with destruction in the increasingly Tory House of Lords. The clash between a democratically elected and left-orientated Lower House and a conservative Upper House was due to become a recurring constitutional issue, and the efforts of the Queen to mediate between the two Houses were also to recur.

The public was, however, only too well aware of the Queen's continued absence from nearly all the great ceremonial functions of her office. A handbill was posted on the wall around Buckingham Palace: 'These extensive premises to be let or sold, the late occupant having retired from business.' Even the loyal press published cartoons showing an empty throne above captions like 'Where is Britannia?' This made the expense of monarchy into a live issue, which was brought into focus by the Queen's request for what to the man in the street seemed very large amounts of money for her children. She asked Parliament for an annuity of £15,000 for Prince Arthur of Connaught when he came of age in 1871. Almost simultaneously she asked for a dowry of £30,000 and an annuity of £6000 for her daughter Princess Louise on her marriage to the Marquis of Lorne, heir to the Duke of Argyll. Louise was the most unconventional of Victoria's children and Lorne was rumoured to be a promiscuous homosexual. As if this was not enough to put a question mark over the expense of monarchy, the lavish and scandalous lifestyle of the Prince of Wales and the Marlborough House set was unfolded before a fascinated public when Bertie had to appear in court in the Mordaunt divorce case in February 1870. Lady Mordaunt had, unwisely, mentioned the Prince of Wales, among several others, as a possible father of her offspring. Victoria had admonished the judge to give her son an easy time in the witness box and Bertie got away with it. Not so the unfortunate Lady Mordaunt, who was declared insane and spent the rest of her days in an asylum. An actual divorce would have made her many sisters unmarriageable. It was a flagrant case of double standards between the sexes. Not surprisingly, respectable middle and upper working class radicals were now ripe for republicanism. A pamphlet *What Does She Do With It?*, meaning what does the Queen do with the money of the civil list, had a wide circulation.

The organised republican movement of the early 1870s arose, however, not only from anything that was happening in and around the monarchy but also from events abroad. The collapse of the Second Empire, the proclamation of a French republic and the Paris Commune were traumatic events close at hand. For Conservatives they were a wake-up call, which confirmed their fears about the advance of democracy. Among more ideologically orientated radicals, the arrival of a republic across the Channel indicated that the next logical step forward for those of progressive persuasions, after the extension of the franchise that had just taken place, should be the setting up of a republic in Britain. Early socialists, followers of Marx, as well as intellectuals and trade unionists who had taken part in the movement for franchise reform, now turned to republicanism as the next step in their crusade for equality and democracy. This type of ideological republicanism was independent of any dissatisfaction with the Queen and other members of the royal family, though it was clearly helped by such dissatisfaction.

Short-lived and relatively marginal as the republican movement turned out to be, even at this peak of its importance, it worried politicians, courtiers and some members of the royal family. Vicky, the Queen's eldest child, wrote a letter to her mother, signed by all members of the family, urging her to avert a real danger to the monarchy by ending her seclusion. 'Beloved Mama, We have each of us individually wished to say this to you ... but we refrained from fear of offending ... Had not the conviction come upon us all (moving as we do in different circles), with an alarming force, that some danger is in the air, that something must be done ... to avert a frightful calamity.'[3] The letter was probably never delivered. Gladstone devoted an inordinate amount of effort to get the Queen to agree to sending the Prince of Wales to Dublin, where he was to replace the Viceroy, hitherto the ceremonial head of the British administration. He thought it would help to improve the mood in Ireland while at the same time providing official employment for Bertie, thereby distracting him from his frivolous social life. With the overbearing zeal characteristic of him, Gladstone kept pushing this proposal in spite of the Queen's adamant refusal to entertain it. In August 1871, when she had again refused to prorogue Parliament in person, he wrote to Ponsonby, the Queen's Private Secretary: 'Upon the whole, I think it has been the most sickening experience which I have had during near forty years of public life. *Worse* things may easily be imagined; but smaller and meaner causes for the decay of Thrones cannot be conceived. It is like the worm which bores the bark of a noble tree and so breaks the channel of its life.'[4] Gladstone's relations with the Queen never recovered from this episode.

Not long afterwards Gladstone found it convenient to make use of the royal prerogative in pursuit of what was one of the main aims of his government, the establishment of meritocratic procedures instead of patronage in the recruitment of public servants. The purchase of commissions in the army was one of the ways in which aristocracy and birth remained crucial to entrance to the officer corps. It was a widely-held view that the purchase of commissions created a close relationship between military and political elites, for many army officers were younger sons of the landed gentry. After a spell in the army they sold their commissions on, and often got themselves elected to the House of Commons. This close relationship was responsible, so it was commonly believed, for the fact that Britain did not have the kind of politico–military tensions that afflicted so many other countries. It was a problem in France, famously exemplified by Napoleon I, in Prussia and even in the United States. Against this, a *coup d'état* by the military was unthinkable in Britain.

The abolition of purchase thus encountered formidable opposition in both Houses of Parliament. The ex-army officers who populated the Commons backbenches in considerable numbers, particularly on the Tory side, staged a determined rearguard action. They were collectively known as 'the Colonels' and adopted tactics of filibustering to frustrate the government bill. It was an early example of the obstruction later practised with such devastating effect by the Irish Home Rulers. Opposition in the Lords threatened to derail a measure which the government considered vital. A group of progressive army officers, among whom Wolseley was to become the most prominent, backed by Cardwell, the Secretary of State for War, was the driving force behind the change, in the teeth of fierce resistance from the Commander-in-Chief, the Queen's cousin the Duke of Cambridge, and an older generation of officers. Gladstone and Cardwell decided to circumvent the opposition by asking the Queen to use the royal prerogative by revoking the eighteenth-century Royal Warrant on which the purchase system was based. The Queen, amply briefed by her cousin, was doubtful if the abolition of the long-established practice of purchasing commissions would be an improvement, but she could not resist the demonstration that the royal prerogative was still a potent factor. For Gladstone and the Liberals such a use of the royal prerogative went against their principles and there was no shortage of those willing to point this out. For those who felt secure in the knowledge that the monarchy was now constitutional it caused some discomfort. Around this time Sir Charles Dilke made the speech at Newcastle, which can be seen as a high point of republicanism. A prominent young politician with a future had openly associated himself with the movement. The Queen was irate: 'Gross mis-statements and fabrications, injurious to the credit of the Queen, and injurious to the Monarchy, remain unnoticed and uncontradicted ... She does not for a moment doubt the sentiments of the Cabinet on the subject, and *only wishes that they should be expressed ...*' In other words she demanded strong countervailing action by her Prime Minister.

Shortly it came to be seen that the popular roots of republicanism were in fact shallow. The Prince of Wales fell seriously ill of typhoid. The Queen hastened to his bedside at Sandringham. Alfred Austin, soon to become Poet Laureate, marked the occasion in rhyme:

> Flashed from his bed, the electric tidings came
> He is not better, he is much the same.

The crisis came on 14 December 1871, the tenth anniversary of Albert's death, a terrible moment for Victoria. It was the moment when Bertie awoke from his fever and recognised his mother. At the end of February the following year a Thanksgiving Service for the Prince's recovery was held at St Paul's. Bertie's lifestyle might have offended many honest burghers, the Queen's neglect of her public duties and her demands for money might have aroused much discontent, but her drive in an open landau with her son to the cathedral could still bring out the crowds and arouse their enthusiasm. They went delirious when Victoria raised her son's arm, still weak from his illness, and kissed his hand. Republicanism meant little at such moments and remained the preserve of intellectuals and earnest artisans.

It was not quite the end of criticism of the monarchy in general or the Queen's performance in particular in the nearly thirty years that remained of her reign. In the collective memory of the later Victorian age the celebratory moments, especially the two jubilees of 1887 and

1897, have come to predominate. In general the burgeoning of imperialist sentiment went hand in hand with monarchism, but occasionally the old scepticism of religious and political dissent came to the surface again. When Disraeli and the Tories returned to office in 1874, having made the preservation of Queen, state, church and empire a central feature of their appeal, there were those, on the other side of politics, who suspected a plot against the traditional liberties of England. The full extent of the Queen's partisanship was kept hidden, but Disraeli was seen as a populist politician bent on using monarchist sentiment to mesmerise the masses. The Liberal defeat of 1874 had made many of those who believed in progress through enlightenment insecure and less certain that the widening of political participation through extension of the franchise would realise their vision of the future.

When the Disraeli government in 1876 promoted the Bill to confer on the Queen the title of Empress of India fears and insecurities of this kind had something to focus on. In an article entitled 'English Imperialism', the *Spectator* declared in April 1876: 'It is not easy to realise that such a policy as that of the "Imperialists" ... should have ... any root ... in these islands ... Mr Disraeli conceived very early in his career the notion that such a policy – a policy which should magnify the Crown on the one hand, and the wishes of the masses on the other, and should make light of the constitutional limitations on either – was still possible in Europe, and might even have a chance in England ...'[5] It was in fact the Queen who was the prime mover in promoting the Royal Titles Bill of 1876 and for Disraeli it was by no means conveniently timed. It was not difficult, however, to find in Disraeli's novels passages suggesting that the country might be better off without a constitution that had reduced the monarch to the position of a Venetian doge. It was not only Disraeli's too vivid imagination as a romantic novelist that conjured up such visions. In Albert they had come closer to realisation than the orthodox view of constitutional monarchy would have it.

This had been revealed in a surprising way when the biography of her late husband commissioned by the Queen from Sir Theodore Martin began to be published in 1875. The Albert–Stockmar view of monarchy was rather different from what most people had imagined. Disraeli knew all about it: in the 1850s Albert had been 'establishing court influence on ruins of political party ... with perseverance equal to that of Geoge III, and talent infinitely greater. A few more years of it and we should have had, in practice, an absolute monarchy ...', but with Albert's premature death 'all that is changed, and we shall go back to the old thing – the Venetian constitution – a Doge'.[6] No wonder that Liberals began to feel queasy when Disraeli made the Queen an Empress in 1876. Even Salisbury, now Disraeli's Cabinet colleague as Secretary of State for India, was not happy about about introducing so flashy and unEnglish a title as Empress of India and saw little benefit in terms of cementing Indian loyalties to the British connection. He was inclined to feel that Disraeli was too prone to humour the Queen's idiosyncracies, but the Prime Minister told him: 'What may have been looked upon as an ebullition of individual vanity may bear the semblance of deep and organised policy.' The highlighting of its imperial dimension undoubtedly played a part in the renaissance of the monarchy as a popular institution in the last twenty-five years of the Queen's reign.

Among Victoria's motives in seeking an imperial title were the seismic shifts in the European dynastic scene that had taken place in the previous few years. The most important was the elevation of a united Germany into an empire in 1871. It came about as a result of the Franco-Prussian war, which started in July 1870. Within six weeks the French armies were surrounded at Sedan and Napoleon III was taken prisoner. The Second Empire collapsed. It was not the end of the story. French reistance continued in an early example of guerrilla warfare, and Paris was besieged by the German armies. When the German Empire was proclaimed, in the Hall of Mirrors in the Palace of Versailles on 18 January 1871, it symbolised the depth of France's humiliation. Meanwhile, for at least the fourth time in a century, the barricades went up in Paris and there was revolution, the Commune. Much blood was shed before the new republican French government managed to defeat the uprising.

These events, only just across the Channel, naturally made a deep impact on British opinion. At first there was indignation at French bellicosity, which seemed to confirm all the stereotypes of French vainglory that had so often dominated British views of their neighbour across the Channel. As Napoleonic France went down to swift and humiliating defeat, sympathy with French suffering and abhorrence of Prussian arrogance began to gain the upper hand. This emotional roller-coaster was reflected in Victoria's correspondence with her elder daughter, the Prussian Crown Princess. Vicky, for all her reservations about Bismarck, could not but glory in the Prussian triumph. In writing to her mother she expressed some sympathy for what had befallen the French Emperor, whom both she and her mother had in days gone by held in high regard, but 'such a downfall is a melancholy thing, but it is meant to teach deep lessons; may we all learn what frivolity, conceit and immorality lead to! The French people have trusted in their own excellence, have completely deceived themselves; where is their army, where are their statesmen? They despised and hated the Germans whom they considered it quite lawful to insult; how they have been punished!' For a time mother and daughter were at one in such priggish moralising about the French. 'Your 2 elder brothers unfortunately were carried away by that horrid Paris, beautiful though you may think it, & that frivolous & immoral court did frightful harm to English Society (that Papa knew & saw) & was very bad for Bertie and Affie. The fearful extravagance & luxury, the utter want of seriousness & principle in everything . . .', wrote the Queen to her daughter, who had written much the same to her mother.

But the two women were also united in sympathy on a personal level for poor Eugénie, and even for her husband, and the Queen expressed her sympathy very publicly for the exiled Emperor and his wife when they had fled to England. This did not go down well in Germany and was one of the many instances that made life difficult for Vicky as *die Engländerin*. Her husband had again played a distinguished role in the war and had made an important contribution to the difficult negotiations that led to the proclamation of his father as the German Emperor. Bismarck saw to it that he did not receive the credit for either achievement that he ought to have done. Frederick William, like most liberals, would have preferred it if the new German Empire had had a rather more unitary constitution than the convoluted system with which Bismarck endowed it. One of the chief results of these complex arrangements, which had first been adopted in the North German Confederation of 1867, was that the Reich Chancellor was the key figure at the centre of the web. Bismarck had every intention of holding on to this position himself as long as possible and only he could operate it effectively.

Neither mother nor daughter showed signs of being fully aware of

how great a change in the affairs of Europe and the world the foundation of the German Empire had brought about. Disraeli summed it up
when he spoke as Leader of the Opposition at the opening of the 1871
parliamentary session: 'This war represents the German revolution, a
greater political event than the revolution of last century. I don't say a
greater, or as great a social event … Not a single principle in the management of our foreign affairs, accepted by all statesmen for guidance
up to six months ago, any longer exists … The balance of power has
been entirely destroyed, and the country which suffers most, and feels
the effects of this great change most, is England.'

Bismarck soon resumed his place as the *bête noire* in the minds of
Vicky and her mother. The Crown Princess saw more clearly than her
mother the futility of the German Chancellor's next major domestic
project, the Kulturkampf, the fight against the Catholics and the
Vatican. Most German liberals, including even Vicky's husband, welcomed the Kulturkampf, which they saw as a struggle between progress
and enlightenment against Catholic obscurantism. They failed to see
that it was an attack on religious toleration and therefore an offence
against liberal principles. Vicky did realise this, but her mother's anti-
Catholic prejudices were so strong that it blinded her to this aspect.
Wires became crossed in these highest royal circles. Augusta, now the
German Empress, had enjoyed Victoria's favour for at least a quarter of
a century, and no *idée fixe* was more difficult to move from the Queen's
mind than the opinions she had conceived about persons near and dear
to her. But Augusta had decided Catholic sympathies and relations
between her and Bismarck were more poisonous than ever. Nobody fed
the Chancellor's paranoia, voracious at all times, more than Augusta.
Even though her marriage to William I had been a formality for at least
a generation, Bismarck could never feel easy about the influence she
might still exert upon her husband. Vicky came only second in the
gallery of royal women whom the Chancellor detested and feared. It was
a tragedy for Vicky that while she agreed so often with Augusta politically, even over the Kulturkampf, the older woman was so often the
mother-in-law from hell. Vicky found Berlin Court life hard to endure,
yet was drawn into the frantic socialising with which her mother-in-law
covered up her own alienated position. It was a family problem in which
she received little support from her mother.

Another family problem was looming on the horizon, the need to get Affie, the Queen's second son, married off. Marriage had not succeeded in reducing Bertie to a more sober lifestyle and Affie was at least as much of a problem. The Queen often expressed a low opinion of him: 'Yes, Affie is a great, great grief – and I may say a source of bitter anger for he is not led astray. His conduct is gratuitous', she wrote to Vicky in 1868. Bertie's failings were at least mitigated by his general good nature, Affie's were not. He had a foul temper and drank heavily. By 1872 Affie was intending to marry the Grand Duchess Marie Alexandrovna, only daughter of Tsar Alexander II and his Hessian wife Marie. There had been little connection between the British royal family and the Romanovs in Albert and Victoria's days. When contact was necessary, as in 1848, it was made through Leopold in Belgium. The worldwide rivalry between the British and Russian empires, highlighted by the Crimean War, had become deeply embedded in Victoria's view of how the world was structured.

The proposed Russian marriage filled her with alarm, not least because of the religious difference. She took it badly that both her daughters, Vicky in Berlin and Alice in Darmstadt, were in favour of the marriage. The link between Hesse and the Russian Court was a long-standing one, but Vicky had never liked the close connection between the Romanovs and the Hohenzollern. More recently a link between the Courts of St Petersburg and Windsor had in fact been established through the marriages of the Prince of Wales and of the Tsarevitch, later Alexander III, with the two sisters Alex and Dagmar, daughters of Christian IX of Denmark. This link had also imported into the highest royal circles strong feelings of resentment against Prussia, Germany and the Hohenzollers. Neither sister could ever forget or forgive the treatment their parents had received at the hands of the Prussians and Germans. Their father had lost Schleswig-Holstein in the war of 1864. Their mother, Queen Louise of Denmark, was a Princess of Hesse-Cassel, which had been wiped off the map after the war of 1866. Such was the revulsion of the Danish sisters that they avoided Berlin and their Hohenzollern relations if they possibly could.

The Crown Princess of Germany had, however, met the Russian girl, Affie's intended, and found her intelligent. She was also very rich, which would be an advantage to Affie when he became Duke of Coburg.

Victoria had never met her and was offended by the Tsarina's suggestion, supported by Alice from Darmstadt, that she should travel to the
Continent to make her acquaintance. 'I do *not* think, dear child,' she
wrote to Alice, 'that *you* should tell *me* who have been *20 years longer*
on the throne than the Emperor of Russia and am Doyenne of Sovereigns, and who am a *Reigning* Sovereign which the Empress is *not*,
what I ought to do.' No wonder Victoria felt that an imperial title might
be useful in keeping up with the Joneses, when there were so many
emperors, empresses and imperial highnesses around. Notwithstanding
their mother's reservations, both the Prince of Wales and Vicky, with
their spouses, attended their brother's wedding in January 1874 at the
Winter Palace in St Petersburg. Even by royal standards it was an exceptionally lavish affair, with the Russian grand duchesses outshining all
others with their jewels, but leaving something to be desired in personal
hygiene. Queen Victoria liked her new daughter-in-law when she came
to live in England, but the marriage was not a happy one. The Duchess
of Edinburgh, as Marie Alexandrovna now was, was relieved when her
husband resumed his naval duties and she was only too glad to decamp
to Coburg twenty years later, when Affie inherited the dukedom. It was
a marriage that showed once more that dynastic ties were no longer
capable of changing the underlying realities of international politics.

It was followed by the Balkan crisis of the mid-1870s, which brought
Britain and Russia to the brink of war. It was a crisis which involved
Queen Victoria more deeply in the management of foreign policy than
had been the case since Albert's death and made her more fiercely anti-
Russian than ever. The family tie to the Tsar, which had now been
established through Affie, proved fully as awkward as the Queen had
feared. At the height of the crisis, in July 1877, she wrote in her journal:
'Affie, I am grieved to say, has become most imprudent in his language
and I only hope he does not make mischief. It is very awkward with this
Russian relationship just now. This is what I always feared and dreaded.'
She also became hotly party-political, regarding Gladstone as virtually
insane and using her influence as much as she could to support Disraeli's policy of propping up the Turks against the Russians. It was
therefore not only that dynastic ties could no longer prevail against
national interest and nationalist sentiment. The Queen's strong Russo-
phobia showed that on this occasion at any rate she identified far more

with nationalist sentiment than with any dynastic loyalties. In the late nineteenth and early twentieth centuries her fellow sovereigns also became increasingly subject to the pull of nationalist rather than dynastic loyalties. Affie's Russian marriage proved to be only the beginning of closer links between the British royal family and the Romanovs. By the early twentieth centuries these links were no longer as much out of kilter with the relations between England and Russia as they had been for most of the nineteenth century.

There are not many examples in British politics of public opinion being as passionately divided over foreign policy as it was between the beginning of the Balkans crisis in the summer of 1876 and its resolution through the Congress of Berlin two years later. Gladstone's mobilisation of opinion in his crusade against the Turkish atrocities in Bulgaria at first attracted more attention and made it difficult for the Disraeli government to take a strong line against Russian expansionism in the Balkans and designs on Constantinople. In due course there was at least as strong a countervailing tide of patriotic Russophobe opinion, which, from a famous music-hall song, became known as jingoism. This was a sentiment fully shared by the Queen. She could not bear the thought of England being reduced to a 'subservient, second-rate, cotton-spinning power', and to avoid such a dire fate she intervened constantly on behalf of the hawks in Disraeli's divided Cabinet. She worked mainly through the Prime Minister, by no means the most hawkish amongst his colleagues but well able to make the most of the advantage derived from royal backing. It was particularly galling to the Queen that the foremost dove was none other than the Foreign Secretary, Lord Derby, the fifteenth Earl. To complicate matters further Derby was married to the stepmother of Lord Salisbury, the third major figure in the Cabinet, who was gradually shifting from the doves to the hawks. It was rumoured that Lady Derby was retailing the secrets of the Cabinet to Shuvalov, the Russian Ambassador in London, reputedly her lover. Such treason in her immediate backyard was more than the Queen could endure. For Disraeli, now Earl of Beaconsfield, it was very difficult to separate himself from Derby, in view of the great debt he owed to his father in sustaining his career. Moreover, Derby was still thought to carry electoral clout in Lancashire, which had been vital to the Tory victory in 1874.

At least the Queen was at one with her daughter in Berlin in blaming everything on the Russians. On the other hand, Vicky was during this crisis inclined to defend Bismark. She took at face value the German Chancellor's claim to be the disinterested peacemaker and, when the Congress of Berlin in 1878 finally resolved the crisis, the even-handed chairman. Her mother was rather more realistic. She saw that Bismarck was as usual playing his own game and by his neutrality giving the Tsar valuable cover in his war against the Turks. In spite of this the Russians were dissatisfied with the way the German Chancellor conducted the Congress of Berlin. He claimed to be acting as the honest broker between England and Russia, even though his Jewish banker Bleichröder had declared that there could be no such thing as an honest broker. The Russians thought Bismarck should have shown greater gratitude for the neutrality they had maintained when he was fighting Austria in 1866 and France in 1870. At Berlin the Russians were forced to disgorge some of their earlier gains in the war against Turkey, while Britain obtained Cyprus. Disraeli was able to return in triumph from Berlin in July 1878, claiming that he had obtained with peace with honour. It was a slightly more realistic claim than Neville Chamberlain's repetition of it sixty years later, when he returned from meeting Hitler in Munich. Even in 1878 the laurels quickly faded and less than two years later the Disraeli government was soundly beaten in a General Election.

For the Queen the Tory defeat was a terrible moment. She had vowed that she would never have Gladstone back, in whom she 'never COULD have the slightest particle of confidence', 'a most disagreeable person – half crazy, and so excited'.[7] Twist and turn as she might, she could not avoid it. She was a constitutional monarch, even if behind the scenes she did not behave like one. In her immediate family, with her daughter Vicky now her closest relationship, the political component had come to a somewhat paradoxical point. Vicky hated Bismarck, now more than ever, for the Chancellor had cut his links with liberalism and the National Liberal Party in the Reichstag. He had taken a strongly conservative turn, had given up free trade and introduced protective tariffs. He had introduced a draconian anti-socialist law, through which he sought to suppress the growing German Social Democratic Party. It proved to be as futile an undertaking as his attack on the Catholic Church in the Kulturkampf. The Queen continued to join her daughter in regarding the all-powerful Chancellor as the villain of the piece. But Bismarck hated Gladstone, perhaps not quite in the manner and for the reasons that the Queen did, but seriously enough. His great fear still was that on the death of William I, now in his mid-eighties, the Crown Prince and his wife would bring in a 'Gladstone Ministry'. When the Gladstones visited Germany, in the summer of 1881, Vicky went to have tea with them. 'Mrs Gladstone told me you had been to tea with her and Mr G. Was that necessary?', the Queen wrote to her daughter. Later, after one of Vicky's usual diatribes against the German Chancellor, the Queen wrote to her daughter: 'I quite agree in what you say about that dreadful man – it is deplorable. No wonder you dislike Conservatives; but you would not if you lived here. Here they are the only security.' Mother and daughter could not bring British and German politics to a common denominator.

For the Queen, the five years of Gladstone's premiership, from 1880 to 1885, were a sore trial. Even to Bertie, whom she regarded as so unfit to deal with serious political business, she confided: 'this dreadfully Radical Government, which contains thinly-veiled republicans – and the way in which they have truckled to the Home Rulers – as well as the utter disregard of all my opinions which after 45 years of experience ought to be considered, all make me very miserable, and disgust me with the hard, ungrateful task I have to go through'. The fact was that the government did contain Sir Charles Dilke, once a leading Republican, though initially he was, as Under Secretary for Foreign Affairs, not in the Cabinet, and therefore was unlikely to have to meet the Queen face to face. As Under Secretary he had to speak on foreign policy in the Commons, for the Foreign Secretary Granville was in the Lords. The Queen and Albert had once regarded Granville as their friend and as their shield against Palmerston. Now she thought he was 'as weak as water', 'absolutely passé and baissé'. Granville had long been a close political friend of Gladstone and the Queen was perfectly right in judging him well past his best.

The Queen was alarmed by the fact that the Gladstone government appeared to be defending Charles Bradlaugh, a Republican, whose case caused constant parliamentary turmoil in the early 1880s. Bradlaugh was not only a Republican, he was also an atheist and an early supporter of contraception. He was the author of a pamphlet *Impeachment of the*

House of Brunswick, which contained passages such as 'I loathe these small German breastbestarred wanderers ... In their own land they vegetate and wither scarcely noticed; here we pay them highly to marry and perpetuate a pauper prince race.' He was elected as Member for Northampton and refused to take the oath on the Bible when taking his seat. A maverick group on the Tory backbenches, soon jocularly known as the Fourth Party (Parnell's Irish Home Rulers being the third), made the most of this case to embarrass the government and the Prime Minister. The group was led by Lord Randolph Churchill. Lord Randolph thereby put himself forward as a future Tory leader, when the party leadership was in an uncertain state after the death of Disraeli in April 1881. Gladstone, as an apostle of religious toleration, felt compelled on principle to defend Bradlaugh's right to affirm rather than take an oath on the Bible. He was also aware that he could not rely on his backbenches to support the exclusion of Bradlaugh.

To the Queen this was yet another example of the utter unreliability of the Gladstone government, on moral, ethical, political and every other conceivable ground. She instructed Sir Henry Ponsonby, her Private Secretary, who had Liberal sympathies, to warn the Prime Minister that 'with reference to the case of Mr Bradlaugh, care will be taken to prevent its being supposed (erroneously of course) that the Government sympathise with the opinions Mr Bradlaugh is stated to hold.' The Bradlaugh case ran and ran, punctuated by repeated exclusions, re-elections by the voters of Northampton, and even confinement of the controversial Member to the Clock Tower of the Palace of Westminster. It played havoc with the cohesion of the Liberal majority and with the government's control of parliamentary proceedings.

The wedding of the last but one offspring of the Queen in April 1882 occurred while the Bradlaugh case was in full swing. Royal weddings and the attendant demands for a parliamentary grant were always liable to stimulate Republican feelings among those so inclined. It was Prince Leopold, the Queen's youngest son and a sufferer from haemophilia, who was getting married to Princess Helen of Waldeck-Pyrmont, an event tailor-made to lend substance to the complaints made by Bradlaugh in the *Impeachment of the House of Brunswick.* Waldeck was a very minor German principality. The Prince's physical handicap had enabled the Queen to keep him hanging around her Court, something that caused tension between mother and son. She had employed him during the Balkan crisis as a kind of subsidiary private secretary, charged with maintaining communication with the Prime Minister and other hawk-ish members of the Cabinet, bypassing the more liberal Sir Henry Ponsonby. Leopold was determined to get married and to get out from under his mother's skirts, even though his expectation of life could not be long. Victoria had no prejudice against marrying into minor royalty, 'great matches do not make for happiness', she wrote to Vicky. She hated all these marriages in her family anyhow, but if she had to have them she was determined to fashion them to her own requirements. In this case the chosen Princess proved well able to stand up to her formi-dable mother-in-law. When it came to the proposed annuity for the couple, the Queen's demand generated the inevitable anti-monarchist backlash. When the Annuity Bill was introduced, a petition from 14,000 working men was presented, protesting against 'excessive demands for the maintenance of the Royal Family'. Henry Labouchere, later the edi-tor of *Truth* and blackballed by the Queen from Liberal Cabinets, said in the debate that there were at least four members of the current Cab-inet, including Joseph Chamberlain and Sir Charles Dilke, whose declared principles should compel them to vote against the grant. In the event only Dilke abstained, to the fury of the Queen. Forty-two MPs voted with Labouchere. Leopold, on whom his mother conferred the title Duke of Albany, survived his marriage by scarcely two years. He died of a brain haemorrhage in Cannes in March 1884, the second of Victoria's nine children to predecease her. The first to die had been Alice, the Grand Duchess of Hesse-Darmstadt, Albert and Victoria's third child, who had succumbed to diphtheria in 1878. Her death, on the exact anniversary of Albert's, 14 December, had been a terrible blow for the Queen. During his brief marriage, Leopold had, in spite of his frail condition, managed to sire two children, the second of whom, born posthumously, eventually became Duke of Coburg.

Only the youngest of the Queen's children, Princess Beatrice, the baby, was now left unmarried. Her presence had become an absolute necessity for her mother, but even Victoria's powerful will and constant vigilance could not prevent her eventual escape. It began in Darmstadt in April 1884, at the wedding of Princess Victoria of Hesse, daughter of Alice. Ever since the death of her mother in 1878, the Queen had acted almost as an honorary mother to her orphaned grandchildren, especially the granddaughters. The eldest, Victoria, now married Prince Louis of Battenberg, an officer in the Royal Navy and the eldest of the four sons of that Prince Alexander of Hesse, who had contracted a morganatic marriage with the Polish Countess Julie von Haucke.

The wedding of Prince Louis of Battenberg and Princess Victoria of Hesse took place in dramatic circumstances. The father of the bride and widower of Alice, the Grand Duke Louis of Hesse-Darmstadt, had taken it upon himself, shortly before his daughter's wedding, to marry his mistress, a beautiful Russian called Alexandra Kolemine, who had been Countess Czapaska before her first marriage. Queen Victoria was aware of his involvement with the Russian before she arrived in Darmstadt for the Battenberg wedding, though she and Bertie are said to have had it in mind to marry Beatrice to the widowed Grand Duke. By all accounts she was infuriated beyond measure by the Grand Duke's conduct and put the fear of God up her extended family, including the Prussian Crown Prince and his wife, who were present in Darmstadt. None of them had summoned up the courage to tell the Queen about the Duke's marriage, and it had been left to Lady Ely to break the news. Jane Ely was a Lady-in-Waiting who had for years completely subordinated her personality to the Queen and had ministered to her every whim. Victoria succeeded in frightening her grand ducal son-in-law sufficiently to make him annul the marriage to his Russian mistress within weeks of entering it. By this time, however, Beatrice had escaped having to marry her widowed brother-in-law and instead decided to marry Henry of Battenberg, the third of the Battenberg brothers, known as Liko. For months thereafter the Queen communicated with her errant daughter only through notes, even though she was living side by side with her. Then she suddenly relented and agreed to the marriage, provided Liko and Beatrice would live in her Court.

Marrying into the Battenberg clan was becoming a major dynastic issue, pitting the British royal family against the Hohenzollerns and spilling over into politics and diplomacy. The second of the four brothers, Alexander, known as Sandro, had become Prince of Bulgaria, as part of the settlement agreed at the Congress of Berlin. The Russians had had to accept a diminished Bulgaria at Berlin, but the presence of Sandro as ruler in Sofia was thought to ensure their continuing influence there.

His aunt, the Tsarina Marie Alexandrovna, wife of Alexander II and a Princess of Hesse-Darmstadt before her marriage, was very fond of him. Unfortunately his cousin, about to become Tsar Alexander III, after the assassination of his father in 1881, looked down upon him as 'the German' and did not consider the Battenbergs of proper royal blood, because of the morganatic marriage of their father. This was a view fully shared by the Hohenzollern clan. Indeed, even in Hesse-Darmstadt it took seven years for Julie von Haucke to move from Countess to Princess.

This was not the view of Queen Victoria, who could make her own rules in such matters. She had found the father, the original Battenberg, very agreeable when he came to the christening of Alice's first baby in 1863, Princess Victoria of Hesse, who was now, in 1884, marrying his eldest son Louis. When the following year the Princess had her first baby, her grandmother sat with her through the long hours of labour, rubbing her hands. A girl was born, Alice, the mother of Philip, Duke of Edinburgh, husband of Elizabeth II. Queen Victoria had also taken a liking to Sandro, when he went round the European capitals after taking up his precarious position in Bulgaria. The Battenbergs were tall, handsome men who reminded her of Albert. A few years later, in 1886, she wrote of him to her daughter: 'I think he may stand next to beloved Papa, and he is a person in whose judgment I would have great confidence. I think him very fascinating, and (as in beloved Papa's case) so wonderfully handsome.' By that time Sandro had already been driven out of Bulgaria.

It was another proposed Battenberg marriage that caused serious political and diplomatic disturbance, the possible union between Sandro and Victoria, better known as Moretta, the second daughter of Vicky. When this union was first thought of is not clear, but in circles around Bismarck it was assumed that the Queen of England was the real originator. It was suspected that she aimed thereby to estrange Russia from Germany, when Bismarck had just succeeded, in 1881, in bringing her back into the so-called Three Emperors' League of Germany, Russia and Austria. It was one of Bismarck's diplomatic masterstrokes, for in 1879 he had concluded an alliance with Austria, and there was a natural antagonism between Russia and Austria in the Balkans. It was this kind of diplomatic balancing act that gave Bismarck the reputation of being able to keep five balls in the air at the same time. It is unlikely that Victoria was using her granddaughter's marriage prospects primarily for hidden political purposes, but she had no objection to the Battenbergs and was certainly interested in shoring up Sandro's difficult position in Bulgaria. The fact was that from 1883 Moretta was deeply in love with Sandro, and both her mother and grandmother were very concerned to ensure her happiness. It was also the case that by 1883 Sandro was no longer the Russian protégé, which he had been at the start of his career as Prince of Bulgaria. His cousin, Tsar Alexander III, disliked him more than ever and would have liked to have seen him replaced.

The proposed Sandro–Moretta match also had repercussions at the top of the German political hierarchy. It again saw the Chancellor and the Crown Princess locking horns. By the 1880s Vicky had reverted more than ever to being *die Engländerin.* In the correspondence with her mother, but even when talking to those around her, she used 'we', when referring to England and English interests. It was her reaction against the growing illiberalism and chauvinism of the social and political atmosphere in Germany. This was not just the doing of Bismarck, though his determination to maintain his grip on power contributed to it. His was a manipulative style of ruling, demonising all manner of groups, socialists, Poles, Jews, as enemies of the Reich, *Reichsfeinde,* and thus keeping the population permanently in alarm and willing to fall in with his authoritarian ways. Even without Bismarck, the liberal parties would have been greatly weakened by the economic slump of the 1870s, which shook faith in free markets. It was all deeply disappointing to the Crown Princess and her husband, who might have hoped that by now he would have occupied the throne and steered affairs in quite a different direction. Tact was not Vicky's strong point, while her husband sometimes impaled himself on trivialities; for instance, complaining that he did not have a special train at his disposal in the way Bismarck did. It was the result of years of being humiliated by his father and Bismarck. Vicky was intelligent enough to see that, when they came into their inheritance, they would not be wise immediately to get rid of the all-powerful Chancellor, who as the founder of the Reich was a hero to most Germans. Bismarck for his part tried to surround the couple in the Neue Palais with courtiers in whom he had confidence. They in their turn felt spied upon. From time to time there were efforts to reconcile the warring Crown Princess and Chancellor. In the spring of 1885 the old Emperor's health seemed to be failing, he suffered a series of minor strokes and his death appeared to be just round the corner. Bismarck's domestic political situation was at this point relatively strong. Reichstag elections in October 1884 had been fought by a reunited Liberal Party, but it did badly. Bismarck met the Crown Prince and there was said to be an agreement that, upon his accession, Frederick William would keep the Chancellor in office. Bismarck's account of this interview, like so much else in his memoirs, cannot be relied on. However desperately he was clinging to power, he always made it appear that he was not doing so.

Typical of the stand-off between the crown princely couple and the Chancellor were the events surrounding the death of Eduard Lasker, a leading liberal parliamentarian. Lasker, a Jew, had given Bismarck crucial assistance in completing the structure of the Reich as a single market in the 1870s, but had then become one of the Chancellor's most effective opponents in the Reichstag. When Lasker suddenly died on a visit to the United States in January 1884, the American Congress passed a message of condolence, which Bismarck refused to pass on to the Reichstag. Such was the paranoid hatred with which the Chancellor pursued those who had crossed him. Convoluted efforts were made to dissuade the Crown Prince from attending a memorial service for Lasker or sending a representative. It would have caused a breach with the Chancellor that would have been difficult to heal. The Crown Prince and his wife stayed away, but Vicky sent a message of congratulation to another leading liberal, Ludwig Bamberger, who had given the address commemorating his colleague. In Bamberger's own words, German politics were a veritable dog house.

10

Bertie and the Kaiser

The gathering of royalty in Darmstadt for the Battenberg wedding in 1884 was probably the beginning of friction in another relationship that was to run for the next quarter of a century and in doing so cause considerable complications on the European diplomatic scene. It was the relationship between Bertie, the Prince of Wales, then aged forty-two, and his nephew, Prince William of Prussia, the future Kaiser, then aged twenty-five. They were such contrasting personalities that it is hardly surprising that they found it difficult to get on. Bertie in early middle age was still without any purposeful employment and was kept well away from affairs of state by his mother. No doubt she was right in regarding him as indiscreet and lazy, but even she had to admit that he was amiable and loving. Without exaggeration one could call him a voluptuary, but, as he went his way in the stratosphere of cosmopolitan aristocratic society, he had acquired much worldly wisdom and a winning way with all manner of men and even more with women.

Prince William of Prussia was very different. His grandmother Queen Victoria was fond of him as a child, and he was the only one of his grandchildren that Albert ever saw. When he spent time as a small boy at Osborne, to get the benefit of the sea air, his grandmother detected occasional signs of wilfulness and arrogance with servants. The real problems started with his education. In 1866, when he was seven, his mother chose one Georg Hinzpeter, a stern Calvinist doctor of philosophy and classical philology, to be his tutor. She was repeating the mistakes her father had made in the education of her brother Bertie. She was a perfectionist and her boy's obvious imperfection, the withered arm, was an abiding grief to her. When he was only two, she wrote to her mother:

> He is a dear, promising child – lively and sweet-tempered and intelligent; it
> is a thousand pities he should be so afflicted ... it disfigures him so much,

gives him something awkward in all his movements which is sad for a prince; though you know I would rather he was straight in mind than in body but I cannot help thinking of dear Papa who was perfect in both ...[1]

It needed constant exorcising and Hinzpeter was the man to do it. Under him William had a hard time. There were agonising, almost sadistic ways of overcoming the lack of balance caused by the crippled arm, so that eventually the boy could ride a horse. More generally Hinzpeter imposed a spartan regime of constant demands, joyless abstinence from every possible gratification, be it play or food, no praise and ceaseless criticism. Vicky and Hinzpeter became in fact rivals, for the tutor thought he should have sole control of the boy without interference from the parents. Frederick William was a distant father, fond enough of his children, but not often there. Vicky watched over every detail of William's progress, but thought she had to put up with Hinzpeter for the sake of the boy, even though she knew the tutor detested her. All this did not diminish the strong bond of affection between the Crown Princess and her eldest son, which continued when William and his brother were sent to a Gymnasium in Kassel from 1874 to 1877, still accompanied by Hinzpeter.

The relationship between Vicky and William began to change when the Prince came of age in 1877. After a brief period with a Guards Regiment at Potsdam he went to university in Bonn, as his father and grandfather had done. There he spent most his time socialising with the Borussia Student Corps and in neighbouring officers' messes. In 1879, on the orders of his grandfather, the Kaiser, he joined the Guards Regiment at Potsdam. He was turning decisively against his parents, and especially against what his mother stood for, not only their liberalism but her Englishness. Her often tactless insistence on the superiority of everything English, when she was destined to be a future Empress of Germany, must have been highly provoking to her son. Typical of her attitude was a letter she wrote to her Italian-born friend Countess Marie von Dönhoff, after a trip to Italy in 1885:

> I cannot tell you how bitterly I feel the contrast when I come back to the heavy dull stiffness, to the cold ugliness of north Germany and the neighbourhood of Berlin! The moral atmosphere of the Court, the political and official world seems to suffocate me! The ideas, tastes and feelings and habits are so totally different from mine that I feel the gulf between me and them

widen and bitterest and hardest of all is that my son Wilhelm and his wife stand on the other side of this gulf!![2]

William became thoroughly imbued with Prussian military values, and happiest with his regiment and his fellow officers. He professed himself an acolyte of Bismarck, and his grandfather, the soldierly Kaiser, was the member of his immediate family to whom he stood closest.

He married, in 1881, Princess Augusta of Schleswig-Holstein-Augustenburg, known as Dona, the daughter of Fritz Holstein, the Augustenburger whom Bismarck had driven out of the duchies, and the granddaughter of Queen Victoria's half-sister Feodora. Strangely enough, the Hohenzollern clan accepted this union of the future heir to the throne with such a minor Princess, the daughter of a dispossessed former enemy. Vicky had initially approved the match, mainly to get William away from his cousin Ella, the second daughter of Alice of Hesse-Darmstadt. Vicky feared the haemophilia known to be around in the Hesse family, but she soon came to regret Dona as a daughter-in-law. Queen Victoria never had much time for Dona and called her 'a submissive blind wife'. She was indeed extremely limited in her views and prudish in her prejudices, motivated by a narrow-minded religiosity. She surrounded herself with ladies-in-waiting of a similar outlook, who became known as the Hallelujah Aunts. She also bolstered her husband's anti-English feelings. England to her meant immorality, hypocrisy and liberalism. Her main advantage to William was that she in no way threatened him and was the opposite of his dominant, intelligent mother. As a personality the future Kaiser was volatile, unstable and mixed up. He covered his many inner uncertainties with a brash, boastful outward demeanour, which he thought fitting for a future ruler of Germany, but which often made him look ridiculous. He was constantly and restlessly running away from himself. Not surprisingly he often stretched the tolerance of his normally benevolent uncle, the Prince of Wales, beyond its limits, while the nephew made his prudish disapproval of Bertie's life style abundantly clear.

When, as a principal figure on the world stage, William's rash remarks brought him into trouble, he became quickly depressed and thought himself deeply misunderstood. 'Those who oppose me ... I will smash', he said in a speech soon after he became Kaiser and it was characteristic of his rhetoric. He made free with Latin tags like *hoc volo, sic*

jubeo (my wish is my command) or *suprema lex regis voluntas* (the king's
will is the ultimate law), which he inscribed in the Golden Book of the
city of Munich on an official visit in 1891. Uncertainty about where his
national roots lay was one of his many crises of identity, for which his
mother no doubt carried some responsibility. Often he made remarks
that the English blood in his veins was a kind of poison, but at the same
time he was inordinately proud of his English heritage and liked nothing better than to take his ease as a country gentleman in the mansions
of the English aristocracy. Even in that pose he could easily invite
ridicule. His mother, writing in the early 1890s, when her son went every
year to the Cowes Regatta and enjoyed himself, summed up his attitude
to England very aptly:

> The England of wealth, of water sports, of an impressive navy, of the court
> and of the present ministry [Lord Salisbury's Tory government] please him
> greatly, but the true, the inner, the serious England, its significance, its strug-
> gles, its aims he knows not, just as little as he knows his own Germany and
> the better side of the German people.

His uncle lived his life precisely on that side of English life that
appealed so much to the Kaiser, but he moved in it with an easy bonhomie and aplomb quite beyond his nephew. Bertie and Willy also
shared a love of the trappings of monarchy, of uniforms and ceremonial, and both were sticklers for etiquette, but the Kaiser looked down
on the company his uncle kept. He affected to despise the circle of *nou-
veau riche* businessmen, plutocrats and financiers around Bertie, as
Prince of Wales and as King, particularly if they were Jewish. The Kaiser
was never backward in expressing the anti-Semitism deeply rooted in
the Prussian Junker aristocracy. Nevertheless, for at least a century not
a few Junkers had married Jewish heiresses to replenish their coffers,
and in due course the Kaiser acquired his own circle of Court Jews,
Kaiserjuden. Bertie was mentally lazy and might appear intellectually
inferior to his quick-witted nephew. William's intelligence was, however, not anchored in any consistency of outlook or purpose. People
called him 'William the Sudden'. His bombastic and ill-judged pronouncements would have been taken as a joke had they not come from
someone so powerful.

After the Darmstadt wedding in April 1884 Bertie escorted Sandro to

Berlin and apparently helped his sister to persuade her husband, the Crown Prince, into accepting the Prince of Bulgaria as a potential son-in-law, though for the moment he could not go against his father, the Emperor, who had prohibited the match. Initially Frederick William had shared the Hohenzollern disdain for the Battenbergs, for once disagreeing with his wife. When it was seen that the Crown Prince had again come round to the views of his wife in this matter, it was grist to the mill for all those in Berlin who held the couple in contempt. Vicky and her husband were once more humiliated, when it was Prince William, and not the Crown Prince, who, in May 1884, was sent to represent William I at the coming-of-age ceremonies of the Russian Tsarevitch, the future Nicholas II. Prince William fully shared the Russian orientation of Bismarck and his grandfather and was therefore a better representative than the Crown Prince and his wife, with their English orientation, particularly when England had a Gladstone government. In St Petersburg Prince William was able to reassure Tsar Alexander III that there would be no marriage tie between the Hohenzollerns and the Prince of Bulgaria. It was the start of a correspondence between Prince William and the Tsar, in which the Prince traduced the pro-English views of his parents and blamed them all on his mother. For a time Alexander was pleased with Prince William, but the time came when he saw through the duplicity and intrigue of the young man.

Queen Victoria was incensed at her grandson's attitude to the Battenbergs, to the Moretta–Sandro match and then to the marriage of his aunt Princess Beatrice to Liko, Henry of Battenberg, which took place in July 1885. To Vicky she wrote that Willy needed a good 'skelping'; as for Dona, she was 'a poor little insignificant p[rin]cess raised entirely by your kindness'. 'If the Queen of England thinks a person good enough for her daughter, what have other people got to say?' The Queen refused to receive her grandson at Windsor that year and Bertie had the unwelcome task of telling his nephew, who had somewhat reluctantly come to see him in Budapest in the autumn, that he would have to cancel his visit to Sandringham scheduled for the following month. He could not very well go there when he was not welcome to his grandmother at Windsor. William was much offended, but it gave him a weapon against his mother when she blamed him for not being well disposed towards his grandmother, whom he now called an old hag.

The Sandro–Moretta affair continued to cause trouble, even after Sandro had been overthrown at the end of 1886. Soon he was succeeded by another Coburg, Ferdinand of Saxe-Coburg-Kohary. He and his descendants managed to hang on in Bulgaria until the end of the Second World War, in spite of the enormous vicissitudes afflicting that country. As for Sandro, he no longer mattered much at the diplomatic level, but the possibility of a Hohenzollern-Battenberg match still soured dynastic relations and kept Prince William and his Uncle Bertie in a state of imperfect sympathy. Vicky could not let the matter drop and was still reluctant to do so when it became clear that Sandro had lost interest in her daughter. One of Bismarck's many nightmares was that Sandro, after his return to Germany, might replace him as Chancellor, when Frederick William and Vicky became Emperor and Empress. In fact Sandro fell in love with an opera singer whom he secretly married in 1889. After the failure of other, grander suitors to come up to scratch, Moretta, in 1890, married Prince Adolf of Schaumburg-Lippe, one of the smallest still surviving German principalities.

At the time of the Darmstadt wedding in April 1884 Queen Victoria had not only just lost her youngest son, Leopold, she had also lost John Brown, almost exactly a year earlier to the day. She was with difficulty dissuaded from publishing a memoir of Brown, which she had started to write. Randall Davidson, the Dean of Windsor, shouldered most of the hard task of dissuading her. He later wrote of this incident:

> There is a good deal more difficulty in dealing with a spoilt child of sixty or seventy than with a spoilt child of six or seven ... the vagaries or follies on the part of people who had the extreme disadvantage of being free all their life from the wholesome influence of their equals.[3]

At any rate politics gave the Queen plenty to think about, for after four years Gladstone was still Prime Minister. When he returned to power in 1880, aged seventy, he had said it was on a short lease. He kept the threat of his retirement hanging over the political scene for year after year, and a highly effective threat it proved to be in keeping his fractious Cabinet in order. Even at the beginning of this, his second premiership, the Queen thought he looked too ill, old and haggard to carry on for long, and she thought so at frequent intervals during the next few years. The wish was father to the thought. Gladstone found the Queen a sore trial, 'enough to kill any man', but he was far too loyal to give any public hint that she was a political partisan.

In fact the Queen was able to enhance her reputation as a scrupulously constitutional monarch over what proved to be the most important piece of domestic legislation of the second Gladstone Government, the third Reform Act. This gave the vote to men in the county constituencies, mostly the rural labourers, who had not yet been given it in 1867. It therefore substantially established universal male suffrage, although the conditions for getting on to the electoral register remained so complex that it still fell well short of 'one man, one vote'. The Tories naturally saw this Bill as a serious threat to their position, because the English counties were traditionally regarded as their strongholds. It gave rise to a bitter political battle, involving a clash between the Commons and the Lords. The Tories hoped to use their majority in the Upper House to extract concessions from the government. In this situation the Queen played a mediating role, which helped to bring the parties together. It won her many plaudits and confirmed the widespread impression that she was a strictly constitutional monarch. The new electoral system was settled by agreement at an inter-party conference in Downing Street. The present-day electoral system, of roughly equal electoral districts fought on a 'first past the post' basis, has it origins in this agreement of 1884.

Shortly afterwards, in February 1885, the Queen made clear where her real feelings lay. In January 1884 the Gladstone government sent General Gordon to evacuate British troops from the Sudan in face of the revolt of the Mahdi. 'Chinese' Gordon, so known because of his service in the Far East, was something of a religious fanatic, strongly evangelical, the last man to carry out an evacuation. Gladstone knew this, but such was his distaste for imperial adventures that he could not bring himself to face up to the situation. His government had conquered Egypt in 1882, but the Prime Minister, although pleased with the victory of Tel-el-Khebir, was unwilling to draw the logical consequences from this major extension of British imperial commitments. Thus the rescue mission for Gordon was not organised in time and the general was murdered by the Mahdi's troops in Khartoum on 27 January 1885. It was an iconic moment for Victorian imperialism. The picture of Gordon, standing at the top of the staircase in the Governor's Palace in Khartoum, defying the Mahdi's troops who had penetrated at the bottom, became deeply engraved in the national consciousness. The Queen was outraged. She suddenly appeared at the cottage of the Ponsonbys at Osborne announcing in a choked voice: 'Gordon is dead'. She telegraphed to Gladstone and other senior members of the government: 'These news from Khartoum are frightful, and to think that all this might have been prevented and many precious lives saved by earlier action is too fearful.' When a stationmaster handed this implied rebuke, sent *en clair*, to the Prime Minister on his way back to London, Gladstone was furious and contemplated resignation. He remained impervious to the public storm that met him and even paid a visit to the theatre when he was back in Downing Street. He was by this time seventy-five years old, cocooned by his family and entourage, but still lionised by a large part of the public.

Victoria did not have to suffer him much longer. In June his government was defeated on a snap division. The divided Liberal Cabinet was quick to resign, hoping that a general election fought on the new constituencies would bring them back reinvigorated. It was now again the Queen whose choice was decisive in bringing Lord Salisbury to the premiership, which he was to hold for all but three years of the remainder of her reign. In the previous few years the Tory leadership had been divided between Sir Stafford Northcote in the Commons and Lord Salisbury in the Lords. Sir Stafford was seen very much as the Queen's man, a sensible, broad-bottomed, middle-of-the-road politician, and she certainly had given him to understand that she would call on him should the opportunity arise. But, in the great battles with Lord Randolph Churchill and over the Reform Bill, Northcote had lost ground compared with the much sharper Salisbury. The owner of Hatfield and descendant of Elizabeth I's great minister was not one to be unduly impressed by royalty, especially if it in fact consisted largely of minor German princelings. Fortunately Victoria knew nothing of his past mocking comments. When Affie was being considered for the throne of Greece, Salisbury said it looked as if 'a fearful famine of royalties had just set in', whereas fifty years earlier 'the great German supply was then almost untapped, and was believed to be ample for all contingencies'.[4] When in 1885 Victoria saw that Salisbury was the more likely to preserve her from Gladstone, she did not hesitate to turn to him. Northcote was left standing.

This first Salisbury government did not in fact last long. The general election of November produced a Liberal majority, but left Parnell's Irish Home Rulers holding the balance. This was one factor that convinced Gladstone that it was his duty to grant Ireland Home Rule, meaning an autonomous status within the United Kingdom. The Liberal leader had long felt that the state of Ireland was a moral blot on the British escutcheon and, since he had disestablished the Anglican Church of Ireland in 1869, he had already made a number of further attempts to deal with Irish grievances. Home Rule proved to be a bridge too far. The Queen did her best to prevent Gladstone from returning to office after the stalemate of the 1885 elections, but she did not succeed. The third Gladstone government brought in a Home Rule Bill, which failed to pass the Commons but split the Liberal Party. Not only its right wing, led by Whigs like Hartington, later the eighth Duke of Devonshire, refused to accept Home Rule, but more surprisingly a part of the Radical left, led by the Birmingham populist Joseph Chamberlain, also refused to follow Gladstone. Lord Randolph Churchill, still the best public speaker in the Tory Party, coined two memorable phrases on this occasion. He called Gladstone 'an old man in a hurry' and told his party 'to play the Orange card'. In subsequent years most Liberal and Radical Unionists failed to return to the Liberal fold and as a result another twenty years were to elapse before the Liberals won a majority again.

During the six months that Gladstone was in office and Salisbury in opposition she maintained communication with the latter, something that made even her Private Secretary, Sir Henry Ponsonby, distinctly uneasy. As a conveyor of verbal messages she also used Lord Rowton, Montagu Corry before his elevation to the peerage and Disraeli's faithful amanuensis for many years. These communications were very useful to Salisbury at a time of bitter and crucial party warfare. Like many of her subjects, the Queen thought the establishment on Britain's doorstep of an autonomous Ireland that was bound to be hostile would spell the end of the British Empire. None of her partisanship seriously dented the Queen's image as the personification of British power and imperial splendour, to which all her subjects regardless of party were bound to pay homage, a few recalcitrant republicans and the ever troublesome Irish excepted.

The mid 1880s were a time of severe social tension, worse than they had ever been since the early years of the Queen's reign. The word 'unemployment' was entering the language, there were riots in London in February 1886 and more in November 1887. The political classes, in their preoccupation with Home Rule, foreign and imperial policy, were paying only intermittent attention to the grievances affecting the deprived part of the population and they had few solutions to these problems. Even the Queen caught a whiff of these discontents when she drove to the East End a month before her Golden Jubilee. She heard something which she described to Salisbury as 'a horrid noise ... (quite new to the Queen's ears) "booing" she believes it is called'. Salisbury reassured her: 'London contains a much larger number of the worst kind of rough than any other great town in the island; for all that is worthless, worn out, or penniless drifts to London.' He blamed it on the socialists and the Irish, 'very resentful men who would stick at nothing to show their fury'.[5]

None of this prevented the Golden Jubilee of 1887 from turning into a massive celebration of a revitalised imperial monarchy, with a little old lady of nearly seventy at the centre of it all. Not only a large array of kings, queens and princes from all over the Empire had come to London, but most of European royalty, many of whom were the Queen's relations. Victoria had not intended to invite her grandson Prince William and his wife Dona, for Germany was in any case to be represented by the Crown Prince and Vicky and she was hard pressed to accommodate all the visiting royalties. William and Dona's behaviour in the Battenberg affair had done nothing to raise them in the Queen's eyes. Victoria wrote to her daughter: 'You know *how* ill he behaved, how rude, to me, to Liko ... & how shamefully he calumniated dear, excellent, noble Sandro & how shamefully he behaves to you both ... *Bertie wants* me to invite William & Dona, but ... I fear he may show his dislike and be disagreeable.'[6] Nevertheless, Vicky pleaded with her mother that she should invite William, though both mother and daughter saw only too clearly how pernicious a frame of mind he was in and how dangerous the company he kept was. Vicky told her mother that Bismarck was a 'very dangerous' role model for her son: 'a great man, but his *system* is a *pernicious* one ... his *blind* followers & admirers & the many who wish to rise by a servile and abject pandering to his every wish & whim are a *bad* lot ... These are all William's friends now ...'[7]

Vicky was right about Bismarck, but William's friends included at least two prominent figures of whom the Chancellor did not approve. One was Waldersee, at this point Moltke's deputy as Chief of Staff and shortly to succeed him; the other was Adolf Stoecker, the Court Preacher. Waldersee was an advocate of preventive war against Russia, when the Chancellor was doing all he could to remain on good terms with St Petersburg. Bismarck also rightly suspected that Waldersee had the ambition to succeed him as Chancellor. William and Dona met Stoecker at Waldersee's house. The Court Preacher advocated a Christian-Social policy, a nebulous mixture of Christianity, social compassion and anti-Semitism, which he regarded as a more effective way of weaning the working classes away from socialism than Bismarck's policy of welfare measures, such as the introduction of accident and health insurance for workers and eventually of old age pensions. Stoecker, on the other hand, was a populist orator, whose principal way of stirring up the masses was to foment anti-Semitism. Bismarck was not above using Stoecker, but did not wish to be publicly associated with him. He warned Prince William against keeping such company. His early accession to the throne was becoming a possibility, for fate was about to play a terrible trick on Vicky and her husband.

Since the beginning of the year Frederick William had suffered from hoarseness. His German doctors discovered a swelling on his vocal cord. He was subjected to agonising treatment and a cancerous growth was diagnosed. The Crown Prince was confronted with the option of removing his larynx, which would certainly deprive him of speech and was quite likely to kill him. A Scottish doctor, Morell Mackenzie, a world authority on diseases of the throat, was called in. He was the kind of swell doctor who made his reputation by treating prominent patients, but was also said to treat poor patients free of charge. He managed to remove some of the tumour for an autopsy, which led to a mistaken diagnosis that it was benign. The rivalry between the German doctors and Morell Mackenzie forms an unpleasant backcloth to the case. The German doctors preferred to leave the Crown Prince to die in the hands of Mackenzie, while the Scot thought them to be incompetent and not even the best Germany had to offer. The medical rivalries were again used to discredit Vicky. There were scurrilous rumours that she had prevented the removal of the larynx, so that her husband would die and she could marry her Chamberlain, Götz von Seckendorff, who was said to be her lover. Among those who put such rumours into circulation was Friedrich von Holstein, the *éminence grise* of the German Foreign Office, who is credited with having become, after the fall of Bismarck in 1890, the virtual maker of German foreign policy. At this stage Holstein was still hand in glove with the Chancellor and particularly his son Herbert, who was the head of the German Foreign Office, though Holstein was becoming increasingly critical of both of them. Such rumours about the Crown Princess could scarcely have surfaced without the connivance of Bismarck. Seckendorff was certainly a confidant of Vicky's and Bismarck was keen to remove him from the Court of the Crown Prince.

The Crown Prince and Princess were due to attend the Golden Jubilee celebrations just after another autopsy appeared to have shown that the growth was not cancerous. The pathologist making the analysis was Rudolf Virchow, a world famous medical man but also a prominent politician. Since the 1860s he had been one of the most persistent and courageous liberal opponents of Bismarck. His hopes must have centred on the survival and succession of the Crown Prince, though his autopsy was no doubt based on strictly scientific criteria. His father's illness gave Prince William the excuse to ask his grandfather, the Kaiser, to send him and Dona as the official representatives to the Golden Jubilee. William I had forgotten that he had already agreed to send Frederick William and Vicky and in the end both couples went. Prince William brought four gentlemen-in-waiting, when Queen Victoria had tried to limit him to two, and was dissatisfied with the treatment he and his wife received; for instance, that Dona was placed behind the black Queen of Hawaii. It was a hard task for the Queen of England to be the matriarch of such a fractious clan. The political and international ramifications of these family relationships made it even harder.

After the Jubilee celebrations Frederick William and Vicky visited Victoria at Balmoral. The Crown Prince appeared to be better and his mother-in-law, anxious to look on the bright side, thought he spoke in his normal voice. Morell Mackenzie was knighted. The German couple had brought with them boxes of private papers, which they asked the Queen to take into her safe keeping. Beset as they were by the spies of Bismarck and the hostility of their eldest son in Berlin, they felt insecure and had perhaps a premonition of the tragedy that was soon to befall

14. Queen Victoria and Princess Alice with a bust of Prince Albert, 1862. (*Royal Archives*)

15. Victoria, Princess Royal, and Frederick William of Prussia, 1858, four days after their wedding. (*Royal Archives*)

16. Victoria, Princess Royal, with her son William, 1863. (*Royal Archives*)

17. Napoleon III.

18. Group photograph at Coburg, 1894. Seated in front, left to right, the Kaiser, Queen Victoria, the Dowager Empress Frederick. Standing behind the Kaiser is the Tsarevich, soon to be Nicholas II, with his fiancée Alicky. Behind the Tsarevich is the Prince of Wales. (*Royal Archives*)

19. Queen Victoria, with the future Edward VII, George V and Edward VIII. (*Royal Archives*)

20. Tsar Nicholas II with Kaiser William II at Swinemünde, 1907.

21. Queen Victoria's funeral procession, Windsor, 1901. (*Royal Archives*)

them. It was not the last of such secretive transfer of papers from Berlin to Windsor. Frederick William and Vicky then went to the Italian Tyrol and the Riviera to help his recuperation. A further examination by Mackenzie revealed that the Crown Prince was definitely suffering from cancer. Vicky resisted the pressure to return to Berlin, where her father-in-law was now definitely failing. He died on 9 March 1888, less than a fortnight before his ninety-first birthday, and his son, himself a dying man, ascended the throne as Frederick III. The Pandora's box of German politics was wide open.

Frederick III's reign lasted exactly fourteen weeks, until 15 June 1888, and was marked by manoeuvres, intrigues and vicious family feuding. The hope that this reign would usher in a more liberal and tolerant age had already worn thin in earlier years. Even if Frederick III had come to the throne in full vigour and with many years in front of him, it would have been difficult to change the course Germany was embarked upon. This was shaped internally by the rapid transformation of German society from a mainly rural to a predominantly industrial and urban one; and externally by growing national and imperial rivalries, many of them aggravated by Germany flexing her newly-acquired power. Bismarck was a principal maker of this constellation and was still up to a point able to control its external aspects. In domestic politics he had long ceased to be aligned with any forward-moving tendencies and had been reduced to pursuing the sole objective of clinging to power. His social welfare policy had been the one creative initiative of his later years. It failed to take the wind out of the sails of the socialists, as he hoped, but it was soon imitated in many countries, not least in Britain by Lloyd George, Winston Churchill, William Beveridge and others. The nightmare that had so long plagued Bismarck, that Frederick William, driven by Vicky, would come to the throne and replace him with a 'Gladstone Ministry' had vanished, but he was now threatened by another danger. The brash and volatile young Crown Prince, influenced by his ultra-conservative friends, might well dispense with his services in short order after coming to the throne. Bismarck was still a hero to the German masses, but there were many in the political establishment who were longing for an end of his oppressive reign. The Chancellor, who as a ruthless and cynical operator was still second to none, tailored his actions during the brief interlude of Frederick III to survival under

William II. The mortally ill Emperor could only communicate by writing his replies on a pad of paper. His wife tried to keep his spirits up against the odds, but she was no match for the Chancellor.

It was unfortunate that Vicky still persisted in trying to promote the Sandro–Moretta match, when even her mother knew that it was pointless. It seems that neither Vicky nor Moretta were aware that Sandro's interest now lay elsewhere. Bismarck continued to oppose the match tooth and nail, on the by now spurious grounds that it would spoil Germany's relations with Russia, and threatened resignation. There was an improbable rumour around that his son Herbert meant to marry Moretta. The affair produced a rare row between the Emperor and his wife, which forced the frail Frederick to take to his bed for two days. In fact the Russians had lost interest in Sandro, though the Tsar still disliked him personally. Ferdinand of Saxe-Coburg-Kohary had already been installed in Sofia for a year. Bismarck's probable purpose in continuing to oppose the Battenberg match was to curry favour with the Crown Prince when his relations with him were somewhat clouded after the Stoecker affair. Prince William, as he then was, had also prepared an accession proclamation a year before it was needed, such was his eagerness to elbow his parents aside as rapidly as possible. Bismarck advised him to burn it, advice that was bruising to the inflated ego of the arrogant young Prince. William was still fiercely opposed to the Sandro –Moretta match, because of Sandro's tainted blood. He wrote to his bosom friend Philipp Eulenburg: 'The worst thing is the feeling of deep shame for the sunken prestige of my house, which always stood so gleaming and unassailable. But yet more intolerable is that our family escutcheon should be bespotted and the Reich brought to the brink of ruin by the English Princess who is my mother!' Bismarck told Vicky that personally he did not care whether Sandro and Moretta married or not, but in public he kept up his opposition. He used the affair in his press campaign against Vicky, which never stopped. He kept in the background the threat of establishing a regency for the sick Kaiser.

Victoria and Bertie were appalled by what was going on in Berlin and by what was happening to Vicky. The Prince of Wales went to Berlin for the funeral of the old Emperor on 16 March, which Frederick III was too ill to attend and could only watch from a window. Bertie went again to Berlin on 24 May, for the wedding of Prince Henry of Prussia, Vicky's

second son, to Princess Irene of Hesse, his niece by his deceased sister
Alice, which the Emperor attended by a great effort of will. On both
occasions Vicky complained bitterly to her brother about William. The
Queen had advised her daughter to 'send William & his odious,
ungrateful Wife, to travel & find his level'.[8] It was unrealistic advice, and
by 24 April, at what proved to be nearly the halfway mark of her son-
in-law's reign, she went to Berlin herself to support her daughter. Her
arrival was not welcome to Bismarck's government, for it was thought
she was still pushing the Battenberg marriage and sowing discord
between Germany and Russia. In fact she had already advised her
daughter not to push the marriage without William's consent. While in
Berlin the Queen granted Bismarck an interview, which went better than
might have been expected. She allowed the Chancellor to sit, they
avoided the by now moribund issue of the Battenberg marriage, and
Bismarck assured the Queen there would be no regency. Victoria spoke
of the inexperience of her grandson, the Crown Prince, but Bismarck
feigned unconcern. Should Willy be thrown in the water, he would learn
to swim. The parting of the Queen from her daughter was heartrending.

For the last fortnight of his life Frederick III was moved to Potsdam.
Even Bismarck was impressed by the dignity with which carried himself as his inevitable end approached. The Crown Prince's behaviour was
worse than ever. As soon as the lowering of the royal standard to half-
mast over the Neues Palais at Potsdam assured him that his father
was dead and he was William II, troops surrounded the palace and no
one, not even the Dowager Empress, was allowed to leave. Desks and
cabinets were rifled for secret documents, but none were found. Prominent in the search was Frederick III's aide-de-camp, General
Winterfeldt, who had been planted by Bismarck as a spy. William sent
him to London formally to announce his accession to his grandmother.
She received the general as coldly as she could.

The funeral of the Emperor was hurriedly arranged and took place
within seventy-two hours. It did not follow the dead man's instructions.
Again the Prince of Wales hurried to the side of his sister, accompanied
by Alix, in spite of her normal reluctance to set foot in Berlin. It was the
beginning of a number of incidents that soured relations between Bertie
and his nephew. The Prince inquired of Herbert von Bismarck if it was
true that Frederick had intended to make concessions to France over

Alsace-Lorraine, to Denmark over Schleswig-Holstein and to the Duke
of Cumberland over the loss of Hanover. It was perhaps not the most
tactful thing to do. Herbert von Bismarck had already angered the
Prince of Wales by an earlier remark that an Emperor who could not
speak could not be Emperor. Herbert von Bismarck was an unpleasant
man, a heavy drinker who was persistently offensive to his subordinates.
The iron had entered into his soul during many years of working
alongside his father. He had wanted to marry a Princess Carolath-
Beuthen, but because she was the sister-in-law of his father's old
enemy, Schleinitz, once his predecessor as Prussian Foreign Minister,
the elder Bismarck absolutely forbade it and threatened a nervous
breakdown. Herbert became an embittered man, 'that horrid creature',
Queen Victoria called him. Bertie's remarks about the restitutions
Frederick III had planned to make were reported to the new Kaiser and
infuriated him. In a speech on 16 August he proclaimed that Germany
would never surrender territories gained by precious German blood that
were rightfully hers.

Then the Prince of Wales got involved in another quarrel. Sir Robert
Morier was the British Ambassador in St Petersburg. He was a man of
liberal leanings, had been helped in his career by Albert and Stockmar,
and was a friend of Fritz and Vicky. He had recommended Hinzpeter as
a tutor for their son. Now the Prince of Wales told him that Herbert von
Bismarck was spreading lies that, at the time of the Franco-Prussian
War, Morier had passed military secrets given to him by Vicky on to the
French. These stories were all part of the campaign by the Bismarcks to
discredit the Dowager Empress and widen the rift between her and her
son. Morier obtained a denial from the French Marshal Bazaine and at
one point challenged Herbert von Bismarck to a duel. It did not come
to that, but neither did the Bismarcks make any apology or beat any
kind of retreat. They accused Morier of wishing to establish an Anglo-
Russian alliance, at a time when Bismarck had some interest in closer
relations with Britain. The German press, which everybody knew followed Bismarck's directives, attacked the Dowager Empress, Morier and
the Prince of Wales. Bertie and his mother wanted Lord Salisbury, who
was both Prime Minister and Foreign Secretary, to demand an explanation from the Germans, not only for the sake of Morier but also to clear
Vicky's name. Salisbury was keen to avoid damage to Anglo-German

relations and inclined to pour oil on troubled waters. Reluctantly he instructed the British Ambassador in Berlin to ask Herbert von Bismarck for a personal explanation, but got little satisfaction. Morier complained about 'the slobbering way in which everybody is making up to Herbert Bismarck', while Bertie told his mother 'Lord Palmerston or the late Lord Derby would never have permitted such insults heaped on one of your ambassadors to be passed unnoticed'.

Soon another furore was aroused by the publication of excerpts from the war diaries of the recently deceased Emperor, written during the Franco-Prussian War. Bismarck was stung to fury, for he could not bear that anybody other than himself should have any credit for the foundation of the German Empire. Underneath his monumental exterior he was a man of seething passions, which he had to battle hard to control. He declared the diaries forged, when privately he conceded that they were genuine. Professor Geffcken, an adviser to Fritz and Vicky, to whom the publication was traced, was accused of treason and imprisoned while awaiting trial. It was again a petty ploy through which the Chancellor hoped to strengthen his position with the new Kaiser by demonising his father and his still surviving mother. It backfired because Geffcken was released after three months by the German Supreme Court for lack of evidence. The young Kaiser realised that such tactics, forced on him by Bismarck, did not necessarily raise his own standing even with the normally supine German public and could damage the prestige of the monarchy itself.[9]

It was particularly hurtful to Vicky, and her mother and brother, that their once liberal German relations had gone over to the enemy camp. Uncle Ernest, the Duke of Coburg, once a champion of liberalism among German ruling princes, had switched to the winning side by 1866, in true Coburg tradition. He and the writer Gustav Freytag, his protégé, carried toadying to Bismarck a long way. An anonymous pamphlet, probably written by the Duke and published in 1886, accused Frederick William and Vicky of collusion with the French in 1870. The Queen wrote to the Crown Princess: 'What you told me of Uncle E[rnest] and that pamphlet is simply monstrous. I assure you I felt great difficulty in writing to him for his birthday, but I wrote it as short and cool as I could consistently with civility. He is a misfortune like the G.O.M. [Gladstone].'[10] Another pamphlet published by Ernest in 1889 vilified Vicky and her mother. In his memoirs, published in 1887, the Duke of Coburg presented himself as a devotee of Bismarck from the start and the account of his earlier liberal days was severely doctored. The Grand Duke of Baden, Frederick William's brother-in-law, was, in Vicky's eyes, another renegade from the liberal camp. He was once regarded as Germany's most liberal ruler, but he now did his best to bolster his wife's nephew, the new Kaiser, and hailed him as William I's true successor. Admittedly, a year later, the Grand Duke used his influence to strengthen William II's resolve to get rid of the Chancellor.

By the autumn of 1888 relations between the Prince of Wales and his nephew were affected by an episode even more serious than the Morier affair. The Kaiser had apparently resented the way the Prince and Princess of Wales had treated him at Frederick III's funeral. The German Ambassador in London, Count Paul von Hatzfeldt, told Salisbury that they had 'treated him as uncle treats a nephew instead of recognising that he was an emperor'. It did not endear her grandson to Queen Victoria that he paid a visit to Tsar Alexander III within a month of his father's death, when she always meticulously observed periods of Court mourning. It did not please her on political grounds either, though her grandson claimed to be 'putting state interests before personal feelings', for the peace of Europe and in accordance with Bismarck's policy. In fact William went on listening to the anti-Russian faction. He saw Waldersee, the advocate of preventative war against Russia, almost daily, thereby causing Bismarck great alarm. Such was the Kaiser's overweening confidence that he believed he could solve all problems by working his charm on the Tsar, his second cousin. By now the Kaiser's boastful and showy behaviour grated on the dour Alexander III, who did not pay a return visit to Berlin until October 1889. Anti-German feeling continued to run high in St Petersburg.

Then William was due to pay a state visit to Vienna in early October 1888. Bertie was planning to stay in Vienna for most of September, where there would be much hobnobbing with the Emperor Francis Joseph and the Crown Prince Rudolf. Bertie got on well with both of them, particularly with Rudolf, then a young man of twenty-nine. The Austrian Crown Prince found it torture to fit into the rigid, reactionary framework of the Habsburg monarchy in its decline and was well

known for kicking over the traces both politically and sexually.* Bertie
had much in common with the younger man, though one cannot
imagine him committing suicide as a way out.

The Prince of Wales had asked his nephew, the Kaiser, for the exact
date of his state visit to Vienna. He, Bertie, would, if necessary, inter-
rupt a hunting trip so that he could be present to entertain William,
together with Francis Joseph and the Austrian Crown Prince. Bertie
received no reply from his nephew. In Vienna he was shown a programme, which showed him to be absent from the city on 3 October. A
little later Francis Joseph casually remarked that it was the day
William II was arriving. The Prince of Wales immediately said he would
return to Vienna that day, but the Austrian Emperor remained silent.
The Austrians could not afford to offend the Germans. The following
day the embarrassing news was broken to the Prince's senior equerry by
the British Ambassador in Vienna that the presence of the Prince of
Wales during William II's visit would be unacceptable to the German
monarch. Bertie tried through various channels to find out in a dignified way what the Kaiser's grievance against him was, but nothing was
ever vouchsafed. The Prince of Wales, never the soul of discretion,
sometimes made remarks about his nephew which cannot have gone
down well when they came to the latter's ears. The Prince frequently
spoke of his nephew as 'William the Great', who 'needs to learn that he
is living at the end of the nineteenth century and not in the Middle
Ages'. Bertie had to leave Vienna during his nephew's visit, not returning till 14 October. It was just as well that he did not know that the
Kaiser regarded his uncle's withdrawal as a victory and said he preferred
'his rooms to his company'. Herbert von Bismarck reported to his father
that the Kaiser was 'beside himself with joy' at the humiliation he had
inflicted upon his uncle.

Not that the Prince suffered. He had a jolly time with Rudolf, who
himself cordially disliked William. There was a bear shoot in Transylva-
nia, then part of Hungary, though no bears were actually shot, because
they had disobligingly withdrawn into the high mountains. He was
then entertained by the King and Queen of Rumania, where he felt

* Rudolf's suicide at Mayerling, together with his current mistress Maria
  Vetsera, was scarcely three months away.

thoroughly at home. The King was a Hohenzollern, while his son and heir would a few years later marry Bertie's niece, the daughter of Affie. Bertie probably had a better time than he would have had staying in Vienna and entertaining his unsympathetic nephew, but this incident could not easily be forgotten. It caused great indignation in the royal family, which spilled over into diplomacy. Bertie told his mother 'I felt sure how pained, surprised and indignant you would be at William's conduct to me. The more I think the matter over the more unaccountable it seems to me.' To his sister he wrote: 'You know, dearest Vicky, how I have taken his part & stuck up for him in the family', and it pained him to have to tell her 'all this'. Vicky wrote to her mother: 'I am so ashamed ... & feel it more than any rudeness to *me*, as, alas, I am used to that'. Explanations, by Bismarck and Hatzfeldt, that the presence of the Prince of Wales at the Vienna meeting would have caused offence to the Tsar of Russia, cut little ice. Queen Victoria was furious. She wrote to Salisbury:

> It is simply absurd that the Emperor of Russia, the Princess of Wales's own brother-in-law should have been angry at the uncle and nephew meeting ... as regarding the Prince's not treating his nephew as Emperor; this is really too *vulgar* and too absurd ... We have always been very intimate with our grandson and nephew, and to pretend that he is to be treated *in private* as well as in public as his Imperial Majesty is *perfect madness*! ... If he has such notions, he better *never* come here ... The Queen will not swallow this affront ... All this shows a very unhealthy and unnatural state of mind; and he *must* be made to feel that his grandmother and uncle will not stand such insolence. The Prince of Wales must *not* submit to such treatment. As regards the political relations of the two Governments, the Queen quite agrees that that should not be affected (if possible) by these miserable personal quarrels; but the Queen much *fears* that, with such a hot-headed, conceited, and wrong-headed young man, devoid of all feeling, this may at *any* moment become *impossible*.[11]

But interests of state did have to take priority over family quarrels and the Kaiser did come to Osborne in August 1889. A naval review at Spithead was laid on for him and he was made an Admiral of the Fleet. It brought out his ambivalence about his English roots. 'Fancy wearing the same uniform as St Vincent and Nelson; it is enough to make one quite giddy', he wrote. He could turn on the charm when he wanted to and the Queen experienced once more the tender feelings she had always had towards Albert's first grandchild. Victoria felt she almost had to apologise to her daughter for William's friendly reception:

> I will only just once allude to the visit of William ... you must remember that it was not the least for William's sake that he was so well received, though not more than any other great sovereign. It was as your and dear Fritz's son, my grandson and the sovereign of a great country with whom it is more than ever important we should be on friendly terms. This was what the visit meant and that the feeling was good and friendly between the Germans and English, I am sure you can only rejoice at. It was your darling's and your aim.[12]

Were Bertie and Vicky sacrificed to what Lord Salisbury required in the national interest? At least the Queen succeeded in bringing her daughter, soon after her bereavement, to England on a prolonged visit, to give her a respite from the oppressive atmosphere that surrounded her in Berlin. It was against the initial opposition of her Prime Minister, who feared damage to Anglo-German relations. The Queen wired to her Prime Minister: 'She has nowhere to go; everyone expects her to come, and wonders she has not come before. It ... only encourages the Emperor and the Bismarcks still more against us. You all seem frightened of them, which is not the way to make them better ... Please let no one mention this again.' Vicky spent three months in England from November 1888 to February 1889.

If Bismarck had thought that petty and vicious attacks on Vicky and the legacy of Frederick III would strengthen his position with their son he miscalculated. He knew that it was not easy to bridge the generation gap between himself, at seventy-four, and the thirty-year-old Kaiser. He may also have felt it was better not obtrude his overpowering presence on to the younger man. This may have been one reason why he retreated to his estate at Friedrichsruh from May 1889 to January 1890, leaving Herbert to keep an eye on the Kaiser. The old man went only once to Berlin, in October, when Alexander III was at last paying his return visit to the Kaiser. The Tsar was well informed about the in-fighting that went on in the highest political circles in the German capital, much of which revolved round Russo-German relations. Bismarck, on the other hand, found it strange that the Tsar assumed he would not remain in office much longer. 'I am not clear who could have suggested that to him', he said.

Retirement was obviously not in the Chancellor's mind. He was still convinced of his indispensability. The more critical and dangerous the situation was at home or abroad, the more difficult it would be to do without him. It had always been an essential tool of his statecraft to bring on confrontations, forcing all players to take a stand and clear the air. In 1889 a great confrontation with the German working classes was in progress, with massive strikes in the mining areas of the Ruhr and elsewhere in Germany, often accompanied by violence. Bismarck, far from wishing to calm this social conflict, wanted to use it to impose an even more draconian anti-Socialist law, when the existing one ran out in 1890. In February 1890 Reichstag elections produced a shock result. In spite of over a decade of repression, the Social Democrats were stronger than ever, polling nearly a fifth of the vote. Tension between Kaiser and Chancellor had been mounting, with Bismarck brushing aside any conciliatory gesture towards the workers that the monarch was contemplating. After the elections Bismarck still felt that the Kaiser would be too frightened by the election triumph of the Socialists to listen to the many voices telling him to get rid of the Chancellor. He was to be disillusioned. At this stage and so early in his reign William did not want to embark on a civil war with large numbers of his subjects. He would rather be a *roi des gueux*, a king of the beggars, as his ancestor Frederick the Great had once claimed to be.

Three weeks after the elections the Chancellor, who had held sway since 1862, was on his way out. In a desperate effort to shore up his position he tried to form a new coalition in the Reichstag that would support his policies. He had a meeting with Windthorst, the leader of the Catholic Centre Party, who had been one of his most intrepid opponents for twenty years. Windthorst had stood up fearlessly to the overmighty Chancellor, when such defiance of authority was becoming increasingly rare in the new Germany. No coalition with the Centre was feasible and Windthorst left the meeting saying: 'I have come from the political deathbed of a great man.'

The parting from the Kaiser was as bitter as could be. During a crucial interview William complained that Bismarck had met Windthorst without his, the sovereign's, authority. The meeting had been arranged by Bleichröder and 'Jews and Jesuits were always in cahoots', said the young monarch. He then complained that he had been kept in the dark about dangerous Russian troop movements on Germany's eastern border. Towards the end of an acrimonious confrontation the Chancellor referred to secret reports lying on his desk concerning the recent visit of the Tsar to London. William demanded to see them, as Bismarck no doubt anticipated. He read Alexander III's reported remarks about himself: 'C'est un garçon mal élevé et de mauvaise foi'. The breach between Kaiser and Chancellor was irreparable.

Bismarck was given a send-off from Berlin with full military honours; he called it a state funeral first class. The only member of Germany's numerous royal families present was Prince Max of Baden.* Bismarck was raised one more step in the military hierarchy and became a Colonel-General. He was also given the title Duke of Lauenburg; useful for travelling incognito, he said.

None of this lessened the state of bitter hostility prevailing for the remaining eight years of Bismarck's life between him and the Kaiser, and the monarch's current ministers and advisers. When Bismarck fell from power hardly anybody in Germany's ruling circles regretted his departure. Seldom can the departure of a man of such massive stature have caused so little regret. He had clearly outlived himself politically and had no recipe for the future. Soon it became apparent that the Kaiser and those he chose as his advisers had no prescription for the future either and were staggering from one blunder to another. The mood changed and the old man in the Sachsenwald, the area near Hamburg in which Friedrichsruh was situated, acquired, in the eyes of many Germans, the status of a prophet and oracle.

Bismarck had no compunction in exploiting this status to make life difficult for his successors. In order to remain on good terms with Russia while an ally of Austria, Bismarck had in 1887 concluded a secret Reinsurance Treaty with Russia. This treaty was up for renewal at the time of Bismarck's fall and the Russians offered to renew it. Bismarck's successors decided not to do so, because it seemed to them to produce

---

* He was destined to be Chancellor for the last few weeks of the German Empire, in October 1918. On 9 November he announced the abdication of William II before himself resigning.

an impossibly complicated situation. They feared that the Russians could at any time endanger the German alliance with Austria by making the existence of the treaty known to the Austrians. Bismarck out of office castigated the makers of German foreign policy for allowing the wire to St Petersburg to snap and thereby driving Russia into the arms of France. In 1896 Bismarck published the Reinsurance Treaty, which he had concluded nearly a decade earlier. This was regarded by the Kaiser as virtually an act of treason. For most Germans it became an article of faith that the deterioration of their country's international position, leading to what they considered their encirclement, began with the failure by Bismarck's incompetent successors to renew the Reinsurance Treaty in 1890. While still alive Bismarck became one of history's greatest backseat drivers. After his death his ghost loomed large over German affairs. Many Germans were always looking for a heroic and charismatic leader who would perform the kind of miracles that Bismarck had done. They were still thinking along these lines when Hitler offered himself for the role.

A division of Europe into rival power blocs already loomed on the horizon while Bismarck was still in power. He had concluded the alliance with Austria in 1879 and then laboured hard and for a while successfully to keep Russia attached to this alliance. By the late 1880s economic factors, such as the difficulty Germany's high tariff policy created for Russian grain exports to the German market, led to a rapprochement between Russia and France. Even in Russia public opinion counted for something, limited though it was to the articulate classes and by the whims of censorship. There was a strong slavophil, pan-Slav school of thought, which believed that Russia had a mission to lead the other Slav peoples of Europe. It easily took on an anti-Austrian, anti-German direction. Nevertheless, the Russian autocracy and France, the mother of revolutions and the one republic among the major powers, made uneasy bedfellows. When Alexander III paid his first state visit to France in 1891, he was asked what should be done about the playing of the Marseillaise. He is reported to have said 'Can I invent another hymn?' This was beyond the power of even a Russian autocrat, but, after the playing of the first few bars of a purely orchestral version, the Tsar is reported to have shouted 'assez'.[13] In the ensuing years the Kaiser was always harping on monarchical solidarity in his efforts to prise the Tsar and his successor away from the French alliance. State interest was, however, gaining priority over dynastic inclinations. Anyhow, the European royal houses could not easily muster solidarity, however closely related. It meant nothing to Willy's uncle Bertie, who was nowhere happier than in Paris. Marie Feodorovna, Alexander III's wife and Nicholas II's mother, was a Danish princess, and like her sister, Bertie's wife Alix, hated Prussia all her life. At any time even his closest relatives found it difficult to get on with William II. Only a formidable matriarch like Queen Victoria could keep some kind of order in this far-flung and dysfunctional family and her time was running out.

11

The End of the Victorian Era

Even in her seventies Queen Victoria was still the unique personality she had always been. Sir Henry Ponsonby's son Arthur said that she did not 'belong to any conceivable category of monarchs or of women'. She bore no resemblance to an aristocratic English lady, to a wealthy middle-class Englishwoman, nor to any typical Princess of a German Court. Expressions such as 'like Queen Victoria' or 'that sort of woman' could not be used about her. But the fierce fires of her feelings, which had in the past flared up even against her beloved Albert, were now slightly banked. Once more she had to endure a spell of Gladstone in 10 Downing Street, from August 1892 to March 1894, but she took it more philosophically than in years gone by. For one thing, the General Election of 1892 did not give the Liberals either a large or an independent majority. The popular vote for the Tories and their Liberal Unionist allies was larger than the vote for the Liberals and they had together 313 seats, while the Liberals had only 272. Only the support of eighty-one Irish Home Rulers enabled Gladstone to form a government. Gladstone's own majority in his constituency of Midlothian had also been severely cut. The Queen noted in her journal:

> These are trying moments and it seems to me a defect of our famed Constitution, to have to part with an admirable Government like Lord Salisbury's for no question of any importance, or any particular reason, merely on account of the number of votes.[1]

She used stronger language to Ponsonby:

> Independent of the real misfortune for the country & Europe, the idea of a deluded excited man of 82 trying to govern England & her vast Empire with the miserable democrats under him is quite ludicrous. It is a bad joke!

Communication between the Queen and Gladstone, which had never been easy, became even more stilted and devoid of substance than ever.

Both of them were afflicted by the infirmities of old age. Victoria's eyesight was weakening, so was Gladstone's, who was also getting deaf. With a certain satisfaction she noted that he was 'greatly altered & changed, not only much aged, walking rather bent, with a stick, but altogether; his face shrunk, deadly pale, with a weird look in his eye ...' The Queen still made her influence felt in the composition of the Cabinet. She barred Labouchere, as much for the fact that he had cohabited with his wife before marrying her as for being the editor of *Truth*. On the other hand, she helped to persuade the reluctant Rosebery to become Foreign Secretary again. Although Gladstone loyally took responsibility for Labouchere's exclusion, the Queen's interference in Cabinet appointments brought criticism in the radical press. *Reynolds's Newspaper* commented on 28 August 1892: 'in her old age Victoria seems to be resorting to the methods which rendered her German Prince so deservedly unpopular'.[2]

In 1893 Gladstone made one more heroic, quixotic and doomed effort to get an Irish Home Rule Bill on to the statute book. It was his ostensible reason for remaining in politics, but he also had to do it to retain the support of the Irish Nationalist Party. The Bill passed the Commons, using the guillotine, by a majority of only thirty. It was then rejected by the Lords with the huge majority of 419 to 41, apparently to much popular acclaim. Salisbury's theory that the peers had a right to make the popular will prevail seemed vindicated, but nevertheless the vote was another step towards an eventual curtailment of the powers of the Upper House.

Even now Gladstone's retirement could not be taken for granted. It came when, in February 1894, his Cabinet would not follow him in rejecting increased naval estimates demanded by the Admiralty. He was particularly disappointed that Earl Spencer, the First Lord, backed the Board of Admiralty. Spencer, the great-great-grandfather of Diana, Princess of Wales, was known as the Red Earl, because of his red beard; he was one of the few members of the Whig high aristocracy who had stuck with the Liberals over Irish Home Rule. Gladstone would have recommended him to the Queen as his successor, but she did not ask his advice. Her refusal to follow the normal practice of consulting the outgoing Prime Minister about his successor was one of several circumstances that made the process of resignation painful for Gladstone.

The Queen could not bring herself to thank him for his public service of more than sixty years or express any regret at his going. Only to Mrs Gladstone was she prepared to say that she believed her when that lady said, tearfully, that her husband had been devoted to the Queen personally and to the Crown. In his retirement Gladstone had a recurring dream that the Queen had asked him to tea, but she never did. She sent for Rosebery to succeed him, setting aside Earl Spencer and Sir William Harcourt, the Chancellor of the Exchequer, who had perhaps the best claim. Rosebery lasted only fifteen months in Downing Street, though during that time his horse won the Derby. Rosebery was not a happy choice as leader for the Liberal Party, which after his short premiership remained out of office for over ten years.

The Queen had in the meantime acquired another personal servant, who almost, if not quite, filled the gap left by John Brown. He was Abdul Karim, an Indian Moslem, whom she acquired, along with other Indian servants, at the time of her Golden Jubilee. Victoria was fascinated by the subcontinent, especially since she was now the Empress of India, although she never went there. She had thoroughly absorbed her role as an imperial monarch and India was the jewel in the Crown. At Osborne a 'Durbar Room' was created for her by a pupil of the father of Rudyard Kipling. It is dominated by fretted plasterwork and contains a large number of Indian artefacts given to the Queen. Abdul Karim soon advanced to being the Munshi, Indian for secretary, who stood behind her when she was working on her boxes and was even allowed to reply to formal requests made to her from India. He taught her a few words of Hindustani, which she used when she had Indian visitors. When he was in bed with a painful boil on his neck, she visited him twice a day and smoothed his pillows.

The Munshi was almost as much a trial for her family, her secretaries and courtiers as John Brown had been. When on her orders he was given a place among the gentry at the Braemar Games, her son Arthur, the Duke of Connaught, protested to Henry Ponsonby. He did not understand Indian etiquette, said Sir Henry, and 'as H.R.H. did, would it not be better for him to mention it to the Queen. This entirely shut him up'.[3] No one could be sure that the Munshi did not abuse his confidential position and a Muslim so close to the Queen was bound to offend Hindus. The India Office had to be careful in selecting what papers to send to the Queen in case the Munshi saw them. It was a fact that the Munshi pretended that his father was a surgeon when he was only an apothecary in a prison. The Queen dismissed such information, and indeed all attacks on her favourite servant, as motivated by race prejudice. The Munshi was often outrageous in his behaviour and pretentiousness in dealing with other members of the royal household. In 1897, when he had contracted gonorrhoea, the royal household threatened to resign en bloc if he accompanied them on the Queen's visit to the South of France. He still turned up later during the Queen's French visit. Lord Salisbury thought she enjoyed the rows about the Munshi because they brought some excitement into her life, increasingly restricted by the infirmities of old age.

The Queen was still kept busy by her large family spread all over the royal Houses of Europe. Family ties were the obvious antidote to the isolation which surrounded royalty as a result of their elevated status. Within this family Victoria occupied a position almost like a goddess, feared, loved and immensely respected. In 1892 a daughter of Affie, Marie (known as Missy) became engaged to Nando, Ferdinand, a future King of Rumania. His uncle King Carol, the current ruler of Rumania, remarked: 'in politics she may be liberal but in her house she is the greatest autocrat I have ever encountered. She expects to be treated by her children like a supernatural being'. By Rumanian standards Victoria's politics may have been liberal, but there is no doubt that she ruled the adults in her family, particularly her own children, with a rod of iron, but to her young grandchildren she could be remarkably indulgent. They knew her as 'Gangan', were allowed to play around her and build walls with her empty dispatch boxes, but even they were ill advised to take liberties. They remembered her immense regal dignity, but also her captivating smile, silvery voice and sometimes helpless laughter.

There remained the serious business of matchmaking, with its political implications. It was a task in which the ageing Queen still enjoyed the active participation of her daughter Vicky, the Dowager Empress Frederick. Mother and daughter still wrote to each other three times a week in the early 1890s. Close to home the most important male to be married off was Prince Albert Victor, known as Eddy, Bertie and Alix's eldest son and eventual heir to the throne. He had always been a headache for the family, for all attempts to educate him had come up against what was politely described as 'the abnormally dormant condition' of his mind, which deprived him of the power 'to fix his attention to any given subject for more than a few minutes consecutively'. The author of this admission of failure was his tutor, the Reverend John Dalton.* Prince Eddy wanted to marry his exceptionally beautiful cousin, Alicky, daughter of the Queen's second daughter Alice, the Grand Duchess of Hesse-Darmstadt who had died in 1878. Alicky, perhaps understandably, turned him down, even though he was a future King of England. The Queen wrote to her daughter Vicky: 'She shows g[rea]t strength of character, all her family and all of us wish it, and she refuses the g[rea]test position there is.' In 1894 Alicky became the Tsarina of Russia. Eddy refused to consider Mossy, Vicky's youngest daughter and sister of the Kaiser, on the face of it more eligible than Alicky. He then fell in love with and actually got engaged to Hélène of Orleans, daughter of the Orleanist Pretender, the Comte de Paris. The Queen was prepared to approve, but Hélène's father refused to allow her to become an Anglican. Lord Salisbury convinced the Queen that this was an insuperable obstacle. This left Eddy, notoriously unstable, still on the loose.

The Queen then had the bright idea of inviting Princess May of Teck for the delectation of Eddy. Victoria thought she, the future Queen Mary, 'is a dear, good and clever girl, very carefully brought up, unselfish and unfrivolous in her tastes. She is very fond of Germany and is very *cosmopolitan*. I must say that I think it is far preferable than *eine kleine deutsche Prinzessin* [a little German princess] with no knowledge of anything beyond small German courts etc. It would never do for Eddy'.[4] May of Teck was the niece of the Queen's cousin George, Duke of Cambridge, who was still hanging on to the post of Commander-in-Chief, which he had occupied since the end of the Crimean War. George's sister Adelaide, an ungainly but popular member of the royal family, had married Francis, Duke of Teck, a member of the House of Württemberg, and May was their daughter. It did not disturb the Queen that the Tecks had no money, only debts. Eddy and May got engaged in December 1891.

* Father of Hugh Dalton, Chancellor of the Exchequer in the Labour government of 1945.

This was a coup for the Queen in a year that had seen Eddy's father involved in yet another scandal and court appearance. It was the Tranby Croft affair, which arose from cheating at a game of baccarat. The Prince of Wales had not himself cheated, but baccarat was an illegal game and the case cast a lurid light on the lifestyle of the heir to the throne, and on the company he kept. At least that is how it seemed to the more strait-laced of the Queen's subjects. The Queen felt that Eddy's engagement gave hope for the future of the monarchy, if only her son allowed it to survive long enough. It was scarcely helpful that the Kaiser sent his grandmother a letter protesting against anyone holding the honorary rank of a colonel of Prussian Hussars, as Bertie did, becoming involved in a gambling squabble with men young enough to be his children. Vicky, on the other hand, was pleased that May had been elevated. Dona, the Kaiserin, her tiresome daughter-in-law, had in contrast considered May too lowly to marry her brother, another Augustenburg Prince, who was considered virtually unmarriageable in most royal circles.

Before he could marry Eddy suddenly died of pneumonia in January 1892, aged only twenty-six.* This turned out to be fortunate, because his much more suitable brother George, the Duke of York, became heir to the throne. It was even more fortunate that he proved willing to fall in love with May of Teck, whose prospects had been so cruelly disappointed. George followed the example of his aunt, the Tsarina Marie Feodorovna, also known as Minnie. When she was Dagmar of Denmark, she had been engaged to the Grand Duke Nicholas, the heir to the Russian throne. He died suddenly in 1865 and Dagmar was passed on to Sasha, the new Tsarevitch and future Alexander III. Alexander was not an attractive man, so one may think that May of Teck did better by being passed from Eddy to the future George V. Prince George had actually fancied another cousin, Missy, Affie's daughter, who was only seventeen at the time, and thought he had an understanding with her. It may have been due to the influence of her mother, the Russian Grand Duchess married to Affie, that Missy committed herself to Nando, the Rumanian heir to the throne, rather than to George. The Prince of Wales was much annoyed, but Victoria took it more calmly than she

* There was a persistent rumour that he was Jack the Ripper.

would have done in earlier days. She asked Vicky to assure her brother, the Prince of Wales, that it was not Affie's fault. As to Rumania, the Queen felt that it was 'very insecure' and the society 'dreadful'; it could not even be a Protestant wedding.

The Queen and her daughter, the Dowager Empress, had to carry on match making even if it separated them from those whose presence around them gave them essential comfort. The Queen faced this dilemma with her younger children, male and female, Helena, Leopold and above all Beatrice. Vicky, as a desolate widow, also derived comfort from her three surviving younger children, all of them daughters. They shared her outlook and were known to their brother William as 'the English colony'. The Queen of England might demand that daughters should hang around unmarried to do her bidding, but even at Windsor it did not come to that. Vicky certainly had to get her daughters married off, however hard it was for her. When it came to the last and youngest, Margaret, known as Mossy, who in 1893 married Friedrich Karl of Hesse-Cassel, known as Fischy, Victoria wrote to her daughter:

> to me there is something so dreadful, so repulsive in that one has to give one's beloved and innocent child, whom one has watched over and guarded from the breath of anything indelicate ... to a man, a stranger to a great extent, body & soul to do with what he likes. No experience ... will ever help me over that.[5]

Between Moretta and Mossy came Sophie, born in 1870, who married Tino, later King Constantine of Greece, in 1889. She converted to Greek Orthodoxy, something that infuriated the Kaiser and Dona, who ceased to be on speaking terms with the couple. It also brought Sophie into the Danish camp, which was viscerally hostile to Prussia and all its works. Tino's father, George I of Greece, was the brother of the Tsarina Marie Feodorovna and of the Princess of Wales. A political consequence was that the Kaiser was strongly anti-Greek and pro-Turk, for example when the Cretans rose against the Turks in 1896 and Greece proclaimed union with Crete. Not that William could do all that much, for he was, as on many other occasions, restrained by his own officials and diplomats. Nor did irritation with the Kaiser's personality, common among his relations around the royal houses of Europe, necessarily mean that their countries opposed Germany. Dynastic politics was by this time becoming an irritant rather than a determinant.

A more heavyweight dynastic alliance was, however, yet to come. In April 1894 Victoria was again in Darmstadt for a wedding. Again it was two of her grandchildren who were tying the knot. Affie's second daughter, Victoria Melita, known as Ducky, was marrying her cousin, the reigning Grand Duke Ernst Ludwig of Hesse-Darmstadt and son of Alice. It turned out to be one of the first royal marriages to end in divorce, after only seven years. The Queen was thunderstruck when at breakfast the morning after the ceremony she was told that Alicky, the groom's sister, had at last become engaged to the Tsarevich, soon to be Nicholas II. Alicky's taste for Russia had been awakened when at the age of twelve she had attended the wedding of her elder sister Ella to the Grand Duke Sergei in 1884. She spent several months in St Petersburg in 1889, when she may well have lost her heart to the twenty-year-old Tsarevich, who called her *Tetinka*, 'Little Aunt'. Alicky had religious scruples about giving up her Lutheran faith, but once she had decided to overcome them she became a fervent member of the Russian Orthodox Church. In earlier years such a significant Russian connection would have clashed painfully with Queen Victoria's Russophobic feelings. Now she merely noted that 'the position was an anxiety', which turned out to be an understatement. She expressed her real feelings more strongly to Alicky's sister, Princess Louis of Battenberg:

> my blood runs cold when I think of her so young most likely placed on that very unsafe throne, her dear life and above all her husband's constantly threatened ... It is a great additional anxiety in my declining years! Oh! how I wish it was not to be that I should lose my sweet Alicky.[6]

The Kaiser, who was a keen participant in the royal marriage market, may have had a hand in this match. If he hoped that this renewal of the link between Romanov and Hohenzollern would prove politically useful, he was mistaken. He was no more successful in charming Nicholas II than he had been with his father.

It was, however, yet another and more important tie between Windsor and St Petersburg. Over the next two decades it began gradually to fit in better with the realities of power politics. Straightaway the Prince and Princess of Wales became intimately involved with royal events in

Russia. The wedding of Nicholas and Alicky was to take place in late November of that year, 1894, but scarcely four weeks before, on 1 November, Alexander III died. Twenty-four hours before he died Bertie and Alix had left London for the Crimea at short notice, for Marie Feodorovna, Minny, wanted her sister by her side as her husband lay dying. So it came about that the Waleses accompanied the Dowager Empress, the new Tsar and his fiancée, and the coffin of the dead Emperor from Livadia back to St Petersburg and remained with their relations throughout the funeral ceremonies and the subsequent wedding, when Bertie's niece became simultaneously a wife and an Empress. Bertie and Alix played their role as comforters, uncle and aunt, mentor and sister with sensitivity and warmth.

The close link that had now arisen between Queen Victoria and the Tsar of All the Russias weakened the deep anti-Russian feelings of the Queen. Now she could no longer personalise them. When she got worked up about the way Alexander III was treating the noble Sandro, she could call him 'the stupid Tsar', in letters to her daughter, but it was quite different with Nicky and Alicky. 'Dear Nicky is very amiable and quite at home with us', the Queen wrote to Vicky, when the Tsarevich was staying at Windsor with his fiancée Alicky in the summer of 1894. When a few months later Alexander III died, the Queen's reaction was 'what a horrible tragedy this is! And what a position for these dear young people. God help them!' Every death was always a horrible tragedy to Victoria. In September 1896 the Tsar and the Tsarina were again staying with the Queen at Balmoral. The Queen wrote to her daughter: 'Dear Nicky and Alicky are quite unspoiled and unchanged and as dear and simple as ever and as kind as ever. He is looking rather thin and pale and careworn, but sweet Alicky is in great beauty and very blooming.'[7] On the social level, Nicky did not like it much at Balmoral, at least while Bertie was there. His wife's uncle, almost exactly twice his age, dragged him out shooting every day in wind and rain and the twenty-eight-year-old Tsar developed neuralgia. When Lord Salisbury arrived at the castle, Queen, Tsar and Prime Minister got down to serious business. Bertie was not allowed to take part and had to leave. The Tsar wrote to his mother, who still had a great deal of influence over him: 'After he left I had an easier time, because I could at least do what *I* wanted, and was not *obliged* to go out shooting every day in the cold and rain ... Granny was kinder and more amiable than ever.' Salisbury in his conversations with the Tsar found the young man 'conciliatory, straightforward, and honest'. Nicholas changed the subject when the Prime Minister wanted to talk about the dismemberment of Turkey, but he had no objection to Britain remaining in Egypt and said it was absurd to think that Russia was trying to obtain India. The Tsar said how much he disliked his 'nervous' and ill-mannered cousin the Kaiser, who 'would poke him in the ribs, and slap him on the back like a schoolboy'. Another talk two days later did not take matters much further, but in his Guildhall speech in November Salisbury said: 'It is, I think, a super-stition of an antiquated diplomacy that there should be any necessary antagonism between Russia and Great Britain.'

For the Prince of Wales it was not easy to cope with these family rela-tionships, which now linked Europe's most important powers, England, Germany and Russia. Willy and Nicky were the greatest figures in inter-national politics, while he was virtually excluded from the political business of a monarchy the powers of which were more restricted than they were in Russia or Germany. His mother still allowed him only selective access to official papers, for she remained firmly convinced that he had neither the industry nor the discretion required to deal with them. Sympathetic ministers, particularly Rosebery, gave him informa-tion; and Rosebery had actually given him, in 1892, the golden key, specially made for his father, which gave access to Foreign Office boxes. A less good-natured personality than Bertie might have become embit-tered and his relations with his powerful nephews might have become almost impossible. On the whole the Prince of Wales carried it off, some of the time even with the unsympathetic Kaiser. As a leader of cosmo-politan society and fashion he outshone Nicky and Willy by a long way. It was this wide and variously assorted social circle that his Russian rela-tions found difficult to stomach. When Nicholas as Tsarevich was staying at Sandringham in 1894 the financier Baron Maurice de Hirsch was a fellow guest. He tried to interest Nicholas in his philanthropic plans to help persecuted Russian Jews. To his mother the Tsarevich described the house party as 'rather strange. Most of them were horse dealers, amongst others a Baron Hirsch! The Cousins rather enjoyed the situation, and kept teasing me about it; but I tried to keep away as much as possible, and not talk'.[8] Horse racing was an interest that Bertie shared with Baron Hirsch. Nicky was close to his mother, while his domineering father had dismissed him as childish and called him a 'girlie'. It had done nothing for his self-confidence.

On a personal level relations between the Kaiser and the British royal family were not bad in the early 1890s. The Kaiser came to the Cowes Regatta every year, on the large yacht he had acquired, the *Hohenzollern*, with a great entourage of men and ships. Sometimes all went well. About the 1892 visit Bertie told his son George that 'William the Great' had been 'not the least grand, and very quiet, most amiable in every respect'. There was now less tension between the Kaiser and his mother, the cause of much of his unstable identity. She and the memories attaching to her were no longer a threat. She started to build herself a house, Schloss Friedrichshof, at Kronberg, near Frankfurt. It took until the spring of 1894 to complete. She was often away from Berlin, sometimes in Greece, to be with her daughter Sophie, the Crown Princess. Sophie and her husband Tino were still not on speaking terms with William and Dona; a reconciliation had to wait until 1898. The Kaiser occasionally came to see his mother, usually at short notice and with an inconveniently large suite. Bismarck paid an official visit to the Kaiser in January 1894, which was meant to symbolise their reconciliation. It was only outward and Bismarck made the visit as short as possible. He still found time for a brief call on Vicky. When they talked of her husband and his illness, the former Chancellor was moved to say: 'How lovable and magnificent he was throughout his illness' (wie liebenswürdig und grossartig war doch der Herr in seiner ganzen Krankheit).

A calmer family situation was accompanied by a relatively friendly phase in Anglo-German relations in the early 1890s. Attempts were made to reduce friction caused by early German steps to acquire colonies in Africa. Bismarck had taken these steps in 1884, probably mainly for reasons of domestic politics, but he remained reluctant to complicate his game of European alliances by going further down the colonial road. In 1891, under his successor Caprivi and while Salisbury was still at the Foreign Office, there was an Anglo-German Agreement to exchange Heligoland for Zanzibar. Britain could not have defended Heligoland and a possible bone of contention with Germany was removed. Caprivi and his team felt the agreement was a feather in their cap, as it showed that their diplomatic competence could bear comparison with that of the old master, Bismarck. The Queen gave her agreement but added: 'Giving up what one has is always a bad thing.'

It was an indication of things to come that in Germany protests against the Heligoland–Zanzibar agreement produced the first moves towards the foundation of the Pan-German League. This body, although numerically not very large, was a key organisation in the promotion of an ambitious German forward policy in Europe and the wider world. German public opinion was becoming increasingly susceptible to the appeal of *Weltpolitik*, that Germany had arrived a point at which she must play a role in the world commensurate with her increasing strength. Even Bismarck, in his resentful retirement, gave support to this feeling, when in his days of power he had always been careful not to overextend German commitments. In 1895 the famous sociologist Max Weber gave his support to *Weltpolitik* in his inaugural address at Heidelberg. German unification would look like a youthful escapade if it was not now followed by a world policy, he declared. When minds as coolly analytical as Weber's could think in this way, it did not need much to move the excitable and volatile Kaiser in this direction. He was nearly pushed over the brink by the Jameson Raid in December 1895.

That year William's Cowes visit had not gone so well. The Kaiser made one of his sabre-rattling, boastful speeches to commemorate the twenty-fifth anniversary of the battle of Wörth, in the Franco-Prussian War. It was hardly tactful to do so in British waters, on board the cruiser *Wörth*, which the Kaiser had brought along with him for good measure. During these August days at Cowes he also had political discussions with Lord Salisbury, who had just returned as Prime Minister following a landslide Unionist victory in the General Election the previous month. He then took it as a personal insult, when Salisbury, owing to pressing business in London, was unable to meet him for a second interview. No doubt the sixty-five-year-old Prime Minister, weighing over eighteen stone, was glad to be spared the business of climbing up a ladder on to the Kaiser's yacht, but he intended no offence to the yacht's owner. The Kaiser, however, saw this as one of several incidents on this visit when he had been slighted. He resented unfavourable comments that had appeared in the British press, which he thought had been inspired by Salisbury. It all served to bring his recently dormant anti-English animus to the fore again.

Two days after his meeting with Salisbury Willy was dining with the Prince of Wales. They were talking about negotiations in progress concerning the frontier between British India and French Indo-China. Their breakdown could lead to war. The Kaiser suddenly jumped up and thumped his uncle on the back saying: 'So you'll soon be off to India again, and we'll see at last what you are really good for as a soldier!' If there was one thing Bertie was sensitive about it was his lack of military experience. It was one of the Kaiser's more eccentric habits to thump elderly admirals, and such like, on the back or on the behind, making them fall over or playing practical jokes on them. There was a distinct homoerotic tendency in him, as well as a strong dose of narcissism. He enjoyed humiliating others, but he harboured deep resentment at even the slightest sign that he was not being taken as seriously as he took himself. If the Kaiser had been a private person his psychological quirks might have caused amusement as well as irritation. In the powerful All-Highest they were not only annoying but also very damaging.

Britain had its own forward policy in Africa and more substantial bases and assets from which to pursue it than Germany. Cecil Rhodes was aiming at a continuous British territorial control from the Cape to Cairo. German colonial enthusiasts were thinking of a German link from East to West Africa, of which the Caprivi Strip in northern Namibia is a lone survivor. British expansion from the Cape had come up against the stubborn resistance of the Boer republics, but this was being undermined by the presence of large numbers of immigrants, Uitlanders, drawn to the Rand by the lure of gold. The Jameson Raid was an attempt to spark an uprising of Uitlanders against the Boer government of President Paul Kruger, but it was premature and turned into a humiliating failure. The Colonial Secretary in London, Joseph Chamberlain, probably knew that the raid was likely to happen, but an inquiry never established his complicity.

There were also German Uitlanders in the Transvaal and they backed the Kruger government. The Kaiser had already became sensitive about the conflict of interest between Germany and Britain in the Transvaal because of an unfortunate remark made by Sir Edward Malet, for many years British Ambassador in Berlin. Malet had good relations with

William. To mark the Ambassador's retirement in October 1895, the Kaiser had invited him to a shoot, along with the Chancellor, Prince Hohenlohe, and the State Secretary for Foreign Affairs, Marschall von Bieberstein. Malet, normally very cautious, committed what turned out to be a gaffe by saying that the Transvaal was a 'black spot' in Anglo-German relations, which could lead to serious consequences. The Kaiser interpreted this as a threat amounting almost to an ultimatum.

The Malet incident, coming on top of the alleged slurs he had suffered at Cowes that year, made William determined to exploit to the utmost the British embarrassment about the Jameson Raid. He wanted to intervene by force and, since he had no navy capable of challenging the British, he contemplated sending troops. It was made clear to him that this was equally impossible. He therefore decided, in consultation with Hohenlohe and Marschall, to send a telegram to Kruger, congratulating him on having repulsed the raid. Even this was toned down by the German Foreign Office and it finally read:

> Most sincere congratulations that you and your people have been successful, by your own strength and without appealing for the help of friendly powers against the armed band that broke into your land as destroyers of peace and restored peace and defended the independence of your country against attacks from without.

British public opinion and the press were furious and so were the royal family from the Queen down. Vicky had to tell her brother that Hohenlohe, the Chancellor, had replied to her questions about the telegram that 'it was in accordance with German public feeling at that moment'; in other words that it was not just the product of her son's notorious impulsiveness. Hohenlohe was correct about German public feeling, whipped up by the fiercely anti-British tone of the newspapers. Many German officials, including Holstein, were, however, less than happy about the telegram. The German military attaché in St Petersburg was heard to say 'the Kaiser must be *mad, mad, mad!*' Bertie saw the telegram 'as a most gratuitous act of unfriendliness' on the part of his nephew. He advised his mother to give William 'a good snubbing', but Victoria knew her grandson too well to think that would do any good. She wrote to her son that William's 'faults come from impetuousness (as well as conceit); and calmness and firmness are the most powerful weapons in such cases'. Her rebuke to the Kaiser was therefore carefully measured:

> It is considered very unfriendly towards this country, which I feel sure it is not intended to be, and has, I grieve to say, made a very painful impression here. The action of Dr Jameson was of course very wrong and totally unwarranted; but considering the very peculiar position in which the Transvaal stands towards Great Britain, I think it would have been far better to have said nothing.

The Kaiser replied in equally conciliatory tone: 'standing up for law, order [and] obedience to a gracious Sovereign who I revere and adore'. His original draft was a good deal stronger and referred to the bad treatment he had received from the British press when he was at Cowes the previous year. The Queen thought the reply 'lame and illogical'. Whatever the conciliatory efforts on both sides, reinforced by Salisbury, Hohenlohe and their colleagues, the Kruger telegram affair rankled for a long time. It crystallised the latent antagonism between Britain and Germany that had been building up over many issues, political, economic and industrial. It was a prelude to the hostility that arose over the Boer War three years later. As far as the royal family was concerned, it meant that William was not invited to the Queen's Diamond Jubilee celebrations the following year, nor to the Cowes Regatta for several years. This annoyed him considerably, but there was nothing like a final breach, either in royal relations or in the relations between the two countries. How royal personages reacted, even those as important as the Kaiser or the Queen, never made as much of a difference as they themselves thought.

There was, however, a consequence of the Kruger telegram affair in which the Kaiser's role was crucial, and one that would become decisive for Anglo-German relations. It was the building of an ocean-going navy by Germany. One reason why, in spite of his inability to apply himself consistently to the formation of policy, the Kaiser was able to exercise great influence was his power of appointment. Two crucial appointments were made in 1897: Admiral Tirpitz became State Secretary for the Navy, and Bülow became State Secretary for Foreign Affairs, advancing to Chancellor three years later. Both were men willing to pander to the Kaiser's current mood. His inability to do anything more than send a telegram to Kruger after the Jameson Raid had maddened the Kaiser and made him feel powerless in the face what he imagined to be a British threat.

Tirpitz told the Kaiser that 'the most dangerous enemy at the present time is England. It is also the enemy against which we most urgently require a certain measure of naval force as a political power factor ... The military situation against England demands battleships in as great a number as possible'. It was exactly what the Kaiser wanted to hear. It accorded with his deepest feelings about England, her navy, ships and maritime power in general. Tirpitz presented himself as the man who could exploit the public mood in favour of world power and force the Reichstag to vote funds for a navy on a scale that it had previously never authorised. In this respect Tirpitz proved as good as his word. With the backing of the Kaiser, a great mobilisation of popular fervour for a large navy was mounted. The Navy League became the largest of the German patriotic organisations and it was powerful enough to prevent any retreat from the naval building programme, even if the Kaiser and his ministers had at some point wanted to slow it down. It became all but inevitable that Britain would eventually seek agreements with France and Russia to protect herself against what was seen as a direct threat to her naval supremacy.

Bernhard von Bülow was the man destined to provide the political and diplomatic cover for the naval building programme. He was a courtier more than a politician and had done everything he could to ingratiate himself with the Kaiser. In a letter to the Kaiser's friend Philipp Eulenburg, which he was sure the Kaiser would see, he wrote about William: 'He is so impressive! He is, along with the great King [Frederick the Great] and the Great Elector, the most impressive Hohenzollern who has ever lived ... he combines genius with the clearest good sense ... He possesses the kind of fantasy that lifts me on eagle's pinions above all triviality and, at the same time, the shrewdest appreciation of the possible and the attainable. And with it, what energy! What reflectiveness! What swiftness and sureness of conception.'[9] However wildly inappropriate this was as a character sketch, perhaps Bülow really believed it. With his good memory and an intelligence that could dart hither and thither at speed, the Kaiser could impress people, as was not too difficult for someone in so elevated a position. With Tirpitz and

Bülow in office the Kaiser really had established the personal regime that many historians discern in the 1890s, without having to apply himself for tedious hours behind a desk.

His grandmother's Diamond Jubilee took place without him, but it was less of a put-down than it might have been. All European monarchs were discouraged from attending, for it would have taxed the seventy-eight-year-old Victoria's strength too much. Only the Queen's close relations, Vicky and her daughters, and a few others, took part in the processions. The Queen could no longer mount the steps to St Paul's and there had to be an open-air service outside the cathedral. At the many garden parties she had to be pulled through the multitude of guests in a small carriage. She reserved herself for her own people and for the representatives of the Empire, but she completed the programme stretching over many days without faltering. It was another apotheosis, made the more poignant by the realisation that it was unlikely to be repeated, and by the contrast between the little old lady in her bonnet and the splendour of the world-wide power she symbolised. She must herself been conscious of the poignancy of this contrast, for years earlier, after an enthusiastic reception in Liverpool, she had written to her daughter: 'And they looked so delighted only to see their little old Queen'.

In May 1898 her old adversary Gladstone died, to be followed two months later by her former *bête noire* Bismarck. Even now the Queen found it difficult to say the right word to Mrs Gladstone about her late husband and her letter of condolence was distinctly restrained. A warmer message had to be drafted for the press. When the Empress Frederick wrote to her mother cautiously: 'Poor Mr Gladstone was often your minister and though it was impossible always to agree with him, yet he was a great Englishman and it is fitting to do honour to his memory as such', the Queen remonstrated:

> I cannot say that I think he was 'a great Englishman'. He was a clever man, full of talent, but he never *tried* to keep up the *honour* and *prestige* of Great Britain. He gave away the Transvaal, he abandoned Gordon, he destroyed the Irish Church and tried to separate England from Ireland and to set class against class. The harm he did cannot easily be undone. But he was a good and very religious man.[10]

The Queen was more seriously aggrieved when she heard that Bertie and his son, the future George V, were to act as pallbearers at Gladstone's funeral. The Prince of Wales still considered himself a moderate liberal and had always preferred the Liberal leader to Disraeli. He regretted his mother's growing hostility to the G.O.M. Gladstone for his part had been sympathetic to Bertie and had cultivated him socially, to the extent of smoking in his company. He had done his best to find employment for the Prince and to give him access to political information.

After the death of John Brown in 1883 the Queen began to travel abroad more frequently. Brown had hated foreigners and foreign travel. In the 1890s Victoria went frequently to the French Riviera, travelling with a large entourage in a sumptuously fitted saloon carriage. The train stopped so that meals could be taken without disturbance. On what turned out to be her last visit, in April 1899, she finally settled the succession in the duchy of Saxe-Coburg-Gotha. Affie, Duke of Edinburgh, the Queen's second son, had taken over as Duke of Coburg after the death of Ernst in 1893. Victoria had come to Coburg for the inauguration of Affie as a foreign sovereign in April 1894 and so had the Kaiser. Affie did not like Coburg and did not enjoy being a very minor ruler in his nephew's empire. He was never popular, remaining too English, but his wife, the Russian Grand Duchess, whose marriage had never been happy, was glad to get away from her British in-laws. In February 1899 their only son, dying of tuberculosis aggravated by venereal disease, shot himself.

Theoretically the succession in Coburg should now have passed to the Queen's third son, Prince Arthur of Connaught. Prince Arthur was about to be a field-marshal in the British Army and had fought at Tel-el-Khebir. The Kaiser now demanded that he should give up his British rank and join the German army. The last thing Prince Arthur wanted was to go to Germany as a minor ruler, even though his wife was Louise of Prussia, known as Louischen. The Queen, thinking of Albert, felt nothing should be done to risk the Coburg heritage. It was decided that the duchy should go to Charles Edward, the fifteen-year-old son of the late Leopold, Duke of Albany, the Queen's youngest son, who had died as a result of haemophilia in 1884. Charlie Albany, as he was known, had been born posthumously and brought up by his German mother, Helen of Waldeck-Pyrmont. This was thought to fit him well for a German duchy. He was at the time a boy at Eton, and had to be taken away from the school. The Kaiser was very annoyed that he was not consulted

about the Coburg succession. The decision was taken by a chance family gathering around the Queen at Cimiez, in the South of France near
Nice, at which he had not been present. The Queen thought William
had no right to be cross and Vicky told her mother that she had no
reason to apologise. Charles Edward and his mother were in fact well
received at Coburg. Affie, a large man who drank heavily and took little
exercise, died in July 1900, the third of the Queen's children to predecease her. Charlie was therefore a minor when he succeeded as Duke.
He was drawn into the inner circle of the Kaiser, his first cousin, but
twenty-five years his senior. There is a photograph, taken on board the
imperial yacht, showing William, laughing in his best back-slapping,
practical joking mood, sitting on top of the prostrate Duke of Saxe-
Coburg-Gotha who is being held down by someone else.[11] The Kaiser's
bullying and shows of machismo were intended to make Charlie
Albany *plus allemand que les allemands*. The Coburgers were now passionately German and did not want to have to think of their Duke as an
Englishman. On the other hand, Charles Edward maintained his links
with the British royal family, reinforced when his only sister, Princess
Alice, married Prince Alexander of Teck, brother of Queen Mary
and later Earl of Athlone. After the outbreak of the First World War, as
Duke of Coburg, Charles Edward strove to measure up to the role which
German chauvinism expected of a ruling prince. By the 1930s he became
a follower of Hitler.

Right at the end of her reign Victoria had once more to become a
Warrior Queen in the Boer War. As in the Crimean War forty-five years
before, and in spite of her physical disabilities, she inspected troops,
awarded medals and despatched parcels of knitting. As in the Crimean
War, the public expected a walk-over but got defeats and casualties.
There was 'Black Week' in December 1899, a series of defeats. To
A. J. Balfour, Salisbury's nephew and successor, Victoria remarked,
clearly for public consumption: 'Please understand that there is no one
depressed in this house; we are not interested in the possibilities of
defeat; they do not exist.'

The Boer War aroused anti-British feeling in many countries, not
least in Germany. The unexpected reverses suffered by the British army
were noticed with glee. The Kaiser personally did not entirely go along
with this anti-British movement of public opinion and press in his own

country. There had been immediately before the war a high level of irritation between him, his British royal relations and the Salisbury government. Even while there were, on the one hand, discussions about an Anglo-German alliance, there were, on the other, more immediate and acute differences on colonial matters in Africa and in the Pacific. The Germans wanted their 'place in the sun', as Bülow put it, and were desperate to catch up with the older colonial powers. It was all a matter of honour and prestige, because they derived only meagre material benefits from the widely dispersed real estate they eventually managed to pick up. This was, however, scarcely appreciated at the time. The price Germany, the latecomer among nations, paid in disadvantage to her diplomacy and foreign policy was formidable. In 1898 it was the small Pacific island of Samoa that became the focus of Anglo-German colonial differences. The Kaiser wrote a bitter letter of complaint to his grandmother about the way Germany had been treated by Lord Salisbury:

> This way of treating Germany's feelings and interests had come upon the People like an electric shock and has evoked the impression that Lord Salisbury cares for us no more than for Portugal, Chili [sic] or the Patagonians, and out of this impression the feeling has arisen that Germany was being despised by his Government, and this has stung my subjects to the quick. This fact is looked upon as a taint to national honour and to their feelings of selfrespect.[12]

It was all 'on account of a stupid island which is a hairpin to England compared to the thousand of square miles she is annexing right and left unopposed every year', the Kaiser added. The Queen and her Prime Minister had by this time arrived at much the same estimate of the mercurial and unpredictable Kaiser, but they did their best not to allow his vagaries to damage inter-state relations. Salisbury agreed with the Queen 'that it is quite new for one Sovereign to attack in a private letter the Minister of another Sovereign, especially one to whom he is so closely related'. Salisbury produced a long memorandum justifying his conduct, without giving anything away, which the Queen forwarded to her grandson. In her accompanying letter she said, 'I doubt whether any Sovereign ever wrote in such terms to another Sovereign, and that Sovereign his own Grandmother about her Prime Ministre [sic]'. She added that she had 'never personally attacked or complained of

Prince Bismarck, though I knew well what a bitter enemy he was to England and all the harm he did'. The Queen knew that her grandson was a cross they all had to bear.

When the Kaiser was forty, on 27 January 1899, she wrote in her journal, 'I wish he were more prudent and less impulsive at such an age!' She knew he was an inveterate intriguer. A few weeks later she had to warn her granddaughter's husband, the Tsar: 'I am afraid that William may go and tell things against us to you, just as he does about you to us. If so, pray tell me openly and confidentially. It is so important that we should understand each other and that such mischievous and unstraightforward proceedings should be put a stop to.' Private and public affairs were inextricably intertwined, but royal personages thought of themselves as shaping the destiny of nations more than they were actually able to. Politicians, public opinion, the press, economic factors, the advance of technology, even the masses, had all become players on the stage of history and were limiting the scope of monarchs and dynasties. Albert had often deplored the influence of the press. His grandson William cursed it even more roundly. He read the London press more thoroughly than he did the newspapers of his own country and blamed it for misrepresenting his benevolent intentions towards England. He adorned the clippings prepared for him with copious marginal comments, as he did diplomatic documents. It was just one of the many manifestations of his inability to keep quiet or keep his own counsel. As for Queen Victoria and the Kaiser, there was a bond between them that neither could ever quite forget. To her congratulations on his fortieth birthday he replied: 'I fully understand how extraordinary the fact must seem to you that the tiny, weeny little brat you often had in your arms and dear Grandpapa swung about in a napkin has reached the forties!'

Political and familial tensions meant that the Queen did not invite her grandson to her eightieth birthday celebrations in May 1899, but the Kaiser did visit the British royal family in November 1899, defying anti-British feeling in Germany. He was accompanied by Bülow and there were again discussions about an Anglo-German alliance. They were inconclusive, but it was by no means the end of the proposal. One of the factors that might have worked in favour of an Anglo-German alliance was the common cultural heritage of the two countries and that the predominant religion in both countries was rooted in the Reformation. At the turn of the century 'race', whatever it might precisely mean, was looming large in the public consciousness. Catchwords like 'the white man's burden' or 'the yellow peril' were on many lips and appeared on many printed pages. Such ideas fuelled the imperialist visions of a man like Joseph Chamberlain, the British Colonial Secretary, who became a principal driving force behind the promotion of an Anglo-German alliance around the turn of the century. At a time when Chamberlain was arguing for an Anglo-German alliance, in May 1898, even Vicky tried to influence her son, something she had long given up, by making the case for religious and racial affinity: 'the *immense* importance of an alliance – between the 2 great Germanic and & Protestant nations, wh. for 50 years has been the dream of so *many* true patriots'.

High-flown fantasies always made a strong, if often short-lived appeal to the Kaiser. He was a fervent admirer of another Chamberlain, Houston Stewart, the English son-in-law of a famous promoter of Teutonism, the composer Richard Wagner. Chamberlain's *The Foundations of the Nineteenth Century*, published in 1899, became a bible for all believers in the Aryan race down to Hitler. The Kaiser thought that it was 'the greatest and most significant work that has ever been written and of such value that every word should be printed in gold'. He was able to give full vent to his racialism when the Boxer Rebellion broke out in 1900 and the German envoy in Peking was murdered. The uprising was a reaction to the Western influence in China. When sending off the German contingent in the punitive expedition mounted by the European powers against China, the Kaiser made a speech that outdid his usual level of bombast and bellicosity:

> Show yourselves Christians, happily enduring in the face of the heathens ... Anyone who falls into your hands falls to your sword! Just as the Huns under King Etzel created for themselves a thousand years ago a name which men still respect, you should give the name of German such cause to be remembered in China for a thousand years that no Chinaman ... will dare to look a German in the face.

The Kaiser was never to shake off the memory of his 'Hun' speech. The European expedition to take revenge on Chinese xenophobia did not prove to be a shining example of the solidarity of the white race. The

Germans bore the brunt of the tensions that arose, because the Kaiser had insisted that the elderly Waldersee should command the international force sent to China.

Towards the end of 1900, Queen Victoria, who had still shown remarkable stamina in carrying out her duties earlier in the year, was visibly failing. When in January 1901 it became clear that she was dying the Kaiser left the bicentenary celebrations of the Hohenzollern kingship and hurried to London, from where he went together with his Uncle Bertie to Osborne. On this occasion the Kaiser behaved impeccably, remaining in the background. Most members of the royal family would have preferred him to stay in Germany but were reconciled to his presence. Even the future Queen Mary, hardly a soft touch, wrote: 'Wilhelm has been too dear and nice and so full of feeling. We were all quite glad that he was here and dear Grandmama knew him and spoke to him.' It appears that the Queen, intermittently conscious, was pleased to see her grandson. During her last hours he kept up her pillow with his immensely strong right arm.

Victoria died on 22 January 1901. Her coffin went from the Isle of Wight to London on 1 February. Her funeral was at Windsor the following day and on 4 February she was laid to rest beside Albert in the Mausoleum she had had built at Frogmore in Windsor Great Park. The Kaiser was present throughout these obsequies and his presence was very well received by the British public and press. His prolonged absence in England was rather less welcome in Germany. In his toast before leaving on 5 February he had planned to say:

> I believe that the two Teutonic nations will, bit by bit, learn to know each other better, and that they will stand together to help in keeping the peace of the world. We ought to form an Anglo-German alliance, you to keep the seas while we would be responsible for the land; with such an alliance no mouse could stir in Europe without our permission.

Bülow cut this passage from his master's speech. The Chancellor did not believe that Germany should actively court the British. Once the German navy was large enough the British would have to seek a German alliance on German terms. That time never came.

12

Descent to Armageddon

Queen Victoria had been a focal point for the royal houses of Europe. Her presence as the revered matriarch had kept a lid on the personal incompatibilities and animosities that divided these royal families, as they divided many more ordinary ones. Now she was gone it left Edward VII, Nicholas II and William II as the major figures on the dynastic scene. Nicky was married to Bertie's niece Alicky, who was also the first cousin of Willy, Bertie's nephew. Thirteen and a half years after the Queen's death their countries were involved a war that brought about the end of the three great European imperial dynasties, Romanov, Hohenzollern and Habsburg. Monarchy ceased to be the normal form of government in Europe. The close family relationships between the leading royal houses of Europe could not prevent the war and this in itself puts their significance into perspective. It can even be argued that these relationships made the European power rivalries at times more difficult to manage than would have been the case without them.

Edward VII inherited a constitutional monarchy from his mother, but at least in domestic affairs his influence was not what hers had been. His main interests were foreign affairs and the armed forces, but quite apart from that he was not a man for desk work. The Queen's conscientious attention to her boxes, which had continued almost to her dying day, was not for him. He was never content with his own company and his large circle of friends knew it was their task never to leave him to himself. He dreaded boredom and his ceaseless immersion in society kept that danger at bay. When it reared its ugly head, there was 'an ominous drumming of his fat fingers on the table, or an automatic tap, tap, tap of one of his feet', according to his biographer, Sir Philip Magnus.

The King's influence was exerted mainly by word of mouth and he depended much upon a circle of trusted friends, who collectively may have performed for the King a service similar to that performed by Prince Albert for his mother. One of them was his private secretary, Sir Francis Knollys, later Lord Knollys. Another was Lord Esher, the *éminence grise* of Edwardian politics, whose role defies any constitutional or legal definition. Esher was a snob and a toady, and a hidden homosexual, but he played a vital part in greasing the wheels of government. Later generations owe him a debt for his work on the royal archives. Esher was intimately involved with the reorganisation of British defence arrangements, which the Boer War had shown to be woefully inadequate. One result was the establishment of the Committee of Imperial Defence, a permanent committee of the Cabinet. It was a constitutional innovation of considerable significance as well as a political factor of great importance in the run-up to the First World War. Esher preferred to stay out of the political limelight, but everybody knew he had the King's ear. Two other members of the King's inner circle held important public offices: one was Sir John, later Lord Fisher, the First Sea Lord from 1904 to 1910 and father of the Dreadnought battleships; the other was Sir Charles Hardinge, later Lord Hardinge of Penshurst, Permanent Secretary of the Foreign Office from 1906 to 1910, who accompanied the King on most of his many foreign trips. In the background was Sir Ernest Cassel, the German-Jewish financier, who converted to Catholicism. He managed the King's as well as Esher's finances. His daughter married a young man about the King's Court, Wilfred Ashley, the grandson of Lady Palmerston. The only offspring of that marriage, and heiress to Sir Ernest's great wealth, was Edwina, later Lady Louis Mountbatten. Also in the background, discreetly helping to smooth access to the monarch, was his *maîtresse en titre*, Mrs Keppel. Edward VII exerted his impact on affairs in a very different manner from his mother, but this did not necessarily reduce it. When he came to the throne the young Winston Churchill, aged twenty-six, asked his mother, who knew the new King well: 'Will it entirely revolutionise his way of life? Will he sell his horses and scatter his Jews ...? Will he become desperately serious? Will he continue to be friendly with you? Will the Keppel be appointed 1st Lady of the Bedchamber?'

The King's impact was undoubtedly most marked in foreign affairs, but what it exactly amounted to is hotly disputed. At one extreme there is the view, which became commonplace in Germany, that he was the author of Germany's encirclement. On 30 July 1914, two days before the outbreak of war, the Kaiser wrote this marginal comment, on hearing of Russia's mobilization: 'He [King Edward] is stronger after his death than I who am still alive.' The Kaiser believed that Nicholas II had played him false, but that ultimately the war was the work of his uncle. In a momentary access of realism William knew that his country was entering a war in unpropitious circumstances. He was incapable of admitting even to himself that the encirclement was largely self-inflicted and that Edward VII was not the author of the links that had sprung up between the countries that felt menaced by Germany. The most that can be said is that men like Esher and Hardinge, who had constant access to the King, largely shared the alarmist view of German ambitions that was also held by other key figures in the Foreign Office.

It may well be that the increased publicity to which royalty was exposed in the press, now accessible to an ever greater mass public, as well as the modern medium of photography, enhanced the King's image as an important policy-maker. According to Lord Northcliffe, the newspaper magnate, the space devoted to royalty quintupled after King Edward came to the throne. He spent more time on the Continent and in fashionable spas than any other monarch. One of his favourite haunts was Marienbad. It was also the place to which Campbell-Bannerman, the Liberal Prime Minister from December 1905 till his death in April 1908, went every year for his wife's health. An illustrated paper published a picture showing the King in earnest conversation with his Prime Minister in the gardens of the Kurhaus, while a ring of visitors stood at a respectful distance. The caption read 'Is it Peace or War?' When the Prime Minister's Private Secretary showed his master this picture, Campbell-Bannerman is said to have asked: 'Would you like to know what the King was saying to me?' and then said: 'He wanted to have my opinion whether halibut is better baked or boiled!' On the other hand, the King talked about something more substantial in 1908 when, again at Marienbad, he sat in full view of the public on the balcony of his hotel in deep conversation with the French Prime Minister Georges Clemenceau.

Contradicting the view of Edward VII as an important policy-maker, there is the verdict of A. J. Balfour, who was the King's Prime Minister from 1902 to 1905, made to Lord Lansdowne, the Foreign Secretary from

1900 to 1905: 'during the years which you and I were his Ministers, he never made an important suggestion of any sort on the larger questions of policy'. There were one or two episodes, which may have stuck in the minds of Balfour and Lansdowne and given them a jaundiced view of the King's activities in foreign affairs. One occurred when the King attended the funeral of his sister Vicky, the Empress Frederick, in August 1901. She had for some time been suffering very painfully from cancer of the spine, but the seriousness of her illness had been kept from her mother. Following the funeral of Empress Frederick there was to be a meeting between the Kaiser and the King, in the context of the discussions that were taking place at the time about an Anglo-German alliance. Lansdowne was not wedded to the policy of 'splendid isola-tion', which by and large had been at the core of Salisbury's conduct of foreign affairs. The King asked Lansdowne for a short note on the points which might be raised in his talk with his nephew. Bertie was in an emo-tional state after the burial of a sister to whom he had been very close. He impulsively handed the Kaiser Lansdowne's note, which he had stuffed in his pocket. It did no great harm, but the Germans tried to cause trouble shortly afterwards when the King met his wife's nephew, the Tsar, in Copenhagen. The incident of the King handing over what was intended to be a confidential briefing note has often been cited to underscore his alleged naivety as a diplomat.

The episode that may also have been in the minds of Lansdowne and Balfour was the affair of the Shah of Persia's Garter. The Shah was induced to pay a visit to Britain on the understanding, conveyed by the British Ambassador in Teheran on his own authority, that he was to be given the Order of the Garter, as his father had been by Queen Victoria. This was at a time when there was intense rivalry between Britain and Russia over Persia. The King guarded his prerogative about the award of honours jealously and had warned Lansdowne that he had no intention of giving the Garter to the Shah, an unpleasant and cor-rupt potentate, and that the Garter would not in future be conferred on non-Christians. These conflicting positions caused a tremendous eruption of ill-feeling with the Shah and his entourage and between the King and his ministers. At one point the furious King threw the box containing a Garter star without the Cross of St George, specially designed for the Shah by Messrs Garrard, out of the porthole of his cabin in the royal yacht while it was anchored in Pembroke Dock. Fortunately it fell into the yacht's pinnace and was retrieved. The Cabinet stood by Lansdowne and nearly resigned en bloc. The King was at first advised by Knollys to remain firm, but Balfour went to work on the Private Secretary. The monarch eventually, on conditions, gave way. When Balfour and Lansdowne years later reminded each other of the insignificance of the King's contribution to foreign policy, the Great War had started and made the Shah's Garter seem trivial. It may have seemed to them in retrospect that Edward VII was mainly interested in the trappings of monarchy.

Historians have tended towards the Balfour view of the King's influence on foreign policy, but more recently this verdict has been slightly modified. History, as it came to be written in the twentieth century, concentrated on large impersonal forces and on the structure of affairs, minimising the impact of accident and personality. The history of diplomacy, which once bulked large, itself became unfashionable and the part played by royal personages and their relationships almost disappeared from view. There is nowadays something of a reaction against this impersonalisation of history and biography is again widely read. No one would now claim that politics and diplomacy can be ignored in international relations. In the intricate clockwork mechanism of diplomacy the relationships between monarchs and their courts played a role that cannot be airbrushed out. This does not mean that one has to take at face value the unadorned personalisation of issues that emperors and kings themselves habitually adopted. It was inseparable from their trade.

Those who have emphasised the importance of the King's role in foreign policy have usually highlighted his contribution to the Entente Cordiale between Britain and France. Bertie had always been a Francophile and the European situation that had arisen early in the new century made him believe that the time was ripe for a better understanding between Britain and France. The two countries had nearly come to blows in September 1898, when Kitchener won a famous victory over the dervish armies at Omdurman only to learn a few days later that a French expedition had reached the upper valley of the Nile from the west. Anglo-French rivalry over the control of Egypt flared up again, but this time the French had to retreat. Four years later intelligence reached the King, partly from a dynastic source, his brother-in-law King

George of the Hellenes, that leading French politicians were ready for some kind of agreement with Britain. At the time the prospect of an Anglo-German alliance was receding as the German naval building programme quickened. The Kaiser had paid a visit to Sandringham in November 1902, but little of political significance was achieved. After William left the King remarked: 'Thank God, he's gone.' Now that he was his nephew's equal as a sovereign the King felt that the time had come for him to match the Kaiser's frequent and spectacular foreign journeys as a head of state. Paris would become the most important stop on the King's progress around Europe.

The preparations for a visit by Edward VII to Paris in 1903 were made in secrecy, with the usual channels, the Foreign Office and the British Ambassador in Paris, bypassed. A channel that was used was the Portuguese Ambassador in London, the Marquis de Soveral, and the King of Portugal, a Coburg descendant. Soveral was a member of the King's inner circle and was known as 'the blue monkey', because of his swarthy appearance. When Lansdowne heard of the proposed visit, he was at first sceptical, because he feared that the King would encounter hostility from the French public. This might well have been the case, had not the King performed so well during his stay in Paris. After the affair of the Shah's Garter, Lansdowne did not want another collision with the monarch and reluctantly gave his consent to the visit. The King was, however, accompanied in Paris not by a minister, but only by Hardinge, who was then an Under Secretary in the Foreign Office. Royal visits are rarely reported in derogatory terms, but the King clearly had to make an effort to warm the atmosphere in Paris. The temperature gradually rose from small crowds and polite applause to milling multitudes shouting 'Notre bon Edouard!' The Entente Cordiale was not made by Edward VII, but in an age when the public mood counted he helped to prepare it.

The King and his ministers were anxious that the Anglo-French rapprochement should not appear to be directed against Germany. At a banquet at the British Embassy, marking the end of his 1903 visit, Edward was seen to single out for attention the German Ambassador in Paris, Prince Radolin. The Ambassador was a close friend of Holstein and had twenty years earlier been Bismarck's eyes and ears at the Court of Vicky and her husband. In June 1904 the King paid a state visit to the Kaiser. On William's insistence it took place in Kiel rather than in

Berlin, so he could show off the new German fleet. The Kaiser telegraphed to his aunt, the Grand Duchess of Baden: 'The King's visit passed off very satisfactorily and I hope it will be a further support for peace.' The Kaiser was always keen to impress his relations, and the other German kings and princes, with his successful appearances on the world stage. The Grand Duke of Baden and his wife, once the rulers of Germany's most liberal and progressive state before unification, had adjusted to the Bismarckian Empire. Like most other German lesser princes, they had become disenchanted with the Kaiser's bombastic rhetoric and condescending behaviour towards them. As it was, King Edward had at that moment reason to make himself pleasant to the Germans and their ruler, and the King was always willing to try. Britain was suspicious again of the Russians and their policy in the Far East, which soon afterwards led to the outbreak of the Russo-Japanese War. Since 1902 Japan had been Britain's formal ally. The visit to Kiel was a damage-limitation exercise, following the Anglo-French agreement of April 1904, which became known as the Entente Cordiale.

The kaleidoscope of international diplomacy was constantly shifting. There were sometimes big, fundamental changes, like the Anglo-French Entente Cordiale, but these were surrounded by minor shifts, adjustments and counterploys. Dynastic relationships, underpinned during this pre-war decade by close family ties, were an accompaniment to the ceaseless machinations of ministers, diplomats and foreign offices. In the dynastic arena the King of England, the Tsar of Russia and the German Kaiser remained the central figures, with the Emperor of Austria bringing up the rear. On paper the Tsar had the most autocratic power, but in practice the Kaiser was more significant. He also remained the greatest irritant. In 1905 the Germans precipitated the first Moroccan crisis, probably the most serious international crisis before 1914, when the Kaiser landed at Tangiers at the end of March 1905. William had at first been reluctant to go, for he feared the diplomatic repercussions. It was also brought home to him that he might be in danger of assassination if he exposed himself in such an insecure area. The architects of the intervention were Bülow and Holstein and one of their aims was to disrupt the Anglo-French entente by demonstrating to the French that the British could do little to help them. They were also taking advantage of the fact that France's other ally, Russia, was even less

capable of acting. She had been humiliatingly defeated by Japan on land
and on sea and revolution had broken out in St Petersburg in January
1905. It therefore looked to the Germans that they were in a strong position and, if it came to war, they would have to fight on only one front.
There could be little doubt that they would be in Paris even more
quickly than they had been in 1870.

Once the Kaiser, on board the liner *Hamburg*, arrived off Tangiers, he
decided, with the impulsiveness characteristic of him, to go on shore
with a large retinue. He entirely disregarded the precise instructions
given to him by Bülow, to exercise restraint, and talked big about Germany's stake in Morocco. He returned to the liner well satisfied with his
performance and elated by having again moved to centre-stage in world
affairs. The next day, April Fool's Day, he met Prince Louis of Battenberg at Gibraltar and again talked big. The world would eventually be
divided between Teutons and Slavs, and 'as to France, we know the road
to Paris and we will get there again if needs be. They should remember
that no fleet can defend Paris'. It was entirely in character of the Kaiser
to think that such talk would go down well with a senior officer of the
Royal Navy, who was also the husband of his cousin, Princess Victoria
of Hesse-Darmstadt. When it reached King Edward, it did not go down
at all well:

> I consider that the Tangiers incident was one of the most mischievous &
> uncalled for events which H.M.G.E. [German Emperor] has ever under-
> taken. It was a gratuitous insult to 2 Countries – & the clumsy theatrical part
> of it – would make me laugh if the matter were not a serious one. It was a
> regular *case* of 'Bombastes Furioso'! I suppose G.E. will never find out as he
> will never be told how ridiculous he makes himself – in all he said to you
> there is throughout a want of sincerity.[1]

Thus the King to Prince Louis.

When this Moroccan crisis was settled at the Algeciras conference the
following year, Germany was seen to have derived no advantage from
her initiative. It merely underscored her isolation, or encirclement, as it
was seen in Berlin, and it was not King Edward's doing. The uncompli-
mentary remarks the Kaiser and his uncle, and their respective spouses,
made about each other were legion. 'He is a Satan, you can't believe what
a Satan he is', the Kaiser remarked about his uncle in 1907. 'The fat old

King', Dona called him and the Kaiser said that his wife had 'a fanatical hatred of the British majesties'. The fact that Dona disapproved of the King's relationship with Mrs Keppel did her no good with Queen Alexandra. She despised both Dona and her husband and called the Kaiser 'a mad and a conceited ass'. None of this should be taken too seriously, for King and Kaiser, their wives and families continued to meet, if not with great enthusiasm; and, face to face, relations were on a reasonably amicable level. The positive impact of dynastic ties, at its height in the heyday of the Coburg connection, had clearly gone. It was more important that some of the most influential figures in the Foreign Office were seeing Germany as the disturber of the peace in Europe. They included Sir Charles Hardinge, who was close to the King. Lord Esher took the same view, reinforced by his personal dislike of the Kaiser.

One can compare the dynastic factor in the relations between Britain and Germany with that between Austria and Britain. Catholic Habsburg and Protestant Saxe-Coburg-Gotha were on the wrong side of the religious divide and they were on the wrong side again in 1914. On the other hand, Coburg had always had close links with Vienna and the integrity of the Habsburg Empire had ranked high with Albert and Victoria. Francis Joseph and Victoria called each other 'Du' and the Prince of Wales got on well with the Austrian Emperor. They met many times both before and after the King's accession, sometimes on official visits, sometimes more informally at spas and hunting lodges. After a visit to the imperial hunting lodge at Ischl in 1905 the King wrote to Sir Ernest Cassel: 'I stayed a few hours at Ischl on my way here [Marienbad] to pay the E[mperor] a visit & found H.M. in excellent health & we had some very interesting conversations – Would to God that other Sovereigns were as sensible as he is'. This was a clear reference to the King's less sensible nephew in Berlin. On this visit the King induced the Emperor to take, for the first time in his life, a ride in an automobile. Francis Joseph was not likely to hold against the King his relationship with Mrs Keppel, in the way William and his even more prudish wife Dona did. The Austrian Emperor had his own long-standing mistress, the actress Katharina Schratt. She had been introduced to him twenty-five years earlier by the beautiful but eccentric Empress Elisabeth, perhaps with the deliberate intention of providing the lonely Emperor with a companion, while she herself preferred to roam the world. Anyway, Elisabeth had been assassinated by an anarchist in Geneva in 1898.

Count Albert Mensdorff, the descendant of Victoria's aunt Sophie who had married Count Mensdorff-Pouilly, was the Austrian Ambassador in London and was a close friend of Edward VII and later George V and a second cousin of the former. He had become so Anglicised and was so much in the royal pocket that Vienna occasionally thought he might have to be recalled. Perhaps in order to defend himself Mensdorff wrote, in 1912, to the Austrian Foreign Minister Berchtold, who was still *en poste* in the crisis of July 1914:

> One can talk more fully with the most powerful personalities in the country at a hunting weekend, at the races in Newmarket or Goodwood, during Saturday to Monday visits in the country, than one can by visiting them in their houses and offices; and one can then learn in a few days a great deal worth knowing, when one often fails to have an interesting conversation for six months. All this one only learns by experience.[2]

Edward complained that Mensdorff was idle, spent all his time at house parties and race meetings, even though 'he does not know a horse from a cow'.

In 1908 the King was again going to meet the Emperor at Ischl on his way to Marienbad, but this time Edward wanted to give the meeting a slightly more official character, with political talk and the possible presence of the then Austrian Foreign Minister, Count Aehrenthal. The King did not, however, want to go quite as far as the formality of a visit to Vienna. The context was that Britain and Russia had concluded an entente in August 1907, to some extent a counterpart to the Entente Cordiale with France. Longstanding rivalries, particularly on Persia, and also in Tibet and Afghanistan, were settled. The King did not want the understanding with Russia to be seen as anti-Austrian or even anti-German, and this was the reason for giving the meeting at Ischl a more political character. Mensdorff knew that both King and Emperor were sticklers when it came to wearing exactly the proper uniform with the proper decorations. The wearing of the appropriate outfit would give the meeting just the proper level of formality. Mensdorff wrote to his masters in Vienna:

> King Edward would on arrival like to wear the white [Austrian] field-marshal's uniform. Should his Imperial and Royal Majesty [Kaiserlich und

Königlich, the style of the Emperor of Austria and King of Hungary] be pleased to wear the English field-marshal's uniform, the King would strongly urge that it should be with the long pantaloons and not with the uncomfortable high boots.[3]

Clearly these two elderly gentlemen – the Emperor aged seventy-eight was about to celebrate the sixtieth anniversary of his accession – had to show exactly the same level of formality, but could not be expected to suffer the inconvenience of wearing heavy boots. The Ambassador also mentioned that the King was prepared to bring along Sir Charles Hardinge for talks with Count Aehrenthal. Unfortunately the political purpose of the raised level of formality at Ischl did not achieve the desired objective. Shortly afterwards Austria formally annexed Bosnia, which she had occupied since the Congress of Berlin in 1878. It had not been mentioned by the Austrian Emperor at Ischl, was a blow to Russian prestige and caused tension between Russia and Austria, in circumstances similar to those that led to the outbreak of war five years later. When Mensdorff delivered a letter from the Emperor to the King at Balmoral, in October 1908, he got a severe dressing down. Royal hobnobbing could not, however, remove the underlying power conflicts that would eventually lead to war, and the clash between Russian and Austrian interests in the Balkans was one of the most persistent of these conflicts. Fevered imaginations, like the Kaiser's, could turn it into a racial struggle between Slav and Teuton.

It was a bonus that Nicky and Alicky were not an irritant in the family circle like Willy and Dona. In the affairs of Russia, however, Nicholas II was if anything an even greater disaster than the Kaiser was on the German political scene. Bertie called him 'weak as water', and he was certainly mild-mannered and instinctively polite. Such qualities might have made him into a good constitutional monarch, and made him likeable to his British royal relations, but did not fit him to be an autocrat. Blinkered obstinacy became a substitute for strength and insight. An ideology lay ready to hand in Russia to bolster his obstinacy and inflexibility. It was the old Muscovite notion of the tsardom as a divine institution, rooted for all time in the hearts of the ordinary peasant masses. The Tsar was their little Father under the great Father. Even by the early eighteenth century this notion was beginning to be outdated. Peter the Great had by might and main tried to impose a bureaucratic autocracy on western models on the country. Both Nicholas II and his father were suspicious of this bureaucracy and felt that it came between them and the Russian people. Nicholas had, however, none of his father's strength of character or capacity for business. Able ministers like Witte or Stolypin, who were trying to modernise the country and might have saved the Romanov dynasty, found no support in him. Witte dealt ably with the aftermath of the disastrous Russo-Japanese War of 1904. He tried to work within the semi-parliamentary regime, which the Revolution of 1905 forced the Tsar to introduce. On the day of his dismissal as Prime Minister in 1906, he had had a long interview with the Tsar, at the end of which Nicholas wished him all the luck in the world and embraced him. When he got home he found a written order for his dismissal. Nicholas was too polite and too weak to bear the embarrassment of such a dismissal face to face. In his limited mind he became jealous of a powerful minister like Witte and saw him as a threat to the autocracy that it was the Tsar's mission to uphold. He deluded himself that he was maintaining this God-given autocratic rule by working diligently on very minor tasks, such as dealing with hundreds of petitions from peasants asking for permission to change their names. By filling his time with routine tasks he avoided having to deal with the broader issues of policy, the implications of which he failed to see. He could understand isolated facts, but the interconnections between them were lost on him. On paper the powers of the Tsar remained very great, but Nicholas was unable to exercise them effectively. It was a lethal combination of autocracy and weakness.

The limitations of Nicholas were made more damaging by his wife Alicky, a stronger character than her husband. She had been born in 1872. After the death of her mother in 1878, her grandmother Queen Victoria had had a large hand in her upbringing. Although she came to be hated in Russia as a German, she was in fact very English. When she became the Tsarina in 1894, almost immediately upon her arrival in the country she embraced the mystical view of the tsardom with the fervour of a convert. Her grandmother, for all her prejudices a woman of eminent common sense, warned her: 'You find yourself in a foreign country, a country which you do not know at all, where the customs, the way of thinking and the people are completely alien to you, and nevertheless it is your first duty to win their love and respect.' It did no good, for Alicky was already bitten by the bug of Russian mysticism: 'You are mistaken, my dear grandmama; Russia is not England. Here we do not need to earn the love of the people. The Russian people revere their Tsars as divine beings, from whom all charity and fortune derive.'[4] There is something bizarre about this couple, Nicky and Alicky, who wrote to each other in English, called each other 'Hubby' and 'Wifey' and who ordered furniture from Maples department store, seeking to play the role of semi-divinities in the hearts of the Russian peasantry in the early twentieth century. At the same time the Tsarina, who had taken lessons in Russian but could not speak the language fluently, earned nothing but derision from the westernised, cynical world of St Petersburg high society.

It all got much worse when Alicky, after having four daughters, at last gave birth to a male heir in 1904, the Tsarevich Alexis. He was a haemophiliac and frequently hovered on the brink of death. It was heartrending for his mother and opened the door to Rasputin. The Russian aristocracy, disorientated, sometimes guilt-ridden, often decadent, was at the time dabbling in all sorts of cults, spiritualism, occultism and other forms of the supernatural. The Russian Orthodox Church pandered to such proclivities and gave support to alleged holy men, who claimed powers of clairvoyance and healing. One such was Rasputin and he undoubtedly helped at various times to calm the Tsarevich at moments of acute crisis. The Empress clung to Rasputin, and the Emperor, perhaps against his better judgement, would allow no one to remove him. Censorship was supposed to be abolished after the Revolution of 1905, but the Tsar stopped the press from printing stories about Rasputin. In 1912 a letter from the Tsarina to Rasputin leaked out: 'I kiss your hands and lay my head upon your blessed shoulders. I feel so joyful then. Then all I want is to sleep, sleep for ever on your shoulder, in your embrace.' A sexual relationship between the holy man and the Empress is unlikely, for Alicky was very strait-laced, but Rasputin boasted constantly of his many conquests among society women. The Rasputin affair brought corruption into the highest circles and eventually hastened the downfall of the dynasty.

The Tsar's royal relations in Britain and Germany were well aware that the Tsarist monarchy, for all its outward splendour, rested on shaky foundations. It became obvious after the Revolution of 1905. In 1899 the

Kaiser wrote on a diplomatic report: 'In any case it is still very questionable which [empire] will collapse first, Habsburg or Romanov.' In January 1908, when the Kaiser was told of the preparations to celebrate the tercentenary of the Romanov dynasty in 1913, he commented 'if they are still there!!' No one could escape the conclusion that in an age of nationalism the Habsburg Empire was an anachronism, and the failures of German diplomacy before 1914 were made evident by the fact that this incipient corpse was left as their only ally. The Russian case was less clear-cut. The country was way behind Western Europe in technology, industrialisation and modernisation. Its military weakness was made clear by defeat at the hands of Japan, but it still had large reserves of manpower and natural resources. Its enormous size would always make it difficult to defeat militarily. All in all, Russia was still a great power and worth cultivating. The Germans certainly tried hard and, for all their doubts about the strength of the Russian monarchy, regarded the dynastic approach as promising. Here again the Kaiser's personality was a handicap. Neither Nicky nor Alicky, his cousin, could really bring themselves to like him. Interviews with Willy always got on Nicky's nerves, and when the Kaiser sailed away after their meeting at Reval (now Tallinn, the capital of Estonia) in 1902, the Tsar exclaimed: 'He's raving mad!' Alicky's brother, the Grand Duke Ernst Ludwig of Hesse-Darmstadt, was a German prince who could have served the Kaiser as a useful conduit to St Petersburg and London. The Grand Duke, like his sister, was, however, culturally English and the Kaiser disliked him as a liberal, a distaste that was well reciprocated.

The Kaiser's attempts to woo the Tsar away from the French alliance with arguments of monarchical solidarity reached a climax when the two Emperors met at Björkö, in the Gulf of Finland, in July 1905. It was a moment when Nicholas was easy game, for Russia had been severely weakened by defeat in the Far East, a war in which the Tsar had invested much personal prestige. The Russian monarchy was then itself gravely weakened by revolution, forcing the Tsar to make concessions, something which went against his deepest convictions. The Germans had pressed the Tsar since the previous autumn to accept a mutual assistance pact. He now seemed ready to do so. In a letter to his Chancellor, Bülow, William described in emotional terms the moment when the Tsar agreed to sign the treaty. They were on board the Tsar's yacht *Polar*

Star, and the Kaiser was looking across the water at his own yacht, the *Hohenzollern*. He saw 'the Imperial Standard on her fluttering in the morning breeze. I was just reading the words "God with us" inscribed upon its black cross when I heard the voice of the Tsar next to me 'that is quite excellent. I quite agree!' William's eyes filled 'with shining tears of joy', sweat streamed down his back, and he felt the spirit of his ancestors close at hand. It was quite a state to get into at the reactions of a cousin, whom he had in the past despised as a weakling. It was, however, an indication of how isolated Germany had become and how necessary it was for her to break the Franco-Russian alliance. Occasionally the Kaiser could see things clearly, but he would quickly lapse back into bluster. Neither the Tsar's ministers nor Bülow agreed to the treaty of Björkö. The Russians felt that it was against their national interest to jeopardise the Franco-Russian alliance. Bülow objected to the fact that in its final form the treaty was limited to Europe, when a clash between Russia and Britain in Asia was what the Germans still expected. They were overplaying their hand. On this occasion Bülow threatened to resign. The Kaiser, almost hysterically, begged him to stay, but the bond between them was loosening. William's constant gaffes were undermining his credibility with the German public and Bülow was coming under pressure to restrain his master. There were thus clear limits to what monarchs could do, even in Russia and Germany.

In Britain these limits were obvious, but Edward VII worked within them adroitly and successfully. In June 1908 royal yachts again converged in the Gulf of Finland, again at Reval. The King of England was meeting the Tsar of Russia. It was in the context of the entente negotiated between the two countries the previous autumn. The Tsarist regime was highly unpopular with the radical left wing of the large Liberal majority that dominated the House of Commons, and even more with its ally, the Labour Party. When the Duma, the parliament elected as a result of the 1905 Revolution, was dissolved in 1906, it caused outrage among progressive opinion in Britain. Twenty-nine MPs sponsored by the Labour Representation Committee had entered the House of Commons in the Liberal landslide of 1906, most of them having been given a clear run by the Liberals in an electoral pact. In a debate on the King's forthcoming journey to meet the Tsar, Keir Hardie, the founding father of the Labour Party, accused the monarch of condoning atrocities.

Among those who voted against the King's impending journey was Arthur Ponsonby (later Lord Ponsonby of Shulbrede), son of Sir Henry and brother of Sir Frederick Ponsonby, the royal private secretaries. The King, though acting on the advice of his ministers in meeting the Tsar, was thus swimming against a considerable tide of adverse opinion at home.

He was also under pressure by his friends to bring up some delicate matters with his Russian hosts. The Rothschilds wanted him to raise the subject of the persecution of the Jews; and Sir Ernest Cassel wanted him to talk about the flotation of a Russian loan. In spite of all potential pitfalls, the visit went off very well and the Russian imperial family warmed to their genial guest. Only Alicky, the Tsarina, who was shy and hated big social occasions, was seen sitting on her own in tears at one point. On a personal level the visit was compared favourably to a meeting between the Tsar and the Kaiser the previous August at Swinemünde, because, with William, Nicholas could never be sure 'what might be unexpectedly sprung upon him'. The King greatly pleased his Russian nephew by making him an Admiral of the Fleet. He was criticised for doing so without prior consultation with the First Lord of the Admiralty and thereby acting unconstitutionally. Such were the constraints laid upon a constitutional monarch. The visit caused great alarm in Berlin and an almost hysterical reaction in the German press. The myth of Edward VII as the promoter of encirclement was reinforced.

At this time the Kaiser was suffering a severe loss of credibility in his own country. In 1907 his close friend Prince Philipp zu Eulenburg was accused of homosexuality by the journalist Maximilian Harden, whose journal *Die Zukunft* (The Future) was a prominent purveyor of cultural and social criticism in Imperial Germany. Eulenburg had been highly influential in the 1890s and had had a hand in all the key appointments of that period. He himself had been Ambassador in Vienna and his cousin Botho zu Eulenburg had been Prussian Prime Minister from 1892 to 1894. His estate at Liebenberg had become the venue for meetings and hunting parties of a circle of friends, of which the Kaiser was one. It was a *Männerbund*, devoted to male bonding, and no women were present. That there was a strong homoerotic element in the Liebenberg circle cannot be doubted; and some of the members, including Eulenburg, may at some point have been active homosexuals, a criminal offence under the Prussian civil code. The Kaiser's homosexual tendencies were hidden and unacknowledged, but they may well have accounted for his bombast and excessive assertion of virility. To the members of the Liebenberg circle he was *Liebchen* (darling). The various judicial proceedings arising out of the Harden allegations finished Eulenburg and the Kaiser dropped him like a hot brick. As his mother had found out years ago, he could be impervious to common human emotions. As so often he felt hard done by, for to him the friendship with Eulenburg had been a matter of shared artistic and aesthetic interests, something which held the whole Liebenberg circle together. Bülow and Holstein had had a hand in precipitating the attack on Eulenburg and the Kaiser now became suspicious of his Chancellor.

While the Eulenburg–Harden clash was still proceeding, another imbroglio was in the making, politically more serious for the Kaiser. It was the affair of the *Daily Telegraph* interview. Following a state visit to England in November 1907, the Kaiser spent three and a half weeks privately as the guest of Colonel Stuart-Wortley at Highcliffe Castle in Hampshire. The Kaiser talked a lot, as was his habit, and portrayed himself as misunderstood in England. In fact he was pro-British, he asserted, and did not share his countrymen's Anglophobia. He had prevented a continental alliance against Britain during the Boer War. He had given advice on how to win the war and it was his plan of campaign that had defeated the Boers. The Kaiser's remarks were rolled up into what purported to be an interview and published in the *Daily Telegraph* on 28 October 1908. In Britain the interview evoked only mild interest and amusement, but in Germany it produced outrage. It was seen as an affront to the nation's dignity and another example of the monarch's never-ending gaffes. In fact William had this time taken the precaution of sending a copy of the interview to Bülow before publication. The Chancellor was on holiday and later claimed that he had never checked the manuscript but had sent it on to the German Foreign Office, assuming that it would be adequately vetted there.

Again the Kaiser felt hard done by and deeply depressed. To cheer him up another of his friends, Prince Fürstenberg, organised an entertainment, during which members of the Kaiser's entourage appeared in female dress. Count Dietrich von Hülsen-Haeseler, Chief of the Military Cabinet, cavorted in a ballet dancer's tutu. Transvestite entertainments were common in the Kaiser's circle, but this time the fifty-six-year-old Hülsen dropped dead of a heart attack. At the height of the *Daily Telegraph* crisis it seemed a singularly inappropriate way for the Kaiser to be carrying on. Bülow did little to defend his master over the interview and the Kaiser never forgave him. By the summer of 1909 Bülow was out. His successor, Bethmann Hollweg, was a man of greater substance, but he could not bring about a decisive change in either the external or internal environment of Germany. For all the doubts that had arisen about the Kaiser in even so deeply monarchical a country as Germany, the constitution devised by Bismarck still left the sovereign in a key position. In 1890 Bismarck had fallen, in the last resort because the Kaiser did not want him any more, and in 1909 the same fate overtook Bülow. It was only days before the final collapse of the monarchy in 1918 that Germany achieved a government responsible to the Reichstag, the elected parliament, rather than to the Emperor. William never quite recovered from the combined effect of the Eulenburg and *Daily Telegraph* affairs. He had, according to his lights, given his countrymen what they wanted and he was indeed very representative of them. He had provided a glittering, constantly changing spectacle. He ruled by the grace of God, but he was a thoroughly modern monarch at the same time. He now felt betrayed by those who had been closest to him and in whom he had put his trust.

The last months of Edward VII's reign were overshadowed by what was for a constitutional monarch a severe test. Lloyd George's 'People's Budget' of 1909 had precipitated a serious constitutional crash, when the House of Lords rejected it in November 1909, contrary to normal practice. The peers were not meant to tamper with money bills. The problem of what the powers of the Upper House should be, on the agenda for a long time, became acute. For the King, it was a worrying crisis, for he knew that at some point he might be required by his ministers to create enough peers to override the veto of the Upper House. The passage of the Reform Bill in 1832 was the relevant precedent. William IV had then agreed to create enough peers to enable the Bill to pass the Lords, a threat that was enough to make the existing peers give in. It was, however, an extremely delicate matter to decide at what point exactly the sovereign was obliged to give the undertaking to inflate the peerage sufficiently to enable a Bill reducing the powers of the Upper House to be passed by the Lords. The King would be asked to tempt the existing peers to commit political suicide and to do so by abusing for political purposes the Crown's position as the fount of honours. It was not a pleasant prospect for a man like King Edward who took so high a view of the dignified aspect of monarchy. When he suddenly died, on 6 May 1910, staunch monarchists, and there were many, said that he had been killed by the politicians, in particular by the Liberal politicians, Asquith and his supporters.

It was one of Edward VII's positive legacies that he had discontinued the Hanoverian tradition, carried on by Saxe-Coburg-Gotha, of quarrelling with his son and heir. Relations between him and Prince George, who had become heir to the throne on the death of the Duke of Clarence in 1892, had always been close and harmonious. George V was, however, a very different monarch from his father. He thought of himself as a simple sailor, not 'an advertising kind of fellow', as he used to put it, and in public he had none of the genial bonhomie that had made his father popular. The carrying out of public functions was a stern duty, not an occasion for currying favour with anybody. It took time for George V to win the affection of the public. He was also less of a fully paid up member of the cosmopolitan royal trade union than Edward VII. He was an execrable linguist who spoke virtually no German and whose French was atrocious. As for travel, he much preferred the Empire to the Continent of Europe.

From his early days George had got to know his royal relations. With some of them he was on friendly terms. This was certainly true of Nicholas II and his wife, both of them his first cousins, whose wedding he had attended in 1894. At the time he wrote to his grandmother, Queen Victoria: 'Nicky has been kindness itself to me, he is the same dear boy he has always been to me and talks to me quite openly on every subject.' Everybody noticed how alike the two cousins looked and they were only three years apart in age. Both of them would have made good English country gentlemen; while this was no handicap to George V as King, it was no advantage to Nicholas II as Tsar. The cousins and their families did not see each other very often, but one such occasion was when the Russian imperial family visited Cowes on a state visit in August 1909, returning the visit that Edward VII had paid to Reval in 1908. In spite of continuing opposition in Britain, not confined to the left, to a link with the Tsarist autocracy, the visit was judged to be very successful. A great naval review was laid on, which, so the King said in toasting the Tsar, was not to be seen as a symbol of war but as a means of protecting 'our coasts and our commerce' to serve the interests of peace. The naval building race between Britain and Germany was proceeding apace and the demonstration of naval power in the presence of the Tsar was meant to send a message to Berlin. In the shadow of these public events there was real friendship between the two lookalike cousins, Nicky and George, and their families.

There was with George V little of the antagonism towards the Kaiser that existed between Edward VII and his nephew. As a young man he echoed some of his mother's dislike of William and called him 'William the Fidgety', who interfered in everybody's business. But he was impressed by the way his cousin had mastered his disability and in 1900 asked him to be godfather to his third son Henry, the future Duke of Gloucester. Queen Mary was one of the few royal personages who had some admiration for the Kaiser. He was, after all, a glamorous figure who had held the world's attention for a generation.*

Since Edward VII had been so much demonised in Germany, the Kaiser was reported 'extremely relieved' when he heard of his uncle's death. He came to the funeral and behaved with restraint. He came again in 1911 for the unveiling of the Queen Victoria Memorial outside Buckingham Palace, but his cousin had made it clear when inviting him that it was to be a strictly private visit. There was inevitably some political talk and the Kaiser later claimed that the King had raised no objection when told that Germany was planning another demonstration of strength in Morocco. In July 1911 the Germans sent a gunboat to Agadir and thereby precipitated the second Moroccan crisis. Britain stood by France, and the Germans in the end gained no advantage. In general, George V was less enamoured of the French link than his father. He thought that Sir Edward Grey, the Foreign Secretary, was rather too prone to show regard to French susceptibilities. In spite of his lack of

---

* It was Queen Mary who renewed contact with the Kaiser after a break of nearly twenty years, when, in 1936, after the death of George V, he sent a letter of condolence from his Dutch exile. The Queen responded by sending him a gold box from her late husband's desk.

interest in continental affairs, the King had wanted to embark on a series of state visits to the major European capitals after his accession. He was not best pleased when Grey forced him to accept that an exchange of visits with the French President had to take priority over visits to monarchs. He would have liked to have gone to Vienna first, since Francis Joseph was the longest-serving European monarch. Albert Mensdorff, the Austrian Ambassador in London, continued to have easy access to his royal cousin, as he had done in King Edward's day. As it was, the King never got further down his list of state visits than the French Republic before the war broke out.

George V had come to the throne in the middle of a constitutional crisis, over the powers of the House of Lords, and this overshadowed all else in the early months of his reign. In order to give the new King a breathing space, the politicians agreed to seek a compromise over the future of the Upper House by holding a constitutional conference. Within a month, by July 1910, it had broken down. Behind the question of the peers there loomed the problem of Irish Home Rule. The Irish Nationalist Party, on which the Asquith government now depended for its majority, was bound to insist that a Home Rule Bill would be forced through, as soon as the Lords were no longer in a position to veto it. This made compromise between the parties almost impossible. By the end of the year George V was therefore faced again with the problem that had so disturbed his father, whether to give a so-called contingent guarantee that he would create enough peers to swamp the Upper House, should the Asquith government win a second general election within a year. Without such a guarantee the government would resign and the monarchy's impartiality might be seriously compromised. On the advice of Knollys, his Private Secretary, whose sympathies were with the Liberals, the King gave this guarantee. Knollys did not tell his master that Balfour, the Tory leader, was prepared to take office, should Asquith resign. The guarantee was to be kept secret until a re-elected government was actually confronted with a House of Lords refusing to commit suicide. George V felt this secrecy to be particularly humiliating. As it was, when in the following February Asquith made the King's guarantee public, the peers caved in. The Hedgers, those peers who were prepared to pass the Parliament Act, had it over the Ditchers, those who were prepared to die in the last ditch. The King was spared the humiliation of having to create five hundred new peers and his stewardship of constitutional monarchy seemed fully vindicated.

In 1912 there was another effort to halt the naval arms race between Germany and Britain. Haldane, the Secretary of State for War, went to Berlin for talks. He had studied at a German university and had done much to introduce some of the features of the German higher education system, particularly the technical universities, to Britain. He could therefore visit Germany without attracting the attention a visit from the Foreign Secretary, or the First Lord of the Admiralty, Winston Churchill, would have done. The visit was prepared by Sir Ernest Cassel and Albert Ballin, two so-called Court Jews, who had the ear of Edward VII and William II respectively. The way in which it was arranged can be therefore regarded as a left-over from the dynastic politics of the Edwardian era. Nothing concrete came of Haldane's visit, but at least it showed that Britain and Germany were not irrevocably set on a course for war.

The last great gathering of the royal clans before the war took place in Berlin in May 1913. The only daughter of the Kaiser, and the only one of his children to whom he was close, Princess Victoria Louise of Prussia, was marrying Duke Ernst August of Brunswick-Lüneburg. It could be seen as a reconciliation between the Hohenzollern and the Guelphs, the House of Hanover. These relations had been broken when Prussia had annexed the Kingdom of Hanover in 1866. It pleased the Kaiser enormously to bring his two cousins, the King of England and the Tsar of Russia, together under his roof. As usual, he greatly overestimated the political significance of such a meeting, but he was not alone in this. Grey, the Foreign Secretary, was chronically worried that any sign of an Anglo-German rapprochement would set the alarm bells ringing in Paris. He insisted that it should be regarded as a family gathering and hoped that the simultaneous presence of George V and Nicholas II would dispel French fears. The Kaiser, on the other hand, could scarcely bring himself to leave his two cousins alone together, for fear they might be plotting against him. German newspapers opined that such a gathering, however much it might be labelled 'family and private', could not but have political significance. The Kaiser, with his usual verbal incontinence, complained to the King's Private Secretary about the plans to send a British expeditionary force of 100,000 men to France in case of war. 'I don't care a fig for your hundred thousand', he said, 'There you are making alliances with a decadent nation like France and a semi-barbarous nation like Russia and opposing us, the true upholders of progress and liberty ...' Socially, the meeting was a great success, though it proved to be the last time that George V saw his Russian cousins. Politically, it caused no more than a ripple.

The year 1913 was a year of royal anniversaries. The Kaiser had been on the throne for twenty-five years, Francis Joseph for sixty-five years and the Romanov dynasty for three hundred years. Nicholas II had only 1/128th Russian blood, the rest being German, but he chose to stress the Muscovite heritage of his House. After celebrations of great magnificence in St Petersburg in February 1913, he and the Tsarina went in the summer on a pilgrimage to the places in the old Muscovite Russia from where the Romanovs had originated. They travelled in the sumptuous royal train, but from time to time, because there were no railway lines, they had to travel in a cavalcade of cars along dusty tracks. The local peasants looked on in awe and crossed themselves. Nicky and Alicky assured themselves that their place was secure in the hearts of the real people of Russia.

There was also a dark side to this. The same year, 1913, was also the year of the Beiliss affair, when an innocent Jew was put on trial on trumped up charges of murder. The body of a boy had been discovered in a cave near Kiev and the rumour spread that it was part of a ritual murder campaign by the Jewish population of the city. The Tsarist authorities did not instigate pogroms, but they gave them all but a free run. *The Protocols of the Elders of Zion*, an account of an alleged Jewish world conspiracy, became the staple of anti-Semitic propaganda everywhere. It was in fact a forgery by the Tsarist police. There was a section of the Russian elite and of the articulate classes determined to keep liberalism and modernity at bay. They thought that the anti-Semitism of the peasantry deserved every encouragement and was a manifestation of the healthy instincts of the real people. This was also the view of the Tsar and fitted in with his own prejudices. He and his advisers knew that the real culprits in the Kiev murder case had already been discovered by the police, yet they allowed the trial of Mendel Beiliss to go ahead. The trial ended in acquittal, but it unleashed a wave of protests among liberals even in Russia. In the west it strengthened the disgust with the Tsar and his regime. Distinguished figures such as Anatole France, Thomas Mann, H. G. Wells and Thomas Hardy signed appeals against the anti-Jewish witch hunt.

The twenty-fifth anniversary of his reign did not find the Kaiser's ebullience noticeably dented. What Bülow, who had an Italian wife, had called his 'parlatina', which could be unkindly translated as verbal diarrhoea, had landed him in many embarrassments, but with his volatile temperament his lows were always followed by highs. His oratorical infelicities had covered domestic affairs as much as foreign relations. On numerous occasions he had called for striking workers to be shot and he had famously called the German Social Democrats 'men without a fatherland' (vaterlandslose Gesellen). It was not a judicious remark in a country that had the most prestigious socialist party in Europe. In 1912 that party had become the largest in the Reichstag and won thirty-five per cent of the vote. The nervous bellicosity that characterised not only the Kaiser personally, but German foreign policy in general, was due to a considerable extent to the domestic tensions in Germany. The large Social Democratic Party was entirely excluded from playing any part in the executive government of the Reich, and members of it were barred from even lowly positions on the German railways. Recruitment to the German army was inhibited by the fact that the generals feared that it would bring in too many socialists. Against this, it was a much coveted social accolade among the aspiring middle classes to attain the status of a reserve officer and no visiting card failed to advertise the fact. It was with some justice that the Kaiser, with all his contradictions, has been described as reflecting only too accurately the problems of the society over which he presided. He harboured reactionary prejudices, about workers, trade unions, coloured races, Jews, to name but a few, but championed some of the most advanced manifestations of modernity. For instance, he helped to found the Kaiser-Wilhelm-Gesellschaft, now called the Max-Planck-Institute, an exemplary way of linking academic scientific research and its industrial application. It was an institution of this kind that Haldane wanted to serve as a model for Britain. The Kaiser had helped to raise the money for it, a lot of it from wealthy Jewish business tycoons, whom he admitted to his circle. His swiftly changing views and moods defied logic.

Imperial Germany, for all its deep divisions and culture wars, did not look like a country in decline in the decade before 1914. Imperial Russia was in an unstable state and the reforms that might have staved off an explosion had stalled. Yet the country had recovered some of its confidence after the defeat by the Japanese and the Revolution of 1905. Russian military spending was high and the Russian army seemed again formidable. Britain and her Empire clearly did not enjoy the unquestioned ascendancy that she had claimed in the days of Palmerston. Great strikes by miners and railwaymen brought the country to a virtual standstill in the years before 1914. The resistance of Ulster to the impending Home Rule Bill seemed to show that law and order were breaking down. Some commentators thought the old liberal England was dying, but when George V crowned himself Emperor of India at the Delhi Durbar of 1912 it hardly looked as if the sun was about to set on Imperial Britain. Decline and decadence sprang to mind most obviously in contemplating the Habsburg Empire, but events like the annexation of Bosnia in 1908 seemed to show that there was life in the old dog yet. At any rate it would be a long time adying. Paradoxically, Vienna was home to some of the most innovative and revolutionary men and ideas of the twentieth century, Freud, Wittgenstein, Schönberg, Climt, Schnitzler, Kraus, to name but a few. Many of them were Jewish and Vienna was a place where politicians, like the mayor of the city, Karl Lueger, made good use of anti-Semitism as a political weapon. Unbeknown to them all, a young man called Adolf Hitler walked the streets and slept in the doss houses of the city.

When the crisis arrived in July 1914 the monarchs could do little to change its course. As it was, it was only in its final days that the realisation dawned that this was the crisis that might unleash the great war expected and feared for so long. Only a year earlier a Balkan crisis had been peacefully resolved, not least by the joint efforts of Britain and Germany. In July 1914, neither the frantic telegrams exchanged between Kaiser and Tsar, nor the verbal assurances which the Kaiser thought King George had given to his brother Prince Henry of Prussia, who was on holiday in England, were of any great importance. Henry and his wife Irene, daughter of Alice of Hesse-Darmstadt, were both first cousins of George V and did not share the Kaiser's ambivalent feelings about their English connections. The declaration of war between Austria and Britain occurred on 12 August 1914, eight days after the declaration of war with Germany. In the interval Albert Mensdorff, the Austrian Ambassador, was still having tea with the King, entering Buckingham Palace by a back door. Both men hoped that peace would be maintained between their countries, but it made no difference. Mobilisation time-tables, naval dispositions and other logistic considerations were more important than monarchs in this crisis.

The course of the war did not conform to anybody's expectations. Many in Britain thought it would be over by Christmas; few expected Britain to fight a land war that would eventually require the introduction of conscription. Before the war some commentators had thought that the growing economic interdependence of the major nations would make war impossible. Against this, many working inside the military establishments, notably in the German General Staff, thought a major European war was sooner or later inevitable. This became a self-fulfilling prophecy. The Germans had for some time expected to have to fight a two-front war, against both France and Russia. For this eventuality they had a plan, the Schlieffen Plan, named after their Chief of Staff who had retired in 1905. It provided for a swift knock-out blow against France. This would then enable the German army to concentrate on the eastern front and defeat Russia. In the event, the Schlieffen Plan contributed to bringing about British entry into the war, for the plan required the violation of Belgian neutrality. It was a colossal gamble that failed. In many ways the Battle of the Marne, in September 1914, which sealed the failure of the Schlieffen Plan, was the decisive battle of the war. Thereafter it became a war of attrition, the state of technological development frustrating all attempts to return to a war of movement. In such a war of attrition the superior resources of the Allied powers was eventually bound to prevail.

The international dynastic brotherhood that loomed so large in the nineteenth century was torn apart irrevocably by the war. Not only was the Kaiser on the opposite side of his cousins, George V and Nicholas II. Many lesser members of the royal brotherhood also found themselves fighting each other. Ferdinand, the Coburg King of Bulgaria, was a German ally; Charles Edward, Duke of Coburg, became a German general of infantry. Rumania, ruled by a branch of the Hohenzollerns, joined the Allies, as did Greece, whose Queen was a sister of the Kaiser.

The list is endless. When, after the even more destructive Second World War, Winston Churchill was trying to revive the feeling of a common European identity, he said, in September 1946:

> In bygone ages, Europe was linked by many ties together: there were the Romans, there was the Empire of Charlemagne, there were the bonds of Christendom, there were aristocratic ties which were cosmopolitan, the great association of reigning houses which in the days of Queen Victoria gave something in common between countries. But all has disappeared this time.[5]

In Britain a wave of Germanophobia was unleashed in 1914. To have a German-sounding name was dangerous and it was inadvisable to have a dachshund or drink hock. When Winston Churchill was taxed with drinking wine from the Rhine, he said 'I am interning it'. The two most prominent British victims of Germanophobia were Prince Louis of Battenberg, the First Sea Lord, and Haldane, the Lord Chancellor. Prince Louis was married to the King's first cousin and, although born in Germany, had made his career in Britain and in the Royal Navy since the age of fourteen. He had done everything to put the fleet on a war footing in August 1914, yet was accused of secretly helping the enemy. He decided that it was better for the sake of the navy to resign. Jackie Fisher, now Lord Fisher, returned to the post from which he had retired four years earlier. Haldane, a ponderous and prolix Scot, had been partly educated in Germany and his conversation was interspersed with references to Goethe and Hegel. At a dinner party in 1912 he had casually remarked that 'Germany was his spiritual home'. The remark made the rounds and, in the paranoid atmosphere of 1915, forced him out of office. Yet without him there would have been no British Expeditionary Force to send to France. The King felt deeply for Prince Louis; 'there is no more loyal man in the country', he wrote in his diary. He conferred the Order of Merit on Haldane, whom his father had called 'a damned radical lawyer and a German professor'.

Whatever the King's personal feelings, the monarchy could not afford to be out of step with public sentiment when the casualty lists were daily lengthening. Since 1914 there had always been some anti-war feeling on the left, on the whole outside the political mainstream, and sometimes it was coupled with republicanism. George V did not like it when compelled to strip the Kaiser and other German members of his family, such as the Duke of Coburg, of their British honours and commands. A visible token of this process was the removal of their banners as Knights of the Garter from St George's Chapel at Windsor. Queen Alexandra, once a Danish Princess, entirely approved: 'It is but right and proper for you to have down those hateful German banners in our sacred Church', she wrote to her son.

Worse was to come. By 1917 the war was pressing hard on all classes of British society. The German had decided to unleash unrestricted submarine warfare early in 1917. It risked bringing America into the war, but the German High Command believed they could starve Britain out before the American contribution to the Allied war effort could become effective. It was a great miscalculation. The Admiralty had resisted the introduction of the convoy system, but were now forced to bring it in. The tonnage lost to the U-Boats began to decline significantly, but it was a close run thing. The arrival of Lloyd George in 10 Downing Street, in December 1916, signalled that the war would be prosecuted with total determination to final victory.

In this charged atmosphere George V decided that it was time to jettison the German family names of the royal family. It was not the bravest of decisions and it is likely that Lord Stamfordham, as Sir Arthur Bigge now was, the King's Private Secretary, had a large hand in it. His whole life was dedicated to the protection of his master and of the monarchy as an institution. He seems to have suggested the name Windsor. Battenberg became Mountbatten, and the Tecks, Queen Mary's family, returned to the name Cambridge. (Francis of Teck, the Queen's father, from a morganatic line of the House of Württemberg, had married a daughter of Queen Victoria's uncle, the Duke of Cambridge.) The Kaiser, on hearing about the change of name, was reported to have said 'I will go and see *The Merry Wives of Saxe-Coburg-Gotha*'.

The year 1917 was the climacteric of the war, a year of earth-shaking events. Perhaps the greatest was the fall of the Russian monarchy in March 1917, February by the Russian calendar, leading by November (October by the Russian calendar) to the Bolshevik seizure of power and Russia's exit from the war. It presented the Tsar's British cousin with a painful moral dilemma. George V heard the news that revolution had broken out in St Petersburg on 13 March, and two days later the British Ambassador informed him that Nicholas had been forced to abdicate.

For Russia's allies this was potentially good news, because it looked as if Russia might at last acquire a parliamentary, democratic regime that would be a more suitable ally ideologically than the Tsarist autocracy. It was thought that the Provisional Government that had come to power under the liberal Constitutional Democrat Prince Lvov would continue the war at the side of the Allies. The so-called Cadet Party, to which Lvov and other members of the Provisional Government belonged, was the moderate face of Russian liberalism. Nobody could be under any illusion that the situation in Russia was stable, but it could not be foreseen that it would swiftly slide into anarchy, to an eventual Bolshevik take-over and to a separate peace.

From the point of view of monarchical and dynastic solidarity the Tsar's forced abdication opened up a more disturbing prospect. Within days it was obvious that the Romanov dynasty and with it monarchical rule was at an end. The Provisional Government wanted to get the Tsar and his family out of Russia as quickly as possible, but there were always others who wanted him to be much more severely dealt with. By 19 March a request from the Russian Foreign Minister, Milyukov, a leading member of the Cadets, reached the Foreign Office in London, requesting asylum in England for the Tsar and his family. Lloyd George and the government decided that asylum could not be refused and stuck by this decision. The pressure to go back on it came from the Palace, from the King advised by Stamfordham. They became aware how awkward the presence of the Tsar and Tsarina would be for their British cousins and how great a threat it might be to the British monarchy.

Events during the war had greatly increased the long-standing hostility to the Tsarist regime among broad sections of the British public. In 1915 the Tsar, under pressure from his wife, but also under the continuing illusion that he still commanded unquestioning loyalty from the ordinary people and therefore from the ordinary soldiers, had taken the disastrous decision of assuming personal command of the army. The home front was left largely to the Tsarina, who was still under the spell of Rasputin. The alleged holy man exercised enormous influence on appointments, patronage and even policy. It was rumoured that he was a German spy and that through him, the Tsarina and the Tsar vital information reached Berlin. Rasputin may well have had some dubious contacts. Among those appointed by the Tsarina to ministerial posts some may have toyed with the idea of concluding a separate peace. The idea that the Tsarina was working towards a German victory was, however, no more true than it was likely that Rasputin was her lover. Even without that, her role in the last eighteen months of the Russian monarchy was disastrous and made a bad situation worse. A lot of this was known in the West and Lord Bertie, the British Ambassador in Paris, reported that there the Tsarina was regarded as a German sympathiser, 'not only a Boche by birth but in sentiment, a criminal lunatic' and the Tsar as 'a criminal from his weakness and submission to her promptings'. It was a not a flattering way for the King's Ambassador to describe the King's cousin, but then Lord Bertie had always been among those members of the foreign service suspicious of Germany. The image of the imperial couple was no better in Britain than in France, and that not only on the left. The King, with Stamfordham his willing agent, soon made sure that the Tsar and his family, wherever they went, would not be coming to Britain.

It is not an episode that enhances the reputation of George V. Lord Mountbatten, a nephew of the Tsarina, maintained to the end of his life that the refusal to give asylum to the Tsar and his family was the fault of Lloyd George, not of the King. Neither the King nor his Private Secretary ever showed any remorse about their role, even though they were deeply shocked by the murder of the Tsar and his family in July 1918. In March 1917 they may have genuinely failed to recognise how great the danger to the imperial family was and they could not have foreseen the triumph of the Bolsheviks. Among those murdered in July 1918 was another cousin of the King, Ella, second daughter of Alice of Hesse-Darmstadt and widow of the Grand Duke Sergei. After the assassination of her husband in the Revolution of 1905 she had become a nun and had founded the only nursing order in the Russian Orthodox Church. Along with other members of the Romanov family she was thrown still alive into a mineshaft. She was said to have implored her sister, the Tsarina, in the autumn of 1916, to send Rasputin away, but her plea had fallen on deaf ears.

It was fortunate for George V that he did not have to face a similar situation over the Kaiser. William was at his headquarters at Spa, in Belgium, as revolution spread like wildfire across Germany in the early days of November 1918. The vast majority of Germans felt by this time that the sooner the Kaiser went the better. They thought that his departure was their only chance of securing a tolerable peace. The Kaiser deluded himself that the army was still loyal to him. A group of younger officers at Spa felt that some spectacular gesture, such as leading an attack from the trenches or even finding death in such an attack, might at least save the dynasty. Such a plan was never actually put to William, who was, however, not lacking in personal courage. When his consent to an announcement of his abdication had at last been wrung from him on 9 November 1918, it had already been pre-empted by the proclamation of a republic in Berlin. William had toyed with plans of putting himself at the head of his army and marching back into the Fatherland to snuff out the revolution. A gathering of generals was hastily assembled at Spa and asked if such a plan was feasible. Almost all of them declared that their troops would march home as a disciplined body, but not in order to restore the Kaiser. The game was up and the only option left was to take the short train ride into neutral Holland early next morning. Even this could not be completed, for Liège was already in the hands of revolutionaries. The final leg of the journey to the Dutch border was made by car. The Kaiser is reported to have said 'I am so ashamed' (Ich schäme mich so). When he finally arrived at Amerongen, at the estate of Count Bentinck, who had agreed to give him shelter, he asked for 'a cup of real good English tea'. The Dutch Government refused to hand him over for trial as a war criminal and he lived until his death in 1941 at a small castle at Doorn, near Amerongen. In his exile he learned little and forgot nothing. He still blamed everybody but himself for his downfall. His private correspondence is studded with calls for the extermination of socialists and Bolsheviks and even for the gassing of Jews.

After the arrival of Hitler in power the Kaiser hoped for a restoration of the monarchy. These hopes were finally dashed when Hitler made himself Head of State in August 1934. In 1915 the Hohenzollern had celebrated the five hundredth anniversary of their arrival in the March of Brandenburg as Margraves. Their ancestral castle was much further south, near Lake Constance and near what is now the Swiss-German border. In the sixteenth and seventeenth centuries they steadily climbed up the ladder of dynastic importance, acquiring real significance as a European power in the eighteenth century, in the reign of Frederick the Great. They had survived their quincentenary by only three years.

The Hohenzollerns ended with something of a bang, the Habsburgs with more of a whimper. The Habsburgs had shaped the fate of Europe for the better part of a thousand years and Francis Joseph had been head of the House for longer than anybody. His reign of sixty-eight years, which began in 1848, was even longer than Queen Victoria's. When he died in November 1916 at the age of eighty-six, the obsequies were heavy with doomladen symbolism. His successor was his great-nephew Charles, aged twenty-nine. Francis Joseph's only son Rudolf had died by his own hand at Mayerling in 1889; the next in line of succession, Franz Ferdinand, had been assassinated at Sarajevo in 1914. Franz Ferdinand's sons were excluded from the succession because his marriage to Sophie, Countess Chotek, who died with him at Sarajevo, was morganatic. So Charles, son of another of the Emperor's nephews, became the heir and, as it turned out, the last reigning Habsburg. Suicides, assassinations, unsuitable marriages were the private disasters that punctuated Francis Joseph's life. They accompanied the many public disasters that marked his reign, such as the defeats of 1859 and 1866. A united Italy and a united Germany arose from these defeats, ending centuries of Habsburg domination. The proud public buildings that sprang up on the boulevards of Vienna in the nineteenth century were designed to contradict a pervasive feeling of decline. Francis Joseph's longevity also served as a counter to *fin-de-siècle* sentiment. It promoted a sense of permanence, and, in retrospect, a nostalgia that outlasted the Emperor and his empire.

The legacy which Francis Joseph left to the young Emperor Charles was unenviable. The Austro-Hungarian monarchy was tied hand and foot to a much stronger ally, Imperial Germany. Even at this late stage there were still military victories to be had from this alliance. The most obvious was the collapse of Russia, sealed by the Treaty of Brest-Litovsk in March 1918. It brought some benefits for the Austrians, for example increased grain supplies from the Ukraine, when the population of big cities like Vienna was on the verge of starvation. A few months earlier, in late October 1917, the Austrians had won a great victory against the Italians in north-eastern Venetia, which brought their troops to within striking distance of Venice. This victory could not have been achieved without the help of a German army, especially despatched to help the Austrians. Nevertheless it required no great perspicacity on the part of the young Emperor to see that he must seek an early peace, even if this meant ending the German alliance. In 1917 he engaged in secret negotiations with France through the Bourbon relations of his wife, the Empress Zita, a Princess of Bourbon-Parma before her marriage. These negotiations got nowhere and only increased the German distrust of their Austrian ally when they became known. There were other initiatives through which the last Habsburg ruler tried to stave off the end of his empire. They consisted chiefly in offering greater autonomy to the component nationalities of the dual monarchy, including the Czechs, the Croats and the Rumanians. Even these limited initiatives were resisted by the two major nationalities of the empire, the Germans and the Hungarians. It was all too little and too late. By the autumn of 1918 the Austro-Hungarian armies were dissolving, with a lot of the troops of Czech or Croatian origin mutinying or simply going home. Even the Hungarians and Austrians were giving up.

The collapse of the three continental empires damaged the idea of monarchical rule beyond repair. The British constitutional monarchy, the most conspicuous survivor, was a monarchy in which the King reigned but did not rule. Nicholas II and William II were men who, at the beginning of the twentieth century, wielded a great deal of political power and did so by the accident of birth. Both of them, in their different ways, were singularly unsuited to the task to which providence had called them. The case of the Habsburg Empire was slightly different. It was a survivor from an age when dynasties could make empires, by inheritance and judicious marriages. When by the time of the French Revolution, territories ceased to be regarded as the patrimony of their rulers and the inhabitants were citizens rather than subjects, the Habsburg Empire became an anachronism. Historical anachronisms can sometimes survive longer than rational analysis would suggest. During the nineteenth century even the most powerful monarchies were gradually subordinated to the requirements of nationhood. The great exception was the Habsburg Empire. The Hohenzollern monarchy, an agglomeration of territories similar to the Habsburg domains, retained its power by hitching the forces of German nationalism to its wagon.

When Albert and Victoria married their eldest daughter to the Prussian Crown Prince, they no longer expected an agglomeration of territories. They hoped, however, that dynasties were still powerful enough to steer the course of events into channels they approved of. Their own marriage had been the greatest achievement of the marriage policy of the small Duchy of Saxe-Coburg-Saalfeld, from 1826 Saxe-Coburg-Gotha. The object of this marriage policy had not been to create a powerful territorial conglomerate but to acquire wealth, status and influence. The long life of Queen Victoria, and her exceptional status, as both Queen of England, a superpower of the period, and matriarch of European royal houses, was the vindication of that policy. On the other hand, a central pillar of the marriage strategy, the union between Vicky, Victoria and Albert's eldest daughter, and the Crown Prince of Prussia, ended in tragedy. No one bore a greater personal responsibility for this than Bismarck. After Queen Victoria's death her descendants became mired in conflicts and the outbreak of war in 1914 severed most of the dynastic links. The collapse of the German Empire in 1918 ended monarchical rule in all the twenty-two German territories where it existed. Ruling families, like the Wittelsbachs of Bavaria, that had been there since the early middle ages, lost their thrones, as it turned out beyond recall.

The eight small Thuringian principalities, of which Saxe-Coburg-Gotha was one, were amalgamated into the Land Thuringia in 1920. Coburg itself, the southern part of the duchy, was absorbed into Bavaria. It was in Munich, the capital of Bavaria, that the Nazi movement had its origin. It began to make waves when an ex-soldier with an exceptional rabble-rousing talent, Adolf Hitler, joined it. The Nazi Party was one of many small groups of the extreme right battening on the disturbed state of Germany after the defeat of 1918. Munich had witnessed an attempt by the extreme left to establish a Communist regime in 1919, which was suppressed with great brutality. Normally the southern part of Bavaria, with a majority of the population Catholic and much of it still employed in agriculture, was a very conservative area. The conservative-Catholic governments that ruled Bavaria after the suppression of the Munich Soviet allowed considerable latitude to extreme groups of the right, such as the Nazis, as a reinsurance policy against further risings from the left. The real stronghold of right-wing extremism was the northern part of the country, Franconia, which only became part of Bavaria in the Napoleonic period and where the majority of the population was Protestant. This is where the notorious Jew-baiter Julius

Streicher had his fief. When he threw in his lot with the Munich-based Hitler, the Führer owed him a debt of gratitude that he was still repaying during the Third Reich. Streicher retained his position as Gauleiter of Franconia when even many loyal Nazis found his antics difficult to stomach. In more normal societies he would have been behind bars.

Coburg was the scene of an early violent rally of Nazi thugs in 1921 and it was the first municipality with a Nazi majority in 1929. Many nationalist and conservative Germans, in denial about the defeat of 1918, were attracted by the apparent virility of Hitler's movement, its virulent nationalism and militant anti-Bolshevism. Among them was the Duke of Coburg, Charles Edward, the grandson of Queen Victoria. Once upon a time he had been Charlie Albany, who had left Eton at the behest of his grandmother in 1899 to become the acknowledged heir to the duchy. In 1918 he was, like all the other German rulers, forced to abdicate; and in 1919 George V stripped him, along with others, of his title as a Prince of Great Britain. In the immediate postwar period Charles Edward became a member of the Bavarian *Einwohnerwehr* (citizen guards) and the Brigade Ehrhardt. These were organisations that inhabited the same political spectrum as the *Freikorps*, extreme right-wing paramilitaries fighting the endemic civil war against the Left in the early days of the Weimar Republic. Among their members were the assassins of leading statesmen of the Republic, including Mathias Erzberger, the Finance Minister, and Walther Rathenau, the Jewish Foreign Minister. Many Freikorps members became Nazis and stormtroopers. The Duke of Coburg then became a leading member of the Stahlhelm, the veterans' organisation linked to the German Nationalist-Conservative Party (*Deutschnationale*) and also a home for many former Freikorps members during the calmer middle years of the Republic.

Charles Edward, in his entry in the German *Who's Who* of 1935, when he was anxious to assert his Nazi credentials, claims to have been reprimanded by the Stahlhelm leadership in 1932 for his open support of Hitler. In 1933 the Nazi government, although to begin with a coalition of Nazis and Conservatives, dissolved the Stahlhelm and most its members were absorbed into the hugely expanded S.A., the stormtroopers. Charles Edward became an S.A. Gruppenführer, roughly equivalent to a major-general, and was on the staff of the Chief of Staff of the S.A.,

Ernst Röhm, then the second man in the Reich after Hitler. The Duke of Coburg was not alone among members of former German ruling dynasties in holding senior positions among the stormtroopers. Prince August Wilhelm, known as Auwi, a son of the Kaiser, had been an S.A. Obergruppenführer even before 1933. Duke Charles Edward was also Reich Commissioner for Automobile Affairs and President of the German Red Cross. He must have kept well out of the way when, on Hitler's orders, Röhm and most of the top S.A. leaders, as well as sundry others, were murdered in the Night of the Long Knives, 30 June 1934. Charles Edward continued to hold honorific posts in the Third Reich, mostly connected with with the NSKK (National Socialist Automobile Corps) and the German Red Cross. The Nazis tried to exploit his links with the British royal family, in particular with the Prince of Wales, later the Duke of Windsor, who was regarded as sympathetic to the Third Reich. Duke Charles Edward was President of the Anglo-German Fellowship, an organisation that supported friendship with Hitler's Germany and the policy of appeasement. Unlike some other members of the German aristocracy, he took no part in the plotting against Hitler later in the war and never regretted his support for the Führer and his regime. At the end of the war he was interned and a denazification tribunal imposed a fine on him. He died in 1954. It was a sad end to the Coburg connection.

Notes

Notes to Chapter 1: Victoria

1. Christopher Hibbert, *Queen Victoria: A Personal History* (2000), p. 6.
2. Christopher Hibbert, ed., *Queen Victoria in her Letters and Journals* (1984), p. 10, quoting Thomas Creevey.
3. Lynne Vallone, *Becoming Victoria* (2001), p. 10.
4. Hibbert, *Queen Victoria in her Letters and Journals*, p. 11.
5. *The Greville Memoirs*, ed. L. Strachey and R. Fulford (1938), iii, pp. 308–11.
6. *Blackwood's Magazine*, 43 (1838), p. 513, quoted in John Plunkett, *Queen Victoria: First Media Monarch* (2003), p. 20.
7. David Cecil, *Lord M.* (1954), p. 328.
8. Elizabeth Longford, *Victoria R.I.* (1964), p. 112.

Notes to Chapter 2: Coburg

1. Hans-Joachim Netzer, *Albert von Sachsen-Coburg-Gotha: Ein deutscher Prinz in England* (1988), p. 45 (translated).
2. Ibid., p. 48.
3. Hans Patze and Walter Schlesinger, *Geschichte Thüringens* (Cologne, 1974–84), v, p. 705 (translated).

Notes to Chapter 3: Albert

1. Hans-Joachim Netzer, *Albert von Sachsen-Coburg-Gotha:Ein deutscher Prinz in England* (1988), p. 59.
2. *The Greville Memoirs*, ed. L. Strachey and R. Fulford (1938), iii, May 1838.
3. Stanley Weintraub, *Albert: Uncrowned King* (1997), p. 80.

4. Netzer, *Albert von Sachsen-Coburg-Gotha*, p. 149.
5. Weintraub, *Albert: Uncrowned King*, p. 88.
6. Netzer, *Albert von Sachsen-Coburg-Gotha*, pp. 155–56.
7. J. Plunkett, *Queen Victoria: First Media Monarch* (2003), p. 33, quoting from HonBle***, *The German Bridegroom: A Satire* (1840), p. 13–14.
8. Stanley Weintraub, *Victoria* (1987), p. 133, quoting *The German Bridegroom*.
9. *The Greville Memoirs*, ed. Strachey and Fulford, iv, p. 323, December 1845.
10. Hector Bolitho, *The Prince Consort and his Brother* (1933), p. 29.

Notes to Chapter 4: Queen and Consort

1. *The Greville Memoirs*, ed. L. Strachey and R. Fulford (1938), ii, p. 39.
2. Theodore Martin, *Life of H.R.H. the Prince Consort* (1875), ii, p. 547.
3. Christopher Hibbert, *Queen Victoria* (2000), p. 167.
4. E. Longford, *Victoria R.I.* (1964), p. 170.
5. S. Weintraub, *Albert: Uncrowned King* (1997), p. 96.
6. Hans-Joachim Netzer, *Albert von Sachsen-Coburg-Gotha* (1988), pp. 192–93.
7. H. Bolitho, *The Prince Consort and his Brother* (1933), p. 31.
8. S. Weintraub, *Victoria*, p. 143.
9. Robert Blake, *Disraeli* (1966), p. 233.

Notes to Chapter 5: Controversy and Conflict

1. Jasper Ridley, *Lord Palmerston* (1970), p. 309.
2. Brian Connell, *Regina v. Palmerston: The Correspondence between Queen Victoria and her Foreign and Prime Minister* (1962), p. 51.
3. Theodore Martin, *Life of H.R.H. the Prince Consort* (1875), i, p. 414.
4. Connell, *Regina v. Palmerston*, p. 65.
5. Palmerston Papers, University of Southampton, RE/H/25, January 1848
6. Günther Heydemann, *Konstitution gegen Revolution: Die britische Deutschland-und Italienpolitik, 1815–1848* (Göttingen, 1995) p. 295.
7. Johannes Paulmann, *Pomp und Politik: Monarchenbegegnungen in Europa zwischen Ancien Régime und Erstem Weltkrieg* (2000), pp. 277–78.
8. Martin, *Life of the Prince Consort*, i, p. 407.

9. Ibid., pp. 450–57.

10. Palmerston Papers, RE/H/25, memorandum of 28 March 1848.

11. Martin, *Life of the Prince Consort*, ii, pp. 314–15.

12. Connell, *Regina v. Palmerston*, p. 119.

13. Ibid., pp. 120–21.

14. Ibid., p. 130.

Notes to Chapter 6: Triumph and Calumny

1. *Disraeli, Derby and the Conservative Party: The Political Journals of Lord Stanley, 1849–69* (1978), ed. J. R. Vincent, p. 90.

2. Christopher Hibbert, *Queen Victoria* (2000), p. 231.

3. *Disraeli, Derby and the Conservative Party*, p. 97.

4. Ibid., p. 111.

5. Richard Williams, *The Contentious Crown: Public Discussion of the British Monarchy in the Reign of Queen Victoria* (1997), p. 101.

6. Theodore Martin, *Life of the Prince Consort* (1875), ii, pp. 545–47.

7. Ibid., iii, p. 121.

8. R. Blake, *Disraeli* (1966), p. 363.

9. *Queen Victoria in her Letters and Journals*, ed. Christopher Hibbert, p. 131.

10. J. Paulmann, *Pomp und Politik* (2000), p. 306.

11. E. Feuchtwanger, *Bismarck* (2002), p. 57.

Notes to Chapter 7: The Prussian Marriage

1. H. Pakula, *An Uncommon Woman* (1996), p. 113.

2. Theodore Martin, *Life of the Prince Consort* (1875), iv, p. 324.

3. B. Connell, *Regina v. Palmerston: The Correspondence between Queen Victoria and her Foreign and Prime Minister* (1962), p. 264.

4. S. Weintraub, *Albert: Uncrowned King* (1997), p. 353.

5. *Queen Victoria in her Letters and Journals*, ed. Christopher Hibbert, p. 115.

Notes to Chapter 8: The Widowed Queen

1. *Disraeli, Derby and the Conservative Party: The Political Journals of Lord Stanley, 1849–69*, ed. J. R. Vincent (1978), p. 180.

2. E. Feuchtwanger, *Disraeli* (2000), p. 127.

3. *Letters of Queen Victoria*, ed. G. E. Buckle (1926), 2nd series, i, p. 117.

4. *Queen Victoria in her Letters and Journals*, ed. Christopher Hibbert (1984), p. 166.
5. H. Pakula, *An Uncommon Woman* (1996), p. 179.
6. Ibid., p. 168.
7. E. Feuchtwanger, *Bismarck* (2002), p. 75.
8. *Letters of Queen Victoria*, ed. Buckle, 2nd series, i, p. 93.
9. B. Connell, *Regina v. Palmerston: The Correspondence between Queen Victoria and her Foreign and Prime Minister* (1962), p. 341.
10. *Queen Victoria in her Letters and Journals*, ed. Hibbert, p. 181.
11. Pakula, *An Uncommon Woman*, p. 221.
12. *Queen Victoria in her Letters and Journals*, ed. Hibbert, p. 192.
13. Ibid., pp. 183 and 191.
14. E. Feuchtwanger, *Gladstone* (1989), p. 119.
15. Pakula, *An Uncommon Woman*, p. 241.

Notes to Chapter 9: The Matriarch of Monarchs

1. E. Feuchtwanger, *Disraeli* (2002), p. 145.
2. R. Blake, *Disraeli* (1966), pp. 490–91.
3. H. Pakula, *An Uncommon Woman* (1996), p. 293.
4. Philip Magnus, *Gladstone: A Biography* (1954), p. 212.
5. Feuchtwanger, *Disraeli*, pp. 178–79.
6. *Disraeli, Derby and the Conservative Party: The Political Journals of Lord Stanley, 1849–69*, ed. J. R. Vincent (1978), p. 183.
7. S. Weintraub, *Victoria* (1987), p. 445.

Notes to Chapter 10: Bertie and the Kaiser

1. T. A. Kohut, *Wilhelm II and the Germans: A Study in Leadership* (1991), p. 37.
2. Lamar Cecil, *Wilhelm II: Prince and Emperor* (1989), pp. 72–73.
3. E. Longford, *Victoria R.I.* (1964), p. 550.
4. Andrew Roberts, *Salisbury: Victorian Titan* (1999), p. 316.
5. *Queen Victoria in her Letters and Journals*, ed Christopher Hibbert (1984), p. 303.
6. *Beloved & Darling Child: Last Letters between Queen Victoria and her Eldest Daughter, 1886–1901*, ed. A. Ramm (1990), p. 47.
7. H. Pakula, *An Uncommon Woman* (1996), p. 442.
8. Ibid., p. 470.
9. L. Gall, *Bismarck. Der weiße Revolutionär* (1980), p. 687.

10. *Beloved & Darling Child*, ed. Ramm, p. 36.

11. Pakula, *An Uncommon Woman*, p. 516.

12. *Beloved & Darling Child*, ed. Ramm, p. 92.

13. J. Paulmann, *Pomp und Politik* (2000), p. 243.

Notes to Chapter 11: The End of the Victorian Era

1. E. Longford, *Victoria R.I.* (1964), p. 518.

2. R. Williams, *The Contentious Crown* (1997), p. 140.

3. Christopher Hibbert, *Queen Victoria* (2000), p. 448.

4. *Beloved & Darling Child: Last Letters between Queen Victoria and her Eldest Daughter, 1886–1901*, ed. A. Ramm (1990), p. 136.

5. H. Pakula, *An Uncommon Woman* (1997), p. 557.

6. *Queen Victoria in her Letters and Journals*, ed. Christopher Hibbert (1984), p. 329.

7. *Beloved & Darling Child*, ed. Ramm, p. 195.

8. Philip Magnus, *Edward VII* (1964), p. 202.

9. G. A. Craig, *Germany, 1866–1945* (1978), pp. 273–74.

10. *Beloved & Darling Child*, ed Ramm, p. 215.

11. J. Röhl and N. Sombart, *Kaiser Wilhelm II: New Interpretations* (1982), p. 39.

12. Andrew Roberts, *Salisbury: Victorian Titan* (1999), p. 720.

Notes to Chapter 12: Descent to Armageddon

1. R. R. Mclean, *Royalty and Diplomacy in Europe, 1890–1914* (2001), pp. 114–15.

2. J. Paulmann, *Pomp und Politik* (2000), p. 128.

3. Ibid., p. 184.

4. Orlando Figes, *A People's Tragedy: The Russian Revolution, 1891–1924* (1990), passim.

5. Speech in Zürich, 19 September 1946.

Bibliographical Note

Royalty leaves more of a trace in history than ordinary mortals and much of the material left by them finds its way into print. Moreover, the Victorians put pen to paper far more frequently than subsequent generations, with their telephones and typewriters, not to mention computers. None more so than the Queen herself, who is calculated to have written about 2500 words every day of her adult life. Had she been a writer or novelist, her complete works would run to 700 volumes. On the other hand, previous generations had far stricter ideas about what should be revealed publicly, even to posterity, and were liable to destroy correspondence and diaries which dealt with aspects of their lives that should remain forever hidden. Thus Queen Victoria's youngest child, Princess Beatrice, selectively transcribed and even altered sections of her mother's journals and then burnt them. Edward VII had massive quantities of his mother's papers and correspondence destroyed, and the process of destruction continued under George V. The Muse Clio, however, often outwits those bent on frustrating her and copies survive of what overzealous descendants had intended for the flames. As for Prince Albert, he was an avid writer of memoranda, for he needed to clarify his thoughts by committing them to paper. He was also a most methodical keeper of his own archives. Biographers and historians therefore have sources in plenty from which to construct their works. Nine authorised volumes of *The Letters of Queen Victoria: A Selection from Her Majesty's Correspondence* were published by John Murray between 1907 and 1932, in three series of three volumes, the first edited by A. C. Benson and Viscount Esher, the second and third by G. E. Buckle. A selection of the correspondence between the Queen and her eldest daughter Vicky, from her marriage in 1858 to the death of the Queen, has been published in six volumes, the first five edited by Roger Fulford (1964–76), the last by Agatha Ramm (1990). A selection of these letters had already been published by Sir Frederick Ponsonby in 1928. When he was Assistant Private Secretary to King Edward he had spirited them away from

Friedrichshof, the Dowager Empress Frederick's castle at Kronberg, at the request of the Empress as she lay dying, so that her son the Kaiser could not get his hands on them. Much of the correspondence between the Queen and her husband and Lord Palmerston is to be found in Brian Connell, *Regina v. Palmerston: The Correspondence between Queen Victoria and her Foreign and Prime Minister, 1837–1865* (1962). Also useful is an edition of the Queen's letters and journals compiled by Christopher Hibbert, *Queen Victoria in her Letters and Journals* (1984).

Biographies are another rich mine of printed sources. Among the many biographies of the Queen, those by Elizabeth Longford, *Victoria R.I.* (1964), Stanley Weintraub, *Victoria* (1987), Christopher Hibbert, *Queen Victoria: A Personal History* (2000), and Walter L. Arnstein, *Queen Victoria* (2003) deserve particular mention. The early years of Victoria are described in *Becoming Victoria* by Lynne Vallone (2001) and in Monica Charlot, *Victoria: The Young Queen* (1991). For Prince Albert, the five-volume biography commissioned by the Queen from Sir Theodore Martin (1875–80) is still useful for the documentation it reproduces. Modern biographies include Roger Fulford, *The Prince Consort* (1949), Robert Rhodes James, *Albert, Prince Consort* (1983), Stanley Weintraub, *Albert: Uncrowned King* (1997) and, in German, Hans-Joachim Netzer, *Albert von Sachsen-Coburg-Gotha: Ein deutscher Prinz in England* (1988). Hermione Hobhouse, *Prince Albert, his Life and Work* (1983), has interesting illustrations. Among the numerous biographies of the Queen's ministers, the books on Melbourne by Lord David Cecil, *The Young Melbourne* (1939), and *Lord M.* (1954), are pieces of literature in themselves. More academic biographies are by Philip Ziegler (1976) and L. G. Mitchell (1997). Norman Gash's standard biography of Peel is available in a one-volume version (1972). There are biographies of Palmerston by Jasper Ridley (1970) and James Chambers (2004). For the Queen's later Prime Ministers, there are the standard multi–volume biographies rich in documentation, *Disraeli*, by Monypenny and Buckle (1910–20), *Gladstone*, by John Morley (1903) and *Salisbury*, by Lady Gwendolen Cecil (1921–32). There are more accessible recent biographies of these statesmen: Robert Blake, *Disraeli* (1966), and more succinctly, Paul Smith, *Disraeli* (1996) and Edgar Feuchtwanger, *Disraeli* (2000); Colin Matthew, *Gladstone, 1809–1874* (1982), and *1874–1898* (1995), and Richard Shannon, also in two volumes, *Gladstone: Peel's Inheritor, 1809–1865* (1982) and *Gladstone: Heroic Minister, 1865–1898* (1999), and, in one volume, Edgar Feuchtwanger, *Gladstone* (2nd edn,

1989) and Roy Jenkins, *Gladstone* (1995); for Salisbury, Andrew Roberts, *Salisbury: Victorian Titan* (1999). Roy Jenkins also wrote a biography of Sir Charles Dilke (1958), whose flirtation with republicanism is mentioned in these pages.

The lives of the Queen's two successors are dealt with by Sir Sidney Lee in his two-volume biography of Edward VII (1925–27) and by Sir Philip Magnus in one volume (1964). Simon Heffer's *Power and Place: The Political Consequences of Edward VII* (1998) focuses on the King's political influence. For George V there are the biographies by Sir Harold Nicolson (1952) and Kenneth Rose (1983). Hannah Pakula's life of Vicky, the Princess Royal and later Empress Frederick, *An Uncommon Woman* (New York, 1995; London, 1996) draws liberally on the archives originally preserved at Kronberg. There is a large literature of memoirs and diaries from men and women in and about the Court. Many quotations in these pages are taken from *The Greville Memoirs, 1814–1860*, edited in eight volumes by Lytton Strachey and Roger Fulford (1938), some from *Disraeli, Derby and the Conservative Party: The Political Journals of Lord Stanley, 1849–69*, edited by J. R. Vincent (1978). For the Queen's later years the reminiscences of Sir Henry and Sir Frederick Ponsonby are particularly valuable: Arthur Ponsonby, *Henry Ponsonby: Queen Victoria's Private Secretary: His Life and Letters* (1942); Sir Frederick Ponsonby, *Recollections of Three Reigns* (1951); also the letters of Lady Augusta Stanley, *Letters of Lady Augusta Stanley: A Young Lady at Court, 1849–1863* (1927) and *Later Letters of Lady Augusta Stanley, 1864–76* (1929), both edited by the Dean of Windsor and Hector Bolitho.

Kaiser William (or Wilhelm) II, the Queen's grandson, who figures largely in these pages, is the subject of an extensive literature. John C. G. Röhl is the author of the most detailed and recent analyses of this controversial personality. His works include the first two volumes of a large-scale biography, *Young Wilhelm: The Kaiser's Early Life, 1859–1888* (1998), and *The Kaiser's Personal Monarchy, 1888–1900* (2004); also *The Kaiser and his Court* (1994), and a collection of essays edited with Nicolaus Sombart, *Kaiser Wilhelm II: New Interpretations* (1982). Among the contributors to this volume are Isabel V. Hull, author of *The Entourage of Kaiser Wilhelm II, 1888–1918* (1982), and Thomas A. Kohut, author of *Wilhelm II and the Germans: A Study in Leadership* (1991), a politico-psychological analysis. There is a two-volume biography of the Kaiser, *Wilhelm II: Prince and Emperor, 1859–1900*, and *Wilhelm II: Emperor and Exile, 1900–1941*, by Lamar Cecil (1989–96); in one volume,

Giles MacDonogh, *The Last Kaiser: The Life of Wilhelm II* (2003), and, more succinctly, Christopher Clark, *Kaiser Wilhelm* (2000). Paul Kennedy, *The Rise of the Anglo-German Antagonism 1860–1914* (1980) has a chapter on dynastic politics. The reactions in the British press to the Kaiser's many visits to England are extensively illustrated in Lothar Reinermann, *Der Kaiser in England* (2001). For those interested in the Prussian and German background, David E. Barclay, *Frederick William IV and the Prussian Monarchy, 1840–1861* (1995), Lothar Gall, *Bismarck: The White Revolutionary*, 2 vols (1986) and, more succinctly, Edgar Feuchtwanger, *Bismarck* (2002), will serve as an introduction. For the Russian background in the reign of Nicholas II, Orlando Figes, *A People's Tragedy: The Russian Revolution, 1891–1924* (1996), Richard Pipes, *The Russian Revolution, 1899–1919* (1990), Robert K. Massie, *The Romanovs: The Final Chapter* (1995), and Dominic Lieven, *Nicholas II: Emperor of All the Russias* (1993), can be recommended. There is information about the links between British and Russian royalty in David Duff, *Hessian Tapestry: The Hesse Family and British Royalty* (1967).

Among the vast literature on British politics in the century covered by this book, some recent titles on the position of the monarchy deserve mention, among them David Cannadine, 'The Context, Performance and Meaning of Ritual: The British Monarchy and the "Invention of Tradition", *c*. 1820–1977', in Eric Hobsbawm and Terence Ranger (eds), *The Invention of Tradition* (1983); *Bagehot: The English Constitution*, edited by Paul Smith (2001); Richard Williams, *The Contentious Crown: Public Discussion of the British Monarchy in the Reign of Queen Victoria* (1997); Antony Taylor, *'Down with the Crown': British Anti-Monarchism and Debates about Royalty since 1790* (1999); Margaret Homans and Adrienne Munich, ed., *Remaking Queen Victoria* (1997); and John Plunkett, *Queen Victoria: First Media Monarch* (2003). Among the equally vast literature on the diplomatic history of the long nineteenth century, the dynastic aspect is specifically discussed in Roderick R. McLean, *Royalty and Diplomacy in Europe, 1890–1914* (2001), and in German Johannes Paulmann, *Pomp und Politik: Monarchenbegegnungen in Europa zwischen Ancien Régime und Erstem Weltkrieg* (2000).

Index